Warriors of the Prophet

Warriors
of the
Prophet

The Struggle for Islam

Mark Huband

Westview Press
A Member of the Perseus Books Group

Copyright © 1998, 1999 by Westview Press, A Member of Perseus Books Group

Published in 1999 in the United States of America by Westview Press, 5500 Central Avenue, Boulder, Colorado 80301-2877, and in the United Kingdom by Westview Press, 12 Hid's Copse Road, Cumnor Hill, Oxford OX2 9JJ

Find us on the World Wide Web at www.westviewpress.com

Library of Congress Cataloging-in-Publication Data
Huband, Mark.
    Warriors of the Prophet : the struggle for Islam / Mark Huband.
        p.   cm.
    Includes bibliographical references and index.
    ISBN 0-8133-2780-6 (hc); 0-8133-2781-4 (pb)
        1. Islamic fundamentalism.   2. Terrorism—Religious aspects—
    Islam.   3. Terrorism—Islamic countries—History—20th century.
    4. Islam—20th century.   I. Title.
    BP60.H8   1998
    320.5'5'0917671—dc21   98-12261
                                                                       CIP

The paper used in this publication meets the requirements of the American National Standard for Permanence of Paper for Printed Library Materials Z39.48-1984.

10   9   8   7   6   5   4   3

For Stephen Smith,
In remembrance of many miles traveled together

Contents

Note on Transliterations   ix
Acknowledgments   xi
Glossary   xiii
Introduction   xv

1 The Road from Kabul: Afghanistan   1

An Arab Army for the Afghan War, 3
Afghanistan and the Politics of Islam, 5
America Traps the Russian Bear, 9
The Secret Army, 11
Warriors of a Holy War, 14
The Endless War, 16
A Nation at the Crossroads, 20
The Battle for Central Asia, 22

2 The Abyss of Darkness: Somalia   25

Order Out of Chaos, 29
From Unity to Disintegration, 33
The Islamists Voice Their Message, 36
The Arab Army Joins the Fray, 38
A Land Set Adrift, 42

3 The Torn Heart: Algeria   46

"Algeria Is My Country," 47
Empires of the Orient, 50
The Road to Catastrophe, 55
Battle for the Soul of a Nation, 59
Travels with a Sheikh, 65
"The Hour of Total Change," 69

4 The Community of Muslims: Egypt   73

The Scholars of the Islamic Revival, 76
The Muslim Brotherhood, 81

Death, Defiance, and the Call to Jihad, 86
The State of Islam, 89

5 The Myth of the Golden Age: The Maghreb and Arabia   94

Politics in the Wilderness, 97
The Building of a Nation, 103
Men of Deeds, Men of Words, 112

**6 The Iron Hand of the State:
   North Africa and the Middle East**   117

Words, Actions, and the "Total Project," 121
A Long, Slow Death, 128
"Unto You, Your Moral Law,
   and Unto Me, Mine," 134

7 The Book and the Gun: Sudan   140

The Land of the Mahdi, 143
The Corridors of Power, 147
"They Have Learnt Silence and Patience
   from the River and from the Trees," 154
The Dangerous Game, 159

8 From Dual Containment to Double Standards   166

Baghdad's Last Smile, 170
The Islamists' Twilight, 183

Conclusion   194

Notes   199
Index   221

Note on Transliterations

THE VARIETY THAT EXISTS within the languages of the Muslim world is as marked as the influence of dialects on the core of Arabic itself. While there is a degree of homogeneity within the Arabic-speaking world, Arabic speakers from one part of the Muslim world can find the language as foreign to them as a foreign language when they travel to other parts of that world. With a few exceptions the languages of the Muslim world are written in Arabic, though with wide differences of stress and pronunciation. To facilitate an easy reading of a language that a western audience finds complicated, I have avoided over-use of punctuation—commas, hyphens, apostrophes, and the like—that would affect the pronunciation and have used spellings that will allow the reader to pronounce with ease the few Arabic words I have found it necessary to use. The spelling of names is as given to me by the person named. In some words I have inserted repeated letters—such as "i" or "y"—in order to stress the sound or indicate a long vowel and to achieve accuracy with regard to the sound of the word as pronounced in Arabic.

Acknowledgments

MANY PEOPLE CONTRIBUTED HOURS of their time in my pursuit of the information, opinions, and experiences that form the central elements of this book. For the chapter on Afghanistan I would like to thank Quentin Peel and David Gardner, foreign editor and Middle East editor of the *Financial Times* respectively, for sending me there. I am also indebted to Patrick Fuller of the International Committee of the Red Cross, Denise Meredith at the British Red Cross, and Jean-Luc Paladini of the ICRC in Kabul for their valuable help in allowing me to reach Afghanistan. I would also like to thank the staff of the ICRC offices in Peshawar and Mazar-I-Sharif for their assistance. For the chapter on Somalia, I would like to thank David Shearer, Steve Rifkind, and the staff of the Save the Children Fund for their kind hospitality during many months spent living in Mogadishu in 1992–1994. For chapters referring to Morocco, Algeria, and Tunisia, I would like to thank Professor Mahdi Elmandra at Mohammed V University, Rabat, for his valuable insights and helpful comments; Francois Burgat for his guidance and readiness to share his wealth of knowledge; and Tareq Ramadan for his advice and contacts. I am grateful to Barbara Plett for her immensely helpful comments on the first few chapters of this book, and, for the chapter on Egypt, to individuals within and outside the country, who prefer anonymity. At Westview Press I would like to thank Barbara Ellington, who had the idea for this book, and Laura Parsons, Elizabeth Lawrence, and Norman Ware for their sensitive treatment of this subject. I am most indebted, however, to my wife, Marceline, and my children, Olivier and Zara, for allowing me the time to complete this book.

Mark Huband

Glossary

ARABIC IS THE LANGUAGE OF ISLAM, and consequently no study of Islam is possible without reference to Arabic words, which are in many instances essential to the Muslims' own understanding of their religion. Debate over words, concepts, and ideas in Islam lies close to the heart of the current debate over the role of the religion; hence an understanding of some of these highly contentious concepts is important. Listed and briefly explained below are key words that appear in this book. This is not an exhaustive list of all the numerous Arabic words that have relevance to the study of Islam but is limited to words used in the text. At points where these terms are referred to in the text, I have also provided a brief explanation of them to facilitate easier reading. Nevertheless, the following list may prove helpful.

Allah   the name given in Islam to God.

Caliphate   or *kalifate*, the political embodiment of Islamic rule. The successors to the Prophet Mohammed held the title "caliph."

Din   the pursuit of religious belief as a way of life, as opposed to the pursuit of a worldly existence.

Emir   the political leader of an Islamic community. In the 1990s, the term has been applied to the military leaders of Islamist organizations.

Fatwa   a legal ruling issued by an Islamic scholar.

Fiqr   or *fiqh*, the totality of Islamic law as expressed in the words of Islamic jurists.

Fitan   sedition, in application to the lay authority.

Haj   the Muslim pilgrimage to the holy city of Mecca, which all Muslims—men and women—with sufficient resources are urged to perform once during their lifetime. Men who have performed the haj may take the title *al-haj*, women *al-haja*.

Ijma   the consensus of the entire Muslim community upon which a legal decision is then delivered. Such judgments could, some twentieth-century Muslim scholars argue, be soundly based on what was deemed best for the community.

Ijtihad the process of personal reflection on the meaning of the Holy Koran, allowing individual interpretation of the words and actions of the Prophet Mohammed.

Islamism the ideological belief in the requirement to enact the political tenets of Islam as the basis of political life.

Jihad struggle in the defense of Islam.

Kufr a term used to describe what is unislamic.

Madrassa an Islamic school in which study centers on developing a profound knowledge of the Holy Koran, with students—*talib* in Arabic—often learning the text by heart.

Mujahideen fighters in a jihad or holy war. Such individuals may also be referred to as *jihadis*.

Mujtahid Muslim scholars qualified to use their knowledge of the Holy Koran as a source for legal decisions.

Salaf the early Muslims. Literally, the *predecessors*, whose acts and beliefs provided a model for later generations of Muslims. Later Muslims, inspired by the interpretative insights of these early Muslims, attempted to follow their example and developed a movement known as the Salafiyya school of thought.

Sharia literally, the Islamic *way* or *path*. To follow this path is to abide by Islamic law as derived from the Holy Koran.

Sufism the Islamic mystic movement, whose practices center on devotion to earlier Muslims renowned for their piety and, in some cases, their supernatural powers, called *baraka* in Arabic.

Sunnism and Shiism the two schools of Islam. The division of Islam into Sunni and Shia has its roots in the political rather than theological differences among the followers of the Prophet Mohammed in the years immediately after his death in A.D. 632. For a fuller explanation of this division, see Chapter 2, note 17.

Tajdid renewal of the Islamic religion. This process is viewed by modern Islamists as essential to retaining the religion's relevance to contemporary society.

Talib student, often a pupil at an Islamic school or *madrassa*.

Tawhid the theory of Allah's overriding supremacy and the secondary importance of worldly authority.

Ulama the established body of religious scholars. Their thoughts and writings are often closely tied to the requirements of incumbent political authorities in need of religious sanction for political acts.

Umma the global community of Muslims, which transcends nationality and nation-states and links all Muslims into a single community.

Introduction

WHEN A MASSIVE BOMB EXPLODED outside the Alfred P. Murrah federal building in Oklahoma City on 19 April 1995, killing 168 people, CNN reporters invited experts on world terrorism to give their immediate opinions on who may have been responsible. It appeared to one particular expert that all the signs pointed to Islamic militants. The heartland of the American Midwest had finally been scarred by the consequences of poor U.S. relations with the militants of the Islamic world and with the governments of particular Islamic countries who were assumed to be those militants' supporters.

The readiness with which this particular commentator could reach such a conclusion, his comments beamed by satellite to, as CNN's advertisement says, "over 210 countries and territories around the world," was a watershed. No logical conclusion could be reached other than that the enemies of the West had had their way. The outcome of the subsequent investigation, trial, and verdict is now well known. What remains contentious is why the Islamic world was the first to be accused.

Several years earlier, a bomb had shattered the heart of New York when the World Trade Center became the target of a terrorist attack, indeed carried out by Islamic militants. Why assume, therefore, that the Oklahoma City bomb was the work of the same, or similar, people? Was it the influence of what Samuel P. Huntington calls "Muslim conflict propensity,"[1] which led analysts to conclude that violent terrorist acts could only be committed by Islamic militants? If so, what is it within Islam that had created such a tendency? Did the West understand that aspect of the world's fastest-growing religion? And if not, what was it doing to widen its knowledge and create suitable conditions for peaceful coexistence?

The West's view of Islam is important. Western attitudes toward the Islamic world, from precolonial times to the present day, have had an enormous impact upon the direction the religion has taken. Western attitudes toward Muslims—the people of the Islamic world—have a tremendous influence on the political direction the Islamic world has taken throughout the twentieth century. But is the impact of Western actions really appreciated by those in the West who form the links—diplomatic, political, and military—between the Islamic and Western worlds? It would seem rarely the case. Although Western countries have their allies in the Islamic world, these alliances are superficial and exposed as such when subject to strain. It is rare for the United States to accede to the wishes of its Arab "friends" in the Middle East if such accessions are at the expense of Israel.

Central to the relationship between the Islamic world and the non-Islamic world is the legacy of an entwined and complex history. Opinion about the current relationship of the West with the Islamic world, particularly the Middle East, is formed by the media. And yet that relationship was really formed almost two centuries ago, perhaps even longer, when the Arab lands were first beginning to be occupied by European colonialists. Although decades of recent history, and self-images formed over the centuries, have forged the heart of what is now the Islamic world, the Western media has skimmed the surface of a long period of interaction. But no other area of the world, when being covered by the Western media, is so in need of constant reference to history as is the Islamic world. These references are missing, perhaps because the knowledge simply is not there.

A deeper Western understanding of the Islamic world must begin not with a view to Islam's interaction with other cultures but with a knowledge of how it relates to itself. Analysis of Islam's relationship with the outside world inevitably follows, due to its close proximity to the predatory Europeans who conquered, ruled, exploited, and departed. But while one examines how the non-Islamic world has profoundly influenced the course of Islamic history, one should also look closely at the reality on the ground. There exists, beyond the reach of the Western observer, journalist, analyst, and commentator, an Islamic reality that has emerged independent of the Western cultural onslaught. There is a history that barely relates to the political events in the Islamic world as they are presented in the West. The Islamic world has evolved, although the West generally views it as alternately stagnant, regressive, or fanatical. At points Islam, like the many constituent parts of what is considered "the West," is indeed all these things. It is also much more. The Islamic world is host to dynamic experiments in living. Within one Arab city, Cairo, 18 million people—Copts, Muslims, Orthodox Greeks, Hindus, and Jews—live in harmony; the city suffers barely any violent crime. How many Muslim cabinet ministers are there in Western governments? Few. But in the Egyptian government, the Coptic Christian minority is represented.

What history has brought the Islamic world to where it is today? The aim of this book is not only to explain the evolution of Islamic thought and activity in a variety of countries but also to allow the main players in what has become known as the "Islamic Revival," or "Resurgence," to explain for themselves, as far as possible, what has taken place. As I have said, the impact of Western understanding, or the absence of it, is of great importance. This book is an attempt to allow the Islamic activists of the 1990s to balance what the West thinks it knows about Islam with their own views of their own experience.

"Political Islam" is the belief that has been attributed to the Islamic organizations that have emerged during the twentieth century. "Islamism" has come to be viewed as the ideology of those practitioners of "political Islam" now active in the Islamic world. As will become clear, no understanding of their beliefs, evolution, and current activities is possible without a sound knowledge of the history that produced them. As a result, this book is part history, for the simple reason that to omit a historical perspective would leave the reader more rather than less confused about the issues, people, and organizations being examined.

Complementing this historical perspective are firsthand accounts of different countries, events, and conversations with individuals, which I believe reveal accurately the current phase through which the Islamist movement is now passing. These accounts are not intended as mere illustration. The reality on the ground has been a key element in the evolution of beliefs. Islam is a living religion, and intrinsic to it are practices that enforce the renewal and review of beliefs. Far from being a religion written in stone 1,300 years ago, which so-called "fundamentalists" are seeking to *return* to, Islam is a religion whose internal variety is a source of dynamism as well as a source of conflict. It is also important to be able to personalize and characterize a religion that, to most people in the West, remains a mystery. I hope that by describing in detail the conversations, people, places, and events I have experienced as a journalist in the Islamic world, I will provide a form of access to a distant and largely unknown territory.

It is my assumption that critics of this book will highlight the fact that it deals more with the militant and radical end of the Islamic spectrum than it does with the mainstream. As I attempt to show in Chapter 6, the radicals' agenda has influenced at least some aspects of mainstream religious practice. However, it is admittedly the case that I have concentrated on examining the views and activities of the "revivalists" rather than those of the establishment. Why is this so? Because the militant organizations represent the latest stage in the evolution of Islam. Although the governments of the Islamic world repudiate the Islamic credentials of many of those they label "fundamentalist," they are also aware that the phenomenon of Islamic fundamentalism is a real and lasting chapter in the evolution not only of their religion but of their society as a whole. I have generally avoided using the word "fundamentalist" largely because it has lost any real meaning other than as a convenient label used by the media. Instead, I have used the phrases "Islamism" and "Islamist," which both distinguish the practitioners of political Islam from the conservatives and highlight the fact that the Islamist is not just a religious believer but also a politician. Muslims believe in the fundamentals of their religion, but Islamists have formed political organizations in an effort to install those fundamentals within the political fabric of society. Therein lies the distinction.

Conflict has dominated the relationship between these two tendencies within Islam. It is no real surprise that Islam in Western eyes is associated with violence. The views of scholars such as Huntington illustrate how such views have reached the heart of the academic establishment. But this conflict still cannot be used, as was at first tried, to explain why a bomb went off in Oklahoma City. The violence in Algeria, or Upper Egypt, or Afghanistan has its roots in the historical and political facts currently reigning in those countries. Islamism is not irrational. Elements within some Islamist movements are extremist and have committed grotesque acts of violence. The question is whether such acts are to be seen as part of the Islamist agenda. On numerous occasions I have written newspaper dispatches concerning the violence in Algeria. It has been very difficult to talk of "Islamic violence." What is "Islamic" about attacking an Algerian baby with an ax? When two brothers yelled "Allah Akbar" ("God is great") before throwing a petrol bomb into a bus carrying German tourists in central Cairo on 18 September 1997, was the bombing an act of religious faith? Of course not.

It is vital to remember that the Islamic movements are made up of individuals with their own histories, experiences, and views on society. For the most part they live in countries that have failed to satisfy their economic, social, political, educational, and individual needs. Their disappointments have been accompanied by an awareness of the cultural richness of the religion into which they have, as a matter of course, been raised. The tension between these two feelings is dramatic. But among these millions of people there are a million interpretations of what it means to believe. Faith lies at the heart of Islamism. But it is society that has nurtured the particular Islamist movements, creating varying and often greatly opposed views within an Islamist phenomenon that has emerged throughout the Islamic world but that it is nevertheless a mistake to view as united, homogenous, and intent upon returning the Islamic world to the practices of the past. I hope that this book will help bring reality a little closer, so that the next time a bomb explodes our first reaction is not to blame foreign religious extremists but at least to first ask why practitioners of that religion would want to do such a thing, and if they are found to be blameworthy then ask whether it really is their religion that has inspired them.

1

The Road from Kabul

Afghanistan

KARIM OMAR stroked his neatly trimmed beard as the rain beat hard against the window of the terraced house in north London. He had returned from Afghanistan two weeks earlier, to the European city he called the "new Peshawar." He had been reluctant to meet me, concerned that if he talked about his politics it might lead the British government to threaten him with expulsion. We were introduced by a mutual friend in whose house we met, and I agreed not to use his real name. Then, for two days, he told me his story. And, as he did, a door opened before me revealing the global underworld of Islamist dissidents who are seeking to apply the political tenets of their religion as the essential elements of life in the Muslim world.

It had been to Peshawar, the elegant town in northwest Pakistan, that Karim Omar and thousands like him were drawn in the quest to assert a new Islamic identity. Of Syrian origin, he was one of thousands of young men dispatched by the religious establishments of most Islamic countries to fight the Soviet Union following its invasion of Afghanistan in 1979. He was typical of the Islamist youth, the foot soldiers of the Islamist ideology. Frustrated in their own homelands, beleaguered by poverty and political stagnation, they had suddenly been offered the chance to fight a war they hoped would give purpose to their unsatisfied zeal. This opportunity would transform ideas into reality, ultimately implanting the roots of a new radicalism deep into the communities to which they, the Arab Afghans as they became known, would eventually return.

The story Omar told me brought together a thousand fragmented incidents, organizations, and individuals. The activists of political Islam, linking the Muslim countries of North Africa with those of Southeast Asia, were portrayed as joined by a unity of purpose, which had been fostered initially in Peshawar in the mid-1980s. Their camaraderie intensified across the border on the other side of the desolate Khyber Pass, on the battlefields of Afghanistan. And now, he said, they are spread throughout the world, from the Philippines to New Jersey.[1]

Since their role in the Afghan war ended, many of these combatants have settled in Western cities, their homelands barred to them by ruling regimes virulently opposed to the Islamists' potent political agenda. London has become one of several centers for those exiles determined to foster a revival of Islam as a political system in their own countries. Meanwhile, other of these youths or their protégés have become the militants of the Egyptian al-Gama'a al-Islamiyya or Islamic Group, the Algerian Armed Islamic Group, and fledgling organizations in Morocco, Saudi Arabia, and Tunisia. They remain intent upon replacing the same regimes that once applauded their departure for the Afghan war.

It was not until 1984 that Arabs began arriving in Afghanistan in significant numbers. By then the Mujahideen,[2] as the Afghan Islamic resistance was called, had been fighting the Soviet army for almost five years. "At its height there were around fifteen thousand who came from Saudi Arabia, five thousand from Yemen, between three and five thousand from Egypt, two thousand from Algeria, around one thousand from the Gulf, a thousand from Libya, and several hundred from Iraq, particularly from Iraqi Kurdistan,"[3] said Omar. He continued:

> Between 1982 and 1984 there were only around two hundred Arabs in Afghanistan. But in 1986 there was a sudden influx. There had been a lot of publicity among Arabs, particularly by a Palestinian, Sheikh Abdallah Azzam,[4] who had left Jordan in 1982 for Saudi Arabia, and then traveled to Islamabad later that year. He was a doctor of Islamic science, and a veteran of the Palestinian cause in the 1960s, who had been educated by the Muslim Brotherhood. There are many *jihadis*, but they're not all revolutionary.

The term "jihad" refers to the holy war through which Islam has, from its early history, both spread outward from its Arabian birthplace and defended itself when under threat. Omar went on: "Azzam was a revolutionary. He went often to the United States to speak on behalf of the cause. And Osama Bin Laden did the same in Saudi Arabia."

For all the Arab Afghans, the key figure linking their distant, Arabic-speaking countries with the Afghan people, who speak Pashtun and Dari, was the Saudi Arabian Osama Bin Laden. A one-time follower of the Muslim Brotherhood[5] who arrived in Afghanistan in his mid-thirties, he was the son of a wealthy Saudi family that had made its fortune in the construction industry, building, among other things, mosques.

"Osama is important in the past and for the future. He has passed through many stages. Osama represents the method. He is between the moderates and the armed groups. In Afghanistan he was closest to Hekmatyar, Rabbani, and Younes Khales,[6] and when he went back to Afghanistan[7] he stayed with Younes Khales and his commanders, and when the Taliban took Nanghahar he became close to them," Omar explained.

An Arab Army for the Afghan War

Arab recruitment to the Afghan Mujahideen, the fighters of the jihad, was transformed when the fledgling Arab force defeated a Soviet operation to seize an Afghan mountain village, Jadji, in early 1986. Both Bin Laden and Azzam were in the village, and with a group of fighters they sustained a forty-five-day siege by the Soviet forces, who were eventually forced to withdraw. Omar described the situation:

> It was the only time the Arabs had a direct battle with the Russians. Many Russians were taken alive and killed. Osama still has the weapon he took from the Russians during that battle. The people who are closest to him are the people who fought with him there, and during the six months after that battle Arab numbers in Afghanistan increased from three hundred to around seven thousand. It was a turning point. Osama visited mosques in Saudi Arabia, and Azzam traveled, giving the cause greater publicity, mainly to explain to people how they could get there. The young Arabs would go and get their visas at Pakistan embassies wherever they lived, and then get money from the people at the mosques where they prayed. It was an easy trip. Everybody wanted to go, even if they weren't going to fight. They arrived in Peshawar with the telephone numbers of the people they should contact, and cars were sometimes there to meet them at the airport, and there were houses in Peshawar for each nationality. We were given Afghan clothes, and then we were sent to train, either in Pakistan or Afghanistan, for between one and three months. Then we went to the front.

Saudi Arabian Airlines gave 75 percent discounts on flights to Peshawar to men going to join the Mujahideen. At times, the Pakistani embassy in Riyadh was delivering up to 200 visas a day to the young recruits.

"Some came with the intention of staying one month. Quite a lot of Saudis would come for their holidays. If you had spent some time with a whore in Bangkok, you would come to fight the jihad to purify yourself. For the Arabs Afghanistan was like a university which introduced a new ideology and school of thought. The ideology of jihad resistance," Omar continued. "It was a gathering point for all the armed resistance. Now the Islamic movement is going through a renaissance, and all the Islamic schools met each other, for the first time, in Afghanistan. It's one very important point. The different trends met each other for the first time, and made it like a university, an open room for discussion. For nearly ten years."

Karim Omar is particularly clear about one issue: Democratic Islam was rejected in Afghanistan. The Arabs found there that they could use force to beat the Russians. Omar was from the Syrian Islamic movement, while some people had experience fighting in other countries. Others, meanwhile, had experience in using computers, communications equipment, and numerous other specializations. In some camps, mostly English-language military training manuals were translated into Arabic. One such work was a U.S. military manual, the *Black Book*, which Omar said contained details of terrorist operations and which was fully translated into Arabic in Afghanistan.

> The West has just started to discover this lately, and it was why they didn't want to arm the Bosnian Muslims, because they didn't want to create the Bosnian Arabs after having created the Arab Afghans. But this is what you find now. In every Islamic conflict now you will find some Afghan Arabs. In the Philippines, in Kashmir, Tajikistan, Burma, Bosnia, in Africa. This, in addition to a bigger presence in their own countries. The bulk of them went back to their own homes. To Western eyes they became terrorists. In their homes they are still considered heroes. What is bothering the Western politicians is that the Afghan Arabs went from being individuals into being a school of thought. The next generation of Afghan Arabs has been born. And the third generation, although they didn't go to Afghanistan themselves.

These Arab Afghans are now a major security issue, because they are not known, Omar told me. Some spent ten years in Afghanistan, not leaving the country until the mid-1990s. Since their departure, many have influenced other people in their home countries. Many are religious leaders—imams—who on any given Friday can influence the views of hundreds of people who flock to hear them preach in mosques across the Islamic world. Others are tribal leaders in countries such as Saudi Arabia and Yemen.

"In Egypt [the government] is fighting the children of the Arab Afghans," Omar said. "The children are perhaps fighting for tribal reasons. The reason is simple: the government makes them suffer. Even those who disagree with the Arab Afghans view them as heroes. Even the secular parties. It's no longer an Afghan Arab movement. It's a social movement."

Afghanistan and the Politics of Islam

For centuries, political power in Afghanistan has drawn its ultimate authority from Islam. But the divine hand is subject to the rigid tribal interests of Afghan society. During the nineteenth century, tribal chiefs were traditionally empowered by the tribal assembly, the *jirga*, to rule primarily in accordance with customary law, except where Islamic law, or *sharia*,[8] naturally took precedence. Thus, the Afghan chiefs were distinct from those in many other Islamic societies, where leaders were empowered by the council of religious leaders, the ulama. The tribal chief was, therefore, bound primarily to uphold tribal tradition. It was the *jirga* itself that was conferred with this power of nomination of the chief as a sacred duty, derived from Allah. It was the *jirga*'s role as an intermediary empowered to nominate the tribal chief that cemented the direct link between the religion and the practice of political power. The ulama merely sanctioned the nomination of the *jirga*.

The intermediate role of the *jirga* also meant that the ruler was empowered by the people he ruled, theoretically guaranteeing a degree of popular influence over him. To have been nominated by the ulama would have distanced rulers from the ruled. The late nineteenth and early twentieth centuries were dominated by attempts by Afghan rulers to modernize their country by centralizing power. They initially attempted this by claiming direct authority from Allah through the Prophet Mohammed. Then, during the reign of King Amanullah (1919–1929), divine authority was pushed aside in favor of popular sovereignty, based on the equality of all citizens and individual rights rather than the rights of clans or tribes. The third Anglo-Afghan war, which ended with Amanullah's accession and which secured Afghan independence from Britain in 1919, was preceded by a declaration of jihad issued by the king himself against the infidel British. Amanullah's victory, and the British withdrawal, greatly enhanced his religious and political credentials. However, throughout his reign it was the assembly of tribal chieftains with their divine authority, the *Loya Jirga*, that was the only body able to make constitutional changes or introduce new taxes. Amanullah's attempts at modernization had, by 1928, earned him widespread unpopularity. His wife was photographed with her face uncovered during a foreign tour, which was portrayed as an insult to the entire nation in a broad swathe of anti-Amanullah opinion. The Shinwari tribe of northeastern Afghanistan launched a revolt when they were deprived of their tribal "right" to collect taxes from trade caravans passing through their "territory." The revolt against modernization spread, and the king was brought down a year later. Central authority, as Amanullah had forged it, slipped away, and the tribal *jirga* with their religious authority re-asserted their influence.

Forty years later, the rift between the central authority and the rural fiefdoms remained in force. In the late 1970s, the influence of Islam on Afghan politicians was as great among the leaders of the Mujahideen as it was among the leaders of the Marxist government they were try-ing to overthrow.

The coup d'état that brought the Peoples' Democratic Party of Afghanistan (PDPA) to power in 1978 inspired the Mujahideen leaders to form their alliance in neighboring Pakistan. The PDPA bore all the hallmarks of a Marxist regime in terms of the social reform program it intended to carry out as well as the terminology it employed to forge a break with the country's past.[9] It introduced the concept of a class struggle by referring to Afghanistan's classes of "feudals" and "ex-ploiters" versus "toiling workers and peasants."[10]

But within a year of taking power, the PDPA's strategy had changed. Efforts were made to highlight the convergence of the government's revolutionary principles with those of the Islamic *sharia,* the Islamic law as written in the Holy Koran and as refined by Islamic scholars since Islam's birth in the seventh century. The purpose of this strategy was to portray the growing Mujahideen resistance as unislamic. It was a clear sign of the key role that religion plays in the Afghan political arena.

The PDPA leadership realized that by appealing to the religious con-servatism of ordinary Afghans, the Mujahideen had a potent weapon. After the Soviet invasion of December 1979, which was ostensibly carried out to bolster the PDPA regime, the government lost its re-maining credibility in the eyes of ordinary people. The Mujahideen re-alized that the most potent weapon in its armory was its ability to portray the Soviet invasion as a threat to Islam. The PDPA was deter-mined to respond and sought Islamic credentials of its own, by ini-tially celebrating the Iranian Islamic revolution as a victory against imperialism. In 1980 it drew up an interim constitution, which ap-peared to extend religious freedom to all the various strands of Islam practiced in the country.[11] It then instituted legal reforms allowing cases to be tried and judged in accordance with the *sharia.* Even so, the government refrained from incorporating a defense of Islamic prin-ciples in the constitution and fell short of recognizing Islam as its ulti-mate authority. Instead, political and religious affairs coexisted, the country's religious direction coming increasingly under the guidance of the political establishment, notably the prime minister's office.

Afghan religious practice was usefully portrayed by the Mujahideen as threatened by the atheistic Soviet Union. But the practical response to the Soviet invasion was determined by the complexion of the political alliances formed by clan and tribal chiefs into the Mujahideen. Within their own communities, these chiefs drew their personal credibility in large part from their religious piety. But in their interclan alliances, their importance was based on their success as warrior-politicians rather than purely as defenders of their faith.

Equally, the PDPA itself shed many of the characteristics that earned it the label "Marxist": "Very quickly, in fact, the communist state began to play the tribal game," writes Olivier Roy.[12] "The more the Afghan resistance endowed itself with political structures, the more the communist state went about ridding itself of all that qualified it as *communist* (abandoning the term 'democratic' in the country's name in 1987, recognizing Islam as the official religion, establishing a multiparty system)."

The religious credentials of the individual Afghan factional leaders tended to suffer as political power, individual ambition, and personal rivalries ebbed and flowed. No alliances proved durable. Still fewer saw religious purpose sufficiently powerful to overcome tribal differences, particularly in disputes over authority within the power structure of the Mujahideen.[13] As opposition to the PDPA mounted[14] and plunged Afghanistan into civil war following the Soviet invasion, the PDPA's ability to cling to power, beyond the security provided by its Soviet allies, was dependent upon the weakness of the Mujahideen stemming from its internal divisions and from the personal rivalries between its myriad tribal chieftains, warlords, and militia leaders. The power struggle of the 1980s can, in essence, be viewed as having this tribal element at its heart. The different factions exerted political power within their tribal areas and retained the prewar tribal structure among their forces. The Islamic element was a unifying call that identified the tribes as having one enemy, but it was not an ideological element that filtered down to alter the practice of local politics. Even so, the desire to view the struggle as one between the atheistic and the theocratic, the modern and the traditional, the PDPA and the Islamists, was strong. And it was this interpretation that the Arab Afghans chose to believe, lured by its resemblance to the polity promoted by the Prophet Mohammed 1,300 years earlier.[15]

The Soviet invasion was an attempt by Moscow to ensure that its southern neighbor's traditional nonalignment was not disturbed by events elsewhere in the region. The Islamic revolution in Iran had overthrown the West's key ally, the Shah. American hostages were held at the U.S. embassy in Tehran, and the balance of power in central Asia was thus overturned. Moscow was awaiting an American reaction, which it was expected would turn the spotlight to Afghanistan, with the prospect that a pro-American government would somehow be installed.[16] In fact, although both the United States and its regional ally Pakistan were anticipating Soviet expansion into Afghanistan, they were apparently not planning a move to preempt whatever the Soviet government may have had in mind.[17] The Soviet analysis is generally considered to have been faulty. Nevertheless, by 1981, the Soviet troop presence in Afghanistan had reached 105,000, its expenditures on troops, supplies, food (including an average of 250,000 tons of wheat per year), and administration rising to $5 billion a year. Military supplies to the PDPA government accounted for much of these expenditures.[18]

The composition of the Afghan Mujahideen movement was notable for its relative lack of middle-class intellectuals, who had dominated Afghan politics across the political spectrum during the previous two decades and who had agitated for change much earlier. From the reign of King Amanullah, modernizing policies based on nationhood and individual rights had been supported by the middle class, who had often been the only ones to understand the purpose of such ideas. The rise of the Mujahideen as the most active opposition to the PDPA provided a national platform for local politicians drawn from within Afghanistan's rural tribal structure, a factor that reasserted traditional power at the expense of the urban middle class who had sought to create national institutions. Only the Mujahideen leadership was drawn from among the majority of the intellectual class of Kabul University.[19] They found themselves leading an army of peasants. Upon leaving Afghanistan as refugees, the intellectuals largely went further afield than Pakistan or Iran, from whose refugee camps thousands of Afghans were then drawn to the Mujahideen. It was from the camps that they formed into seven military-political parties, all to varying degrees drawing their inspiration from Islam, the most influential being the Hizb-i Islami led by Gulbeddin Hekmatyar. Aside from the parties, there were local military commanders who occasionally allied themselves with larger factions; the most prominent of these leaders was the Panjshir valley commander, Ahmed Shah Massoud.

The pattern of foreign assistance to the Pakistan-based Mujahideen resistance to the PDPA resulted from a combination of circumstances that established common ground between those with the resources to help and those with the contacts through which the aid could be effectively channeled.

Pakistan's ties to the Afghan Islamists had evolved along with its relationships with its neighbors—India and Afghanistan. Afghanistan's Islamists were the only Afghan group to have opposed the splitting off of East Pakistan into independent Bangladesh, and they had supported Pakistan politically during its 1971 war with India. The Islamists had also opposed the campaign for self-determination by the Pashtuns in northwest Pakistan, which would have reduced Pakistani control over its semiautonomous Tribal Areas within the North-West Frontier Province. This area of Pakistan, dominated by the Pashtun tribe, had defied British colonial attempts to administer it. At independence and the partition of British India into India and Pakistan in 1947, the Pakistani government did little more than inherit the status quo. Only in 1997 did the Islamabad government announce that the Tribal Areas would have the opportunity to vote in Pakistani national elections. Even so, the area that borders Afghanistan continues to be controlled by tribal chiefs and their well-armed militias.

Pakistan's Islamic party, the Jamaat-i Islami, led by the influential Islamist scholar Mawlana Sayyid Abul A'la Maududi until his death in 1979, cemented these ties with the Afghan Islamists as Afghanistan's instability during the late 1970s worsened.

Meanwhile, Saudi Arabian aid to the Afghan refugees in Pakistan began to be channeled via the Saudi Arabia–based Muslim World League (Rabitat al-Alam al-Islami) through the Jamaat-i Islami.

America Traps the Russian Bear

The installation of the military regime of General Zia ul-Haq in Pakistan in 1977 was followed by a program of Islamization. In 1981, the U.S. government approved a $3.2 billion program of assistance to Pakistan, allowing Islamabad to further pursue its overriding interest, which was to achieve internal security by provoking instability among its neighbors. General Zia's aim was to ensure Pashtun dominance in Afghanistan so as to dilute calls for a Pashtun state in western Pakistan.

Support for the Afghan Mujahideen was a key element in this strategy, coinciding with the U.S. determination to actively confront the Soviet forces through surrogates. American and Saudi financial assistance for the purchase of weapons intended for the Mujahideen was channeled through the Pakistani intelligence service, the Inter-Services Intelligence (ISI), in which there was a significant Jamaat-i Islami presence. The Pakistani government recognized the seven Mujahideen parties, and the Muslim World League funded the recruitment of members of the Muslim Brotherhood to staff the Saudi Red Crescent and Islamic Co-ordination Council in Peshawar, where the Afghan parties had their headquarters in exile.

U.S. military aid to the Mujahideen mounted rapidly, from $30 million in 1980 to $250 million in 1985.[20] The Americans built upon the ties that had already been established by their Saudi ally, as well as those between the Muslim World League relief organization and the Islamist opposition in Pakistan. From 1986 to 1989, total provisions for the Mujahideen reached $1 billion. American assistance was matched dollar for dollar by that from Saudi Arabia. Starting in September 1986, the United States also began supplying the Mujahideen with shoulder-held, laser-guided Stinger missiles, the first such provision outside the North Atlantic Treaty Organization (NATO).

Support for the Afghan Mujahideen became one of the major covert operations carried out by the U.S. Central Intelligence Agency during the 1980s. The combined cash funds provided by the CIA and the Saudi Arabians, for what was called Operation Cyclone by the outgoing administration of President Jimmy Carter in 1981, were transferred to special accounts in Pakistan controlled by the ISI's director general, Lieutenant General Akhtar Adbul Rehman Khan.[21] This was in addition to funds provided specifically for purchasing weapons, which accounted for the bulk of the funds made available by the U.S. Congress and spent outside Afghanistan on weapons from the Mujahideen's main suppliers—China, Egypt, Israel, Great Britain, and the United States. The ISI's former director of Afghan affairs, Brigadier Mohammad Yousaf, recounts the procurement procedure:

> Having agreed what [weapons] were wanted, it was up to the CIA to provide [them]. They had to purchase all the items and get them by ship to Karachi or, for a small proportion, by air to Islamabad. Until 1985 it was a firm policy that only communist-bloc weapons could be bought. This was part of pretending that the West, and America in particular, was not backing the Mujahideen with material assistance. So the CIA buyers with their shopping lists were limited as to sources. During 1983 approximately 10,000 tons were received, rising to 65,000 tons in 1987.[22]

The realization that the CIA was on an arms-buying spree spread among countries with a domestic arms industry or with unwanted stockpiles. The CIA would buy and supply weapons as long as they could not be traced back to the agency. Until 1984, most of the weapons came from China. In 1985 Egypt became a main source, though these weapons were of inferior quality. Even India, a close ally of the Soviet Union, in 1984 sold 100,000 .303 rifles to the CIA at a rock-bottom price for use by the Afghan Mujahideen. A large proportion of the Israeli weapons sold to the CIA were those Israel had captured during its 1982 invasion of Lebanon.

Saudi Arabia and Egypt were occasionally used as transit points for weapons flights from the United States, though most loads were transported by ship to Karachi. Other countries, notably Turkey, also saw Afghanistan as a dumping ground for obsolete weapons, which were offered for sale and duly purchased by the CIA through ISI mediation, despite the ISI's objection to the purchase of weapons that were so old as to be virtually unusable.

Brigadier Yousaf was aware that unequivocal political support from anti-Soviet states required the Mujahideen to gratefully accept all offers of weapons, which the Pakistani military advisers to the Afghan resistance were then obliged to incorporate into their battlefield strategy. Yousaf's main task was to liaise with the Mujahideen on the ground inside Afghanistan. He briefed and advised Mujahideen leaders on military strategy and therefore knew what was required to conduct the campaign.

Many of the weapons were ancient, nonfunctional, and, at the least, inappropriate for the war in which they were to be used. American officials insisted, for example, that the Mujahideen accept British Blowpipe surface-to-air missiles (SAMs), which required the firer to stand up while the target aircraft approached. Although the purchase of the weapon was a boost to the British arms trade, it was fairly useless to the Afghans, who found it unreliable and hazardous to use. The British flew the firing mechanisms back to the United Kingdom for modifications when they were discovered to be faulty. But even when they were returned to the Mujahideen, the weapons were deemed ineffective. Several were later captured by Soviet troops and displayed on Soviet television.

The weapons that arrived in Pakistan were transported to warehouses near Peshawar and Quetta in northwestern Pakistan. There, the ISI would allocate them to the Afghan parties, who would in turn distribute them inside Afghanistan. Around 70 percent of the weapons were allocated to the Islamist parties, and the rest to other factions. The bank accounts controlled by the ISI and replenished on a monthly basis by the CIA paid for each stage of transportation and storage and covered the expenses of the Afghan parties. This support was supplemented by funds from individual Arab countries, particularly Saudi Arabia, which were sent directly to the seven Islamist parties.

According to Yousaf, the CIA operatives based in Pakistan, as well as those who visited from the United States or who accompanied CIA director William Casey in his travels, did not have direct contact with the Mujahideen.[23] They neither trained nor advised the Afghan insurgents. Meanwhile, the United States kept its embassy in Kabul open until the Soviet withdrawal in 1989, when it was closed in expectation of a descent into violence if the Soviet-backed PDPA government of Mohammed Najibullah fell.

The Secret Army

The states at the center of Operation Cyclone—in particular, Saudi Arabia—had little or no idea that their war against the Soviet Union had amassed, albeit inadvertently, the nucleus of the reorganized and revitalized Islamic movements of the Arab world that have since become their most virulent opponents. The Pakistani ISI liaised closely with the Afghan opposition parties in Pakistan and their military wings operating inside Afghanistan. But even the ISI seems to have attached little real long-term significance to the influx of the Arabs.

Details of the ISI liaison with the Mujahideen do not specifically identify the role played by the Arabs. Brigadier Yousaf barely mentions the Arab contribution to the Mujahideen forces. He reflects indirectly on the cause of this blind spot when outlining his understanding of the broad American approach to the Afghan campaign; simply put, he interprets the American involvement as a payback for Soviet support for the Vietcong, which had resulted in American defeat in Vietnam a decade earlier.[24]

The realization that there would be unanticipated consequences of the strategy of flooding Afghanistan with arms—termed "blowback" by those involved—was not publicly recognized in the United States until the World Trade Center bombing of 26 February 1993, which led to the subsequent arrest of the Iraqi-born Ramzi Ahmed Yousef, who had fought with the Afghan faction leader Abdul Rasul Sayyaf. Victor Marchetti, a former senior CIA official, observes:

> Afghanistan was a golden opportunity for the weakening of the Evil Empire. But the CIA has had this experience time and time again: Korea, Cuba, Vietnam. In all these clandestine activities, the pressure is so great to get something done and get it done right away that no one takes a long-term view. They hire all sorts of people, some of whom are crazy. When the operation ends, they are inevitably left with people trained in demolition, firearms use or guerrilla warfare, some of whom are suddenly out of a job. But a lot of this was going to happen anyway, whether the U.S. government got involved or not. People were going to come there and fight against the Soviets. There was going to be money. The CIA just gave it shape and direction.[25]

It is difficult to see how the Soviet Union could have been forced out of Afghanistan without U.S. assistance to the Mujahideen. Certainly a "social movement" emerged among the Arabs who went to Afghanistan, a movement supported financially by religious and political leaders from across the Muslim world. But the American financial and logistical support—and the Saudi support that matched it—was the element that turned a local conflict into the pan-Islamic jihad that the Afghan resistance leaders had declared in November 1979. The call to fight in Afghanistan spread from Morocco to Indonesia. Military success, however, was what turned the trickle of recruits into a flood. Far from giving "shape and direction" to this movement, the foreign financiers transformed the entire war by providing the weapons that made such success possible.

American awareness of the existence of the Afghanistan-born Arab movement became more pronounced following the Soviet withdrawal in 1989. Discussion in the West centered on how best to extricate the United States from the system of support it had provided. The anti-Western views of faction leaders like Gulbeddin Hekmatyar could no longer be ignored. Providing lethal assistance to such leaders—to whose factions many Arabs had been attached—became an issue that the United States no longer wanted left in the hands of the ISI. In 1992, measures to neutralize the Arab Afghans began to take shape. Karim Omar explains:

> In 1992 two things happened which caused most of the [Arabs] to leave Afghanistan. When Kabul fell to the Mujahideen the Americans realized it was time to eliminate the Arab presence. They pushed the Afghan and Pakistani intelligence services to carry out the mass arrest of Arabs. The intelligence services in Arab countries were involved too. Then, secondly, the Afghans started to fight each other. It was because of this that most Arabs left. But by then the experience of Afghanistan had had its affect.

Many of the Arabs had not become frontline troops, opting instead to work within the numerous Islamic relief organizations assisting the Afghan refugees flooding into Pakistan. American officials who were on the ground in Afghanistan portray the Arabs as lacking the fighting spirit of the Afghans themselves and as having been deemed unreliable by the Afghan commanders, though this perception has not been borne out by the vitality of the Islamist groups that have subsequently emerged in the countries of the Arab world. Arabs continued to drift to Afghanistan even after the Soviet withdrawal. Ramzi Ahmed Yousef, even before the World Trade Center bombing, was believed by U.S. intelligence to have received training there after 1989. He was also implicated in a plot to simultaneously bomb several passenger airliners over the Pacific, a plan to assassinate Pope John Paul II during a visit to the Philippines, and a plot to kill the Pakistani prime minister, Benazir Bhutto.

But in the years immediately following the withdrawal of Soviet forces from Afghanistan, when many Arabs who had fought there during the 1980s began to drift away, it was in Algeria that the presence of the Arab Afghans became most pronounced. Tayeb al-Afghani, Jaafar al-Afghani, Abdelhak Layada, Abu Abdallah Ahmed, and many other military and political leaders of the Armed Islamic Group and the Islamic Salvation Front in Algeria were veterans of the Afghan war.[26]

Egyptian Islamists led by Mohammed Shawky al-Islambouli—
whose brother Khaled led the group of soldiers who assassinated
Egyptian President Anwar al-Sadat in 1981—have had several bases in
Afghanistan, including one in Nanghahar province, which has remained Hekmatyar's base even since the arrival of the Taliban in Jalal-
abad. In 1990, al-Islambouli played host to Sheikh Omar Abdel Rahman, the spiritual leader of Egypt's al-Gama'a al-Islamiyya, now in jail
in the United States following the trial of those found guilty of bombing the World Trade Center. Among others found to have been involved in the New York bombing were Mahmoud Abouhalima, Ahmad Ajaj, and Siddiq Ibrahim Siddiq Ali, all of whom had seen combat
in Afghanistan,[27] while two other Egyptians, Ibrahim al-Mekkawi and
Mahmoud al-Sabbawy, are also believed to have established bases in
Afghanistan from which to conduct campaigns elsewhere.[28]

Pakistani authorities subsequently became more active in tracking
down the Arab Afghans they had assisted throughout the 1980s. The
arrest of Ramzi Ahmed Yousef in Pakistan and his subsequent extradition to the United States is one such example. Pakistan also extradited
Ali Eid, alleged to be a member of the Egyptian Tal'a al-Fath (Van-
guards of Conquest), the successor to the Jihad group that had carried
out the Sadat assassination.

The clampdown on the Arab Afghans by Pakistani security forces,
with the encouragement of Washington, Cairo, and other governments, was, as Karim Omar says, a key reason why many of the Arabs
left Afghanistan.

Many of these Arabs then began arriving in third countries, particularly Yemen and Sudan.[29] Others joined the Bosnian Muslim forces
based in Zenica and fought alongside the Bosnian 3rd Corps. Meanwhile, Muslims from the former Soviet Union made their way to the
Afghan training camps. Chechens and Tajiks, the latter numbering up
to 5,000 according to Russian officials, were dispatched to Afghanistan
in the early 1990s, after which they returned to their homelands. The
late Chechen separatist leader, Dzhokar Dudayev, sent Chechen forces
for training to Afghanistan prior to the uprising against Russian rule in
Chechnya.[30] Meanwhile, a son of the Egyptian Sheikh Omar Abdel Rahman led Tajik rebels in their fight against the Tajikistan government.

Warriors of a Holy War

The varied meanings, motives, and purposes of a jihad lie at the heart
of any explanation of what has taken place in the Muslim world since
the war in Afghanistan became a holy cause for its participants; these
factors will be examined closely in later chapters.

The repressiveness and inadequacies of most of the governments of the Muslim world provided sufficient political motivation for the emergence of the Arab Islamist movements, which long predated the Afghan war. The evolution of the Afghan war into a jihad involving Muslims from across the Islamic world was also spurred by the fact that, for the first time since the birth of Western colonialism, the most powerful states of the non-Islamic world were not initially in opposition to an Islamic agenda. Instead of undermining the credibility of Islam, the West sent weapons, advisors, money, and support to the Afghan Mujahideen. The democratic parliaments of the Western world applauded the ardor with which the Islamists poured their effort into what was, ultimately, one of many proxy wars that were fought by Third World states on behalf of one superpower or the other, at the culmination of which, as Karim Omar says: "The Russians lost. The Muslims died. The Americans won."[31]

This Western support reversed a thousand years of history, though it only lasted as long as it suited the global strategy of the CIA. By the time the last Soviet soldier departed Afghanistan and retreated across the Amu river to the Uzbek town of Termez, the accommodation had been largely terminated. Alliances responded to the quickly changing political agenda dominated by the crumbling of the Soviet Union and the emergence of new states in central Asia. In Afghanistan, the new reality was characterized by the failure of the Mujahideen to transform jihad into peace.

"The most important thing is for the rules of Islam to be brought to Afghanistan. The purpose of fighting is to bring the Islamic *sharia* to our country." It is that clear. Mullah Amid Khan Motaqi wrapped himself tighter inside a fine wool cloak close to a glowing metal stove in the corner of his damp office in Kabul's Ministry of Information.

"Islam is Islam everywhere. The only difference is that some people are saying it, but they are not doing it practically. Right now we are strong enough to bring peace to our country. We want to solve its problems and avoid its divisions. We are going to keep our borders and national integrity, because we have overcome all these divisions."[32] He offered me a plate of biscuits and filled small glasses with hot tea. Red sparks flickered through holes in the long metal chimney rising up the wall from the stove, crossing the ceiling to a vent in the frosted window.

A religious battle for political ends. A political battle for religious ends. Chaos spread throughout Afghanistan following the Soviet withdrawal. The Najibullah government clung to power until April 1992, when the president sought the protection of the United Nations, in whose Kabul compound he lived until October 1996. The Mujahideen's disparate factions formed a shaky coalition government,

which failed to find unity and instead fragmented. With the disintegration came disillusionment and lawlessness.

Out of this emerged the Taliban, on whose behalf Motaqi was speaking. Following the Mujahideen's expulsion of the Soviet army in 1989,
their seizure of Kabul three years later, and the return of many refugees
from Pakistan, the Taliban emerged in response to the growing chaos in
the southern part of the country around the city of Kandahar, which was
under Mujahideen control. The movement had recently seized Kabul
and brought with it an extremely strict application of Islamic law.

Now Afghanistan's single most important faction, the Taliban
draws its name from the Arabic word *talib*, meaning student. Its
young leaders, all in their mid-thirties, are in essence the refugees of
the Mujahideen's war against the Soviet Union. Many had been among
the millions of Afghans who had fled to Pakistan during the 1980s, living in the refugee camps along Pakistan's western border. Others had
been displaced by the Mujahideen's war; they had remained within the
borders of Afghanistan during the fighting. For those who had spent
the 1980s in Pakistan, the daily life of the refugee camps had been
dominated by the *madrassa*, the Islamic religious schools that had
been established in the camps.

The Taliban's leader, Sheikh Mohamed Omar Akhund, is said to
have been enraged by the worsening abuses committed by militias
loosely attached to the increasingly disunited Mujahideen factions
grouped under the weakening leadership of President Burhanuddin
Rabbani. In 1992 Sheikh Omar and others in Kandahar confronted the
Mujahideen militiamen and gradually took over policing the town. After 1994 their control spread, and the Mujahideen forces were pushed
back in the face of a steady Taliban advance from Kandahar, first to
the west, then northward. On 27 September 1996, twenty-two months
after first pushing out of Kandahar, the Taliban seized the capital. A
new war was launched as the Taliban assumed control over the center
of power. The ousted Mujahideen factions retreated to the north. The
Taliban has since followed a purely military course of action, invoking
this option on the grounds that to follow any other course would be to
deviate from its Islamist creed[33] and to invite failure.[34]

The Endless War

The war had come again, after a week of silence. It was December
1996, and I had traveled to Afghanistan to see the Taliban's power
firsthand. Kabul cowered—a frozen shell of a city, spread like a lake of
rubble on a high plateau just beneath the sky. Beyond the northern

suburbs, snow draped the soaring peaks rising above the Chakadaria valley. Tangled grapevines had lost their leaves. Over the brow of a hill, a herd of goats bleated as they were driven along the road by old men fleeing the frontline fighting a few miles ahead. City buses had been sent to bring civilians from the battle zone. Households wrapped in colored cloths teetered on the roofs of vehicles packed with young and old—women covered, children bewildered, men ponderous, unmoved but anxious, clinging to the steps and windows and roofs of the buses taking them away from the conflict.

Further on, the plateau seemed the most silent place on earth. The sun was bright. The land was pale brown where the vines lay in their tangled winter dormancy. The mud-walled compounds of the Kabul elite's weekend retreats lay deserted in the shelter of leafless trees. All was silent, until the vast valley screeched with the sound of rockets searing the frozen air between the mountains, then shook as the missiles pounded the hills near what was then the former Mujahideen government's stronghold at Jabal es Saraj, where the Chakadaria valley meets the Paghman range and the Hindu Kush scrapes the sky.

A truck carrying a multiple rocket launcher was parked on a slight rise beyond a walled compound where the Red Cross had set up a hospital. Another rocket launcher, its barrels pointed skyward like the pipes of an organ, was parked further along the rise. There was no movement around the vehicles and no obvious signs of preparation. Just the silence, then a roar as a missile surged into the icy air. From over the hill a tank rattled along the road toward the battlefront. A pickup truck sped down the slope just behind it, overloaded with young men, Kalashnikovs, rocket-propelled grenade launchers, and mortars.

"It is the way to Allah," one shouted, as the truck went past.

The Taliban were on the move.

Commander Hafez Abdirashid peered from the small open window of his Russian-made jeep. The engine turned over noisily as he spoke. The driver of the tank sent blasts of black smoke into the air. The young fighters sat silently in the back of the pickup; they had stopped where a rope was slung across the road to mark a checkpoint.

"We are going to apply Islamic *sharia*. The Mujahideen were raping and looting and throwing up illegal checkpoints where they were troubling the people. This is why we're going to annihilate all these things and apply Islamic *sharia* all over the country," said Hafez.

The rope was lowered at the checkpoint and the tank roared across the plateau toward the distant Paghman. Hafez turned his jeep and followed. The pickup truck with reinforcements followed, as another searing volley from the multiple rocket launcher splintered the air. At the checkpoint, three of the Taliban raised the rope and asked to have their photographs taken. A group of old men leading a herd of goats approached from the direction of the mountains.

"We came from Kalikan. The Taliban told us to leave, and they took the women and children on the buses, but told us to walk with our goats. The alliance was bombing from an airplane, from just after dawn. They launched the attack, and so we fled."

They talked on the roadside. Both Kalikan and Estalef had been bombed that morning. Some of the injured had been brought to the Red Cross hospital nearby. An Afghan official there talked about what had happened, saying that three seriously injured Taliban had been brought in. He was silenced by a European who arrived to assess the situation. Further along the road toward Qarah Bagh there were no signs of life. The road descended steadily. A jet fighter circled high above the mountains. The village was empty. The forces of the jihad had moved north.

By midday the battle had died down, though it was to restart the following day. On the hill outside Kabul to which the people from the villages had fled, a few now remained, as the sun reached its midday heat but failed to lift the cold. In the suburbs it was as if there were no war. Or perhaps these were merely the suburbs of a war, market stalls offering the wares of wartime, bulbous vegetables transported from some peaceful part of the country. The stump of a huge tree was being slowly chopped with blunt axes, its branches being weighed on a massive pair of scales to ensure that every drop of heat was paid for by weight.

In the bazaar, the eyes of an old woman set in a thin, haggard face caught mine. She was the only woman whose face I had seen since my arrival in Kabul. She passed three other women who were completely covered in a their flowing *byrka,* a cloak falling in faded blue, green, or indigo from their heads down to their feet, broken in its flow only by an intricately woven grille across the eyes and nose and mouth, through which nothing could be seen from the outside. The covered women's hands were gloved, their pace rapid, their world hidden from view. But this other woman was different.

"We have become very poor. Our property was robbed by the last army that came. That's why I'm forced to beg. When the army came to town they looted everything. My house is in southern Kabul and it was completely destroyed, though things are a little better since the Taliban came, only food has become very expensive, for me and my seven children." Poverty completely dominated her life. She stood on the roadside talking to me, breaking all the rules. A woman should not have been seen alone on the street. She should not have revealed any part of her body to any man other than her husband. She should not have spoken with a man who was not known to her. But she talked, while other women scuttled past, the gaze from behind their woven grilles seeming to fall upon her where she stood talking.

"I don't have money to buy a *byrka*," she said. "But nobody creates any problems for me because my face is showing. They think I am weak and poor, so they don't disturb me."

Her presence was a relief from the Taliban's excesses. I had seen a succession of lampposts in the center of the city from which the city's new rulers had hung smashed televisions, which were condemned as agents of decadence and which were destroyed in the street by the young zealots and then strung up by their cables. Women had been beaten in the streets for failing to cover themselves completely, while all women had been suspended from their jobs and female students told that they would no longer be allowed to attend Kabul University. The leadership was about to begin debating whether two 1,500-year-old standing statues of Buddha at Bamian—the tallest in the world—should be pulled down, as they contradicted Islam's ban on statues.

Across the road, beyond a maze of market stalls, was the Ariana money market, a two-story building surrounding a muddy courtyard, where men in groups of two or three stood counting piles of ragged banknotes as they discussed exchange rates and converted foreign currency into Afghanis. From somewhere within the market, a loudspeaker crackled to life. The call to prayer drowned the talk of business. Transactions were rapidly concluded, and some of the men drifted into a room in one corner of the courtyard set aside as a mosque, while others drifted out of the gate onto the street.

There, swinging a long, knotted rope, was the representative of the government department responsible for ensuring that Islamic morals are upheld. With a lunge he brought the heavy knot down onto the back of a man attempting to ignore the call to prayer. A man beside him started to flee, but was caught on the back of the head by the lash. The man wielding it then began to round up all those trying to leave, swinging the rope over his head as he forced twenty or thirty men back through the gate and into the courtyard. Then the road outside was empty, the money market quiet, but for the occasional murmured responses of those at prayer inside.

Mawlawi Abdarab Akhunzada fumbled with a gold pen as he sat at a table large enough to seat thirty or forty people. The thirty-two-year-old second deputy chairman of the central Da Afghania Bank was surrounded by the civil servants who had, until two months earlier, served the Rabbani government as loyally as they were now being expected to serve the young men whose seizure of Kabul had overturned every institution in the city. Akhunzada was discussing whether or not the 250,000 bank accounts held by women would be forcibly closed, taken over by the women's husbands, or left dormant. It would be a decision made by the High Council of the Ulamas, he said, referring to the religious council whose decisions would forge the new Taliban government's religious identity.

"We are going to take special measures for this. First, we are going to see whether we can organize for women to stand in separate queues in the banks. We have a commission that will decide this. Right now the conditions are suitable for that, but for various reasons we aren't in a position to make a decision about this. It will be a decision taken by the higher authorities, and we will do what they say," he said,[35] with calm certainty. Akhunzada said that he had spent twenty-three of his thirty-three years before joining the Taliban movement at a religious school. His education, he said, had not included economics, and it was unclear as to why he had been chosen to reform the central bank.

"It's not only the Holy Koran that must be followed on this, but the other words of the Prophet, the *fiqr*. It needs a lot of scholars who have specialized knowledge to make a decision. It's not clear in the Koran. But the High Council will make any decisions in the light of Islam, because in Islam a person can't give his own views."

Our conversation ended. He silently returned to his adjoining office and his team of male advisers. The bank's four hundred women employees had been suspended on full pay of 200,000 Afghanis per month each while it was decided whether they should be allowed to continue to hold jobs, the religious system having already decreed that women should remain at home.

But the bank official with Akhunzada lingered, gathering his papers. It would be difficult, he said in a low voice, once his youthful and heavily bearded boss had left the room, to Islamize the banking system. Such a system would have to comply with the Koranic ban on the payment or charging of interest on loans, which would significantly reduce bank profits and thereby reduce their ability to lend.

"There's no evidence that it works. It's not a simple task. If they allow women to keep their accounts, then they will have to employ women to serve them in the banks. I was asked to participate in the consultation to make it an Islamic bank. But it will be very difficult. The main difficulty is that, if there is no interest paid by the bank then people won't put their money in it."

A Nation at the Crossroads

The Taliban derides its opponents among the Mujahideen who ousted the Soviet forces by exposing their failure to institute the religious practice of the kind they, the current conquerors of Kabul, view as the only valid version. The religious zeal of the former Mujahideen leader Gulbeddin Hekmatyar is condemned by the Taliban as ineffectual because he lacks the political power to pursue a religious agenda.

Kabul is now under a strict dictatorship. The men of the city smile as they discuss how well they are doing in growing the beards the government has instructed them to wear. Woolen cloaks and embroidered hats have replaced jeans and jackets. Behind the smiles, the change has become entrenched. But despite the extremism of its leaders, the Taliban's ruthlessness is barely out of character with previous Afghan governments. As a response to the lawlessness of the unstable government it ousted, the Taliban can only be viewed as reflective of a widespread realization that anarchy is more unpopular than fanaticism. But for the few who had hoped to pluck the fruits of peace, the coming season looks bleak.

"Afghans had always experienced economic poverty. Now we are moving toward cultural poverty, which is very dangerous." Dr. Amir Hassanyar was experiencing the failure of his efforts to use his chancellorship of Kabul's sixty-three-year-old university to safeguard Afghanistan's intellectual life and prevent its isolation from that of the outside world. The university was largely rebuilt and then reopened under Mujahideen control in 1995, with a student population of 10,000. In February 1997 it was reopened after the Taliban takeover, though only to male students.

> When we reopened the university in 1995, some students came back from Pakistan who had grown up there, in the Pakistani culture. Others came back from Iran. Others were ex-Mujahideen. They are all part of the cultural crisis in Afghanistan. We are losing our Afghan cultural heritage, because they returned with no national pride. Then [when the Taliban arrived], the university was closed, which was a catastrophe. Even before they came, when the [Mujahideen] were in control in Kabul, we had problems. They wanted to separate boys and girls and to influence the subjects we taught. But I knew some of the people in the government, and we were able to overcome.
>
> But the problem for intellectuals remains. We are in a minority. We believe that we cannot live outside human civilization. We believe that the world is moving. But we are not even 1 percent [of the population]. Since 1978 the intellectual stratum has left the country. In this country and society there's no place for them. They are out of place and out of time. We stay out of politics, because it's dangerous for us, but we want an elected government. We want the people of Afghanistan to participate in creating their own destiny. We don't have a nation. It's a tribal society. But we are very proud of our past heritage. We are brave and hospitable. But in the past two decades we have lost what we had.[36]

Outside Hassanyar's office, the remnants of Kabul's intellectual elite had gathered under the leafless trees, waiting to see if the university would be reopened. Hassanyar had said that most of the professors were now to be found in the market, selling potatoes. They all had to report to work once a week, to sign for the pay that they had been told would eventually arrive but that they had not received for the previous two months. A feeling of isolation, of being forgotten, of slipping irretrievably into oblivion, prevailed.

The university is surrounded by devastation. The Rabbani government rebuilt the institution, but the surrounding streets are rubble. Strips of plastic tape flutter in the cold breeze. They mark where the land mines are thought to be. Nobody goes there. There are reckoned to be 2 or perhaps even 3 million land mines scattered across Afghanistan. But there may be many more.

The Battle for Central Asia

The new war has meant that the Great Game, as Rudyard Kipling[37] called the meddling by regional and nonregional states in the affairs of central Asian countries, is now more active than ever. Far from being a one-sided battle with nineteenth-century British artillery in combat against Afghans armed only with determination, the stakes in Afghanistan are in reality higher than they have ever been. With Russia, Iran, India, Uzbekistan, and Turkmenistan now backing the ousted remnants of the Mujahideen once supported by the United States and Pakistan—the latter now regarding the Taliban as the only possible guarantors of Afghan stability—the complexion of the Afghan conflict has been submerged by regional interests.

"The settling of the conflict by agreeing to Pashtun dominance and giving a minor role to the other groups is unlikely because of the role of the sponsors. If the Taliban came into the north there would be tribal bloodshed," said Nikolai Sherchenko, Russia's consul general in the far northern town of Mazar-e Sharif.[38] Eight months later his prediction proved correct, when Taliban forces briefly seized the town and the streets witnessed a particularly vicious bout of slaughter.

If our borders were under threat we would take appropriate measures. And considering the Taliban's actions and their ideology, I believe that they are planning to come here and they are preparing their expansion as far as Samarkand, and we think their coming here would be a threat to the CIS. The Russian role in the region is inevitable, and Russia is consolidating itself, our main interest being to ensure that our main allies in the region are safe. The trade routes to the Indian Ocean would be of great benefit to Russia.

For Russia, the border that the Taliban may not cross is the border with Uzbekistan, where Russia maintains a military presence. That is where I spoke with the consul, who sat behind his desk stroking a small Chihuahua dog as we talked in a barracks house behind the barbed wire of a barren concrete compound.

He rarely makes the two-hour journey to the consular office in Mazar-e Sharif, along a road passing between frozen sand dunes among which huge golden eagles swoop. He prefers the frozen air of the border compound beside the Amu River, from which the last Soviet troops had left Afghanistan a few years earlier. His colleagues, a small team, one of them a great nephew of Count Leo Tolstoy, knew Afghanistan well. They had served there during the Soviet occupation. Now they were back, playing the Great Game again, this time loosely allied with Iran and the former Mujahideen leaders Ahmed Shah Massoud and Burhanuddin Rabbani, who had joined a shaky anti-Taliban alliance with a former communist, General Rashid Dostum.

Russia has ensured that food and other supply routes will remain open into northern Afghanistan. Iran has supplied military equipment to Dostum. India has involved itself in discussions on Afghanistan in an effort to remind its arch rival, Pakistan, that it also carries weight within the regional balance of power. Pakistan remains firm in its support for the Taliban, pursuing its traditional policy favoring the Pashtun—the tribe from which many Taliban are drawn. Islamabad argues that the Taliban have brought security to areas of Afghanistan that, under the Rabbani government, had known only warlordism and chaos. Pakistan, with India to the east, has had to bolster its ally in Afghanistan by attempting to portray the Taliban government as less fanatical and uncompromising than it appears. Pakistani officials characterize Taliban excesses as the result of the country's chaotic condition rather than an innate extremism.

As with the earlier maneuverings of the CIA and the Pakistani regime of General Zia ul-Haq, which had formed the Afghan Mujahideen as an army and sent them into battle, foreign powers are competing in Afghanistan only insofar as their strategic interests are concerned. The question of religious principle is only of consequence because of the role religion has traditionally played in the Afghan political arena. Islam was the ideology that once bound the disparate, tribally based political parties headquartered in Peshawar. But this bond was in fact rarely strengthened by the greater purpose of jihad.[39]

The anti-Soviet jihad allowed Afghans and other Muslims to identify an external enemy, which is an essential element of the holy
war.[40] But the Afghan jihad did not bring with it a strengthening of the
umma, the community of Muslims. Their susceptibility to tribalism
reemerged after victory had been achieved. Even during the course of
the jihad, Roy doubts whether the tribal factions, which had transformed themselves into political parties, had rationalized their intentions beyond that of the main aim of tribal warfare. Rather than seeking centralized state power for themselves, he argues, they sought to
prevent the expansion of their adversaries' power.[41] Jihad, Roy says, "is
an affair between the believer and his God and not between the believer and his enemy. There is no obligation to obtain a result. Hence
the demonstrative, even exhibitionist, aspect of the attacks. It is an
act of faith, the passion of penitents, who are satisfied with nocturnal
fireworks *ad maiorem Dei gloriam*. Jihad is not political."[42]

The apparently deliberate pursuit of inconclusive military activity
is explained as the result of a kind of cowardice. Outright victory by
one party would bring with it the responsibility to create a centralized
state. As the motive for the war is essentially intended to retain tribal
areas and local power, few are prepared to pursue their strategies with
this larger goal in mind.[43]

Afghanistan's anti-Soviet *jihad* was a false dawn for the Islamists,
particularly for the Arabs, despite the very real role it played in bringing them together as a force, which in a variety of ways has since had a
major impact throughout the Islamic world. Perhaps unwittingly, they
had attempted to insert themselves into the politics of an Islamist
movement whose strategy remained rooted in tribal structures, the
fractiousness of which the holy war is supposed to overcome. But after
their departure from Afghanistan, they used their experience to inject
new life into movements elsewhere.

Meanwhile, Afghanistan's headlong plunge into medievalism under
the Taliban has left unanswered the question of whether the strict
pursuit of Islam's rules can forge the Islamic state promised as the re-
ward for religious obedience. The message from Afghanistan's rugged,
war-torn earth bears this out. As I was told in Kabul: "Very few of the
leaders of Afghanistan have struggled for principles. They are struggling for power. So a nation bled, and is still bleeding."[44]

The fallout from that struggle has spread far beyond its borders. Battles now being fought in distant countries have adopted the same terminology. But is it the same war that has since been fought in the villages of Algeria, in the towns of Upper Egypt, or on the streets of
Mogadishu?

2

The Abyss of Darkness
Somalia

TWO DOORWAYS TO THE COURT'S technical room had been cemented up. The light fittings had been ripped out of the ceiling in some long-ago looting spree. The rafters showed through scars in the ceiling where the plaster had crumbled to the floor. A court official took out a sponge to dust off the judge's desk. The audience sat cross-legged on the carpeted floor. The spare-framed, neatly bearded judge, Sheikh Ali Dere, entered and sat with a young guard armed with a Kalashnikov standing behind him, while another guard stood at the door. The judge chewed and spat into the spittoon beneath his desk. The court official told the audience that anybody who did not need to be there should leave. Only witnesses and relatives should stay.

Issa Mohamed Wahiby, the nineteen-year-old defendant, crouched handcuffed on the floor in front of the desk, accused by North Mogadishu's *sharia* court of armed robbery and assault. Beside him sat Hussein Mohamed Abdul Nur, also handcuffed, accused of conning women into buying magic potions supposed to make them attractive to their husbands.

Issa's handcuffs were removed for the hearing, but the security man behind the judge took out a revolver and held it across his chest. Issa, said the prosecutor, had been to the court on three occasions. The previous time, also on a charge of theft, his sentence had been lenient, at least according to the prosecutor: thirty-five lashes. Two other cases were also pending against him.

That day's case had been brought against Issa by a young woman whose scarf he had allegedly stolen, Amina Ali Hassan, who was standing behind him. She was going to present her own case against him. She started crying as she was asked to point out the man who had robbed her. She pointed at Issa, saying, "He held out a knife at me and told me to stop where I was. Then he grabbed my scarf and pointed the knife at my face." She pointed at the sheath of the knife, which was lying on the judge's desk. Then the prosecutor draped the scarf around himself and posed as Amina. Amina played the part of Issa and ran off with the scarf.

"I remind you that the court has forgiven him in the two other cases, hoping that he would change his ways and become a more productive citizen," the prosecutor said, then paused. "Issa," he asked, "What happened? What have you taken from the woman?"

Issa replied: "The scarf. That's the one I grabbed from her."

"Issa," the prosecutor asked, "Do you recognize the sheath?"

"It's mine. I was carrying it," he said, and strapped it around his waist. "I held the sheath in front of her and told her to hand over the scarf. I didn't have a knife. I only had the sheath," he claimed.

The prosecutor called a witness, Said Mohamed Farah, who was told to button up his shirt in court. He pointed at Issa and said that he had apprehended him, and explained that Amina had run to him saying she had had her scarf taken from her by a man with a knife. Said had chased Issa and caught him with a knife, then had accused him of taking the scarf, which Issa had not denied.

Issa bowed his head lower and lower.

"Issa had thrown the knife away," said Said, who further stated that he had had a piece of wood with which to defend himself against Amina's attacker.

The judge asked Issa: "Are you a good Muslim? Do you pray five times a day? Are you fasting for Ramadan?" To all of which Issa replied: Yes.

A second witness was called, who described how he saw Issa throw the knife away. He went on to say that Amina had asked him and the other pursuers to take Issa to the Islamic court.

A third witness was called and was also asked to button up his shirt before giving his testimony. He said that he had not seen Issa holding a knife. Judge Dere then dismissed him, explaining that he was unable to confirm that he had seen a knife, while the other witnesses had seen it. Then Issa himself started to speak, his slit eyes darting from face to face; he confronted the court's hostility with defiance, even courage, as he leaned forward over the judge's desk and harangued him:

"I only fear God. I don't fear any human beings. I captured the lady by threatening her with the sheath. But I had no knife." He picked up the leather sheath from the desk and pointed it at the judge. "Okay, yes I had a knife. But the men who caught me stole 48,000 shillings from me."

Then the third witness interjected: "Actually, when we apprehended Issa last night, he was under the influence. But we didn't take any money from him."

Judge Dere insisted that all three witnesses swear on the Koran that they did not steal from Issa. But Issa's self-defense became more defiant.

"God can cut off my prick and balls if I'm lying that those guys didn't take the money. Okay I was drunk. But what's wrong with drinking? No, I wasn't drunk. I took some drugs and sleeping tablets. Anyway, the man who took the money from me isn't here. I took the drugs because they were tranquilizers and I wanted to sleep. I'd chewed qat^1 and I couldn't sleep, so I took the pills," he shouted at the court.

Judge Dere asked the witnesses to turn to the public. He then asked the public to give their opinion on the credibility of the witnesses. The public replied that they were good citizens.

Issa leaned on the judge's desk, but was told to get his hands off it. A shopkeeper in the audience was asked to assess the value of the scarf. Issa helped the court official hold it up so that the shopkeeper could evaluate it. After some discussion, they agreed that it was three meters long. Then it was passed around the courtroom while the quality of the material was discussed and a value of $1.50 was agreed upon.

Judge Dere entered into discussion with the court officials. He announced that if the value had been only $1.00, then one hand could be amputated. However, as the value was more than $1.00, the case would be subject to further discussion. During this discussion the other accused, Hussein Mohamed Abdul Nur, had his case tried.

Judge Dere then turned to me where I was sitting against one wall of the courtroom and explained:

> If the punishment is severe you should not be astonished. Because in your country you have the problem of racism. So as to not be shocked or even feel sympathy for these criminals, put yourself where Amina was. The law has come from the people. This country has been reduced to rubble because of civil war. Crime went up. Rape was common. Finally we had had enough. And *sharia* means that we can work in all parts of North Mogadishu. Afterward we will see people's reaction to the punishment: if they are unhappy with it, or disgusted, or supportive. And you will see that the punishments fit the crime.[2]

He turned to the two accused. "We believe in mercy. But this man has been given leniency three times. He presents a clear danger to the community and he has testified against himself," the judge said, addressing Issa. Hussein, the con man with the love potions, received a sentence of thirty-nine lashes and imprisonment until he could pay back the money he had extorted. The judge then flicked through the

Koran on his desk. "And for you, Issa, you will have your right hand and left foot amputated."

Issa did not react. Somebody in the audience clapped. Judge Dere asked the audience if they approved of the punishment and they all raised their hands.

Hussein was taken to the sandy parade ground outside the court, where a Soviet-style plaster statue of a couple racing toward the goals of scientific socialism once stood. Now, like all icons, the statue has been toppled for being unislamic and lies as rubble in the sand. Hussein was bound before a gathering crowd and was struck with a stick thirty-nine times before he collapsed onto the sand.

Issa crouched scowling alone in the corner of the courtyard at the back of the court, his slit eyes and slavering mouth perpetually sneering as the court officials prepared themselves.

There was no noise. Tall walls blocked whatever sound there may have been from outside. The court officials beckoned Issa into an empty storeroom, its concrete floor covered in sand and dust. He lay down. Two men wearing white medical coats, their heads bound with white turbans, gently held him down on the floor. A long thin piece of rope was tied around his right wrist, and then extended down to his left ankle. From a wooden box the court official handed the two men two six-inch knives. Very quickly they began simultaneously to saw through Issa's limbs. He did not move, though he once raised up to look at his foot and seemed to grin before lying back down again. The official sawing at his wrist cut away the last piece of flesh within a minute of starting. He lay the hand, which looked like a crab's claw, on the doorstep. But the foot would not give. Issa raised his head, his face expressionless, and peered down again to see his foot attached only by raw tendons. Again he said nothing, then lay back. A jet of blood spurted from an artery. The amputator picked up another knife, which had been lying on the floor, and hacked and then sawed and then finally cut away the last piece of flesh and lay the severed foot beside the hand on the doorstep.

"He didn't even cry," somebody said.

"And they hadn't given him any anesthetic."

Issa was carried out by four men, who held him by the ankles and wrists and took him away in the back of a pickup truck to the hospital. A trail of blood coursed through the lower floor of the court. The hand and the foot were laid beside each other on the steps of the pedestal that had once supported the monument to scientific socialism. People looked on as the hot sun dried the blood that had seeped into the white sand.

Order Out of Chaos

The disorder, both spiritual and social, that was being addressed by the *sharia* court in North Mogadishu is a similar force, according to Islamist scholars, to that to which Allah's message was in its essence applied by the Prophet Mohammed in seventh-century Arabia. Some historians portray that pre-Islamic society as typical of the social reality prevalent throughout the known world at that time[3]—as a medieval, tribally based clan system, in which trade, wealth, and learning nevertheless played their parts. But for the Islamist scholars, the infertility of the Arabian desert is symbolic of the spiritual and religious barrenness that was to be reversed by the birth in Mecca of Mohammed ibn Abdullah in A.D. 570[4] and the spread of Islam from the second decade of the seventh century. Prior to those events, the Islamists argue, tribal conflict dominated political life, while pagan religious practice dominated spiritual life and insecurity prevailed throughout the region.

Chief among the proponents of this view are the Pakistani Islamic scholar and former leader of the Jamaat-i Islami, Sayyid Abul A'la Maududi, and the Egyptian writer Sayyid Qutb, both of whose writings during the mid-twentieth century have influenced the outlook of most late-twentieth-century Islamists:[5]

"Whatever notions they had of morals, culture, and civilization were primitive and uncouth. They could hardly discriminate between pure and impure, lawful and unlawful, civil and uncivil. Their life was wild. Their methods were barbaric. They reveled in adultery, gambling, and drinking. Loot and plunder was their motto, murder and rapine their very habits,"[6] Maududi wrote, until Mohammed, whom he likens to a "diamond shining in a heap of dead stones,"[7] appeared as Al-Ameen, the Truthful and the Trustworthy.

But was it really like that? The question is vital. The influence of Maududi and other writers over late-twentieth-century Islamist movements has been great, particularly regarding the question of perceptions of the past. This question is essential in assessing the relevance of past practices for the present and the future.

The political and social uncertainty of life in pre-Islamic Arabia is not the major issue raised by Sayyid Qutb in tracing the historical passage of Islam, though he asserts that "the life of mankind, under the influence of this welter of [pre-Islamic] confusion, was ground down by corruption and chaos, tyranny and oppression, and hardship and misery. It was a life unfit for human beings, unfit even for a herd of cattle."[8] Nevertheless, for him, faith lies at the heart of the religion's appearance in the lives of the Arabs, life's hardship being worsened by a profusion of "beliefs, concepts, philosophies, myths, superstitions, traditions and customs in which falsehood was mixed with truth, wrong with right, nonsense with religion, and mythology with philosophy."[9] Qutb asserts both the fact of Islam's appearance as a system of law underpinning justice amid the apparent chaos of pre-Islamic Arabia, as well as the satisfaction of man's innate need for religious faith, as the dual gifts the Prophet Mohammed offered the people of Medina. With great clarity, Qutb succinctly condenses his view that these two aspects are in fact indistinguishable, summing up the core of the Islamists' message when he says: "A social system is a product of a comprehensive concept that includes an explanation of the universe, of man's place in it, and of his role and the ultimate purpose of his existence . . . because a harmony between belief and the social system is both an organizational necessity and an intellectual imperative."[10]

Disputing Maududi's representation of the pre-Islamic world, Maxime Rodinson provides substantial evidence that the Islamist scholars of the twentieth century have envisioned pre-Islamic Arabia purely through the veil of Islam's birth.[11] There is an assumption on the part of Maududi, in light of the substantial body of evidence Rodinson presents, that because of the extraordinary event of Islam's appearance, all that preceded it *must* have been begging for an alternative, and that Islam was the phenomenon the people of Arabia had been awaiting.[12] Rodinson in fact gives a very strong impression that pre-Islamic Arabia, while lacking a written code of law, enjoyed an extraordinary degree of security, stemming largely from the fear of reprisal if one group set itself against another.[13] Rodinson writes: "The Arabs certainly did not live in a state of total anarchy for the very good reason that no such conditions have ever existed anywhere."[14] Although this broad claim is doubtful, he presents evidence suggesting that pre-Islamic Arabia was certainly as structured as most other parts of the world known to the Arabs at that time.

The impression that there was a relatively extensive body of accepted social practice—not necessarily law—among the nomadic tribes of the Arabian peninsular in the years preceding the advent of Islam is argued by other scholars. Rodinson emphasizes the degree of social stability prevailing among the Arab tribes before Mohammed appeared. Qutb, however, emphasizes the absence of spiritual refinement and asserts that Islam's emergence was essentially a response to spiritual rather than social needs. William Montgomery Watt takes this argument a step further. Like Rodinson, he portrays pre-Islamic Arabia as structured along tribal lines but ordered by an extensive degree of understanding among the tribes. He also raises the issue of spirituality:

There was some understanding about the area in which a tribe had a right
to pasture, and a strong tribe would maintain its right by force. When a
tribe became too weak to maintain its rights, it could appeal to a strong
tribe for support and protection, and such relationships were common.

The nomadic Arabs are said to have had many gods, but they do not
seem to have meant much to them. They firmly believed that the main
events in a person's life were determined by an impersonal force called
Time or Fate. . . . Their deepest belief seems to have been what might be
called tribal humanism, and this was fostered by the strong tradition of
poetry. . . . There was also what might be called a code of ethics associated with the tribal system. In this, a tribe or clan as a whole was held responsible for the misdemeanors of its members, and the principle of a life
for a life was generally observed. . . . There was also an expectation that
the leading men of a tribe would show some concern for the tribe's
weaker members.[15]

The core of social order lies in the law. The conduct of the *sharia*
court in North Mogadishu reflects the imposition of law on the basis
of an appeal to religion. In areas of Somalia where the *sharia* is not applied, the deterrent element of the law is absent and the legal structure relies upon internal clan discipline, which has largely collapsed.
The establishment there of the *sharia* court system is an innovation,
just as it was in seventh-century Medina. The difference is the absence of the pre-Islamic element—Somalia is a Muslim country, it was
so before the collapse of the state, and those in conflict are of the same
religion though they did not practice the *sharia* before the war. Nevertheless, it is a useful reference if one is looking at the application of
the Islamic *sharia* from social and legal perspectives, as well as at the
practical rationale behind the introduction of a system of law that has
become an article of religious faith.

The fact that neighboring communities share a religion is, as Somalia and Afghanistan have shown, no guarantee against social collapse.
In Somalia, the desire for social order is strong, and Maududi's representation of historical logic—an apparent need met by an appropriate
response—is in many ways more relevant in the Somali case than in
his version of the reality of pre-Islamic Arabia. As a source for the
twentieth-century Islamists' agenda, Maududi's work is relevant to
the social elements of Islamist belief and practice. The reality of Somalia speaks for itself, as does the efficacy of the *sharia*. This is what
makes Maududi an important figure for modern Islamists. The reality
of their lives is such that they, in an atmosphere of social breakdown,
disaffection, political turmoil, and conflict, are seeking to emerge
from the darkness both Maududi and Qutb describe. But these conditions are not, if one believes Rodinson, what Mohammed himself ex-

perienced. The vitality of the message he conveyed on Allah's behalf suggests less a sense of chaos than a sense of mission, less a reaction against what had preceded his receipt of Allah's message than a vision of the future.

The imposition of the *sharia* in certain areas of Somalia[16] illustrates vividly the essentially social goals projected within the Koranic way of life. As portrayed by Maududi, the reality of pre-Islamic Arabia resembles in all ways but one (namely, the pre-Islamic element, as Somalia was Muslim before the current chaos) the collapse of law, civility, and morality prevalent in late-twentieth-century Somalia, whose population is 99 percent Sunni Muslim.[17] Mohammed's specific aim of transcending the political reality of tribalism by inculcating Muslims with a sense of loyalty beyond tribal tradition as a means of ensuring the survival of the Islamic nation—the *umma*—drew the political and religious agendas of Islam into one from the very beginning.[18] The evolution of this process is a key element in the Islamist agenda. The lure of Islam's seventh-century golden age during the lifetime of the Prophet Mohammed, when the Islamic system is reputed to have achieved a perfection that today's Islamists seek to revive, is a theme present in much Islamist writing. It is reliant upon the understanding and interpretation of history projected by writers like Maududi. The French social scientist François Burgat recognizes that the late-twentieth-century Islamists' understanding of their own historical context is subject to significant intellectual shortcomings: "The *Arab* approach to Islamism, better informed, closer to the ground, is naturally less a victim of fantasy than the Western output. Produced locally, its critical potential is certainly much greater. . . . That precious proximity to the subject has nevertheless a scientific cost: its impact on the political landscape, both ethnic and religious, is perhaps also a source of distortion," he says, in reference to the Egyptian writer Fouad Zakariya.[19]

For some historians, the key factor that is ignored by those now aspiring to recreate the Islamic polity as practiced by the Prophet is the fact that Islam has coexisted with other cultures since its appearance in the seventh century. Gustave von Grunebaum describes the modern Islamist's aspiration to recreate the past as "salvation by sameness" in a critique of the work of the Indian Muslim scholar As-Sayyid Abul-Hassan Ali Al-Hasani an-Nadwi.[20] Von Grunebaum accuses an-Nadwi, and by implication other Muslims with this aspiration, of a form of "cultural provincialism," which he says "implies a certain relaxation of creative self-discipline in its directedness toward control of the external world. The loss in scope and depth is to be compensated for by the regained coziness of life in a universe that is thoroughly familiar and amenable to supposedly well-tried rules."[21]

From Unity to Disintegration

Throughout the civil war, Somalia's religious leaders have argued that application of the *sharia* is the sole route by which social order can be restored; they contend that the clan-based political structure, which endured colonialism and dictatorship, has failed to achieve a political resolution on a national level.

The application of Islamic rules in Somalia is less subject to religious debate than debate over the rules' political purpose. If the warlords feel that it threatens their authority, they will forbid it. The more uncompromising critics of the Somali Islamists have occasionally fought them and regularly verbally abused them. These clashes have been due less to anger at the calls being made for a religious agenda than to the fact that the political factions had little to offer that was as attractive to ordinary people as the Islamists' offer of law and, perhaps as a consequence, a degree of order.

In reference to the period of the seventh century known as the Medinese era, when Mohammed and the first Muslims lived in the Arabian city of Medina, Dilip Hiro writes: "By demanding unequivocal acceptance of one God, Muhammad created loyalty which went beyond traditional allegiance to the clan, and this upset the powerful clan leaders, who also resented Muhammad's strictures against their unshared riches."[22] The same can be said about the political reality of Somalia, particularly since the factional leaders have utterly failed to achieve a political solution to the crisis into which the country has plunged. In 1997, Sheikh Ali Dere went on a pilgrimage to the Muslim holy city of Mecca. As of February 1998, he still had not returned to Somalia, though the *sharia* court in North Mogadishu has continued to function. His departure was inspired by his increasing influence, which the factional leader Ali Mahdi Mohamed, in whose territory the court operates, decided was beginning to eclipse his own.

Hiro continues: "The events of early Islam offered precedents upon which subsequent Muslim societies strove to organize themselves. It is to this seminal period of Islam that contemporary Muslims return for answers to such basic questions pertaining to a political-administrative entity as power, legitimacy, relations between ruler and ruled, law and order, and social harmony."[23]

The introduction of the *sharia*, in light of social and political collapse, has to be seen in the context of that collapse. For Islamists from elsewhere in the Muslim world, the application of the *sharia* is only of relevance in a social context, the spiritual element of the religion being of little import.[24] In Somalia, the practical application of Islamic law within a harshly despiritualized environment has emerged out of the chaos. Meanwhile, Somalia's religious leaders, whose awareness of the violence is firsthand, have not refrained from asserting their views, despite possible repercussions from armed bandits, who respond violently to any form of criticism. The voices of the religious leaders do echo those of the first Muslims—if Maududi's version of pre-Islamic Arabia is to be accepted—calling for "order, discipline and modesty in an atmosphere of violence, decadence and lawlessness." Even if one doesn't accept Maududi's version of history, the wish to identify a historical progression, beginning with the emergence from spiritual darkness into a new, more ordered world, is clearly attractive.

In Somalia, the calls for the practice of Islamic *sharia* in the legal system have gained ground throughout the 1990s. Somalia's devolution from a tenuously united nation-state into a war-torn patchwork of fiefdoms controlled by clan chiefs has become Africa's, and perhaps the world's, most vivid example of the devastation bequeathed to developing countries by the end of the Cold War and the termination of the superpowers' strategic interest in the Third World. The process of postcolonial nation building in the opportunistic environment of the Cold War generated experiments with ideologies whose failure brought political catastrophe. The rejection by Islamists of imported Western ideologies, which will be examined more closely in later chapters, has been a key element of their agenda for the past hundred years. What is now under scrutiny is their claim that the application of an ideology that is closer to the traditional faith of the Muslim population—whether in Somalia or elsewhere—can provide a practical, workable alternative to the system it is seeking to replace.

Somalia's recent history is a stark example of how nation building is subject to the twin pressures of tradition and modernity in what ultimately becomes a search for national identity. Throughout his twenty-three-year rule, Mohamed Siad Barre, the Somali president who was overthrown in 1991, exploited the country's geographical proximity to the Middle East as a means of playing the former Cold War superpowers off against each other. During the 1970s he flirted with the Soviet Union, whose military presence in Somalia mushroomed in 1972 when he requested Soviet assistance to contend with the effects of drought and famine. He approved the installation of 6,000 Soviet military advisers in the country and received thousands of tons of military equipment.

In 1974, however, the Soviet Union found that it had a new ideological ally in Ethiopia, with the seizure of power by Haile Mengistu Mariam. Somalia and Ethiopia had long been in dispute over the Ogaden desert, parts of which both claimed for themselves. In return for guarantees of military assistance from pro-Western Saudi Arabia,

Barre expelled the Soviet advisers in 1977, hoping that this move would lead to direct American assistance in his planned fight with the Ethiopians. But the United States was reluctant to provide this assistance, as it believed that such a move would upset Kenya, part of whose northern territory was also claimed by Somalia. In the end no American aid was forthcoming, but Somalia became part of U.S. Persian Gulf strategy, which had been evolving ever since the Soviet invasion of Afghanistan in 1979. In August 1980, the United States signed an air defense pact with Barre, which gave the Americans air and naval facilities at the Soviet-built port of Berbera. The relationship flourished until 1988. Then, Barre, disappointed with the small scale of American assistance, switched sides again, reestablishing his ties with the Soviet Union. He also received substantial weapons supplies from Libya, just before the rebellion led by Mohamed Farah Aideed, which erupted into the ongoing civil war, reached his presidential palace in 1991. At that point, Barre and his remaining followers fled Mogadishu in a column of Russian-built tanks, which roared through the city blasting missiles in all directions, until they reached the village of Afgoy and were out of range of rebel gunfire.

Barre's rapprochement with the superpowers allowed him to manipulate the delicate relationship between Somalia's clans by using money and his overwhelming military might to intimidate, cajole, and abuse his would-be critics. His manipulation of the clans, and the concentration of power around himself and his Marehan clan, created a false unity reliant upon dictatorship. What Somalis have been left with is the transformation of the once functional clan identity into a web of bloody rivalries often on the level of the subclan, exacerbated by desperation borne of psychological and physical insecurity. This in turn has destroyed any semblance of a national polity. It has been accompanied by the presence of thousands of weapons, which have placed authority into the hands of those who are the least capable of exercising it with any sense of what national purpose it may be used for. Somalia is, as Maududi describes pre-Islamic Arabia, an "abyss of darkness."[25]

Only the country's Muslim leaders have remained, in the message they have conveyed, at least partially immune to the daily fact of political disintegration, which has determined the course of events in Somalia. Also, a generally respected class of Somali intellectuals, and the clan elders with whom they have often been identified, have remained the mediators in some intra- and interclan disputes, when the military factional leaders have allowed them to be so. But as the war has evolved, the structure of authority has altered. The factional leaders have usurped the clan elders as political figures, despite the fact that the factions themselves remain clan-based. Only Islam, and its leaders, have remained outside the entanglements of clan politics.

The Islamists Voice Their Message

"Now, the Islamic groups are involved. They are armed and among the people who are supposed to take power one day. Religion is being interfered with. And the [Western] relief organizations—some of the relief organizations—are distributing bibles. And when we see all these foreign troops here, it's like colonial rule. It's preventing Somalis thinking about how they should confront their own problems. The foreign troops should leave. But we know some will be here forever."[26]

Sheikh Mohamed Moalim Hassan, Somalia's most venerated religious figure, sat cross-legged on the carpeted floor of his cool, calm mosque, just off South Mogadishu's Kilometre Four crossroads. For months, beginning in late 1992, I had heard rumors that armed Islamists were attempting either to influence the main factional leaders or to lead their own movements. Central to the Islamist effort was the provision of assistance through the Muslim World League, which had played a key role in Afghanistan and to which many of the Arab Afghans had attached themselves when joining the Afghan Mujahideen. As the Somali famine worsened, having claimed 350,000 lives by mid-1993, the league opened offices in Mogadishu and distributed food aid provided by Saudi Arabia.

"We are doing our best to bring a Muslim government to the country. But if the Muslims are to have a role in the government, they won't make any deals with the military leaders if they refuse to introduce the *sharia*," Sheikh Moalim told me. "Islam is seen as extreme. But if it is going to do harm, then it won't work. The Koran itself has been misunderstood. The Muslim groups have armed themselves and then separated themselves apart. There are no accurate numbers for the size of the armed Islamic groups, but they represent all Muslims."

The armed Islamic groups that emerged on the Somali scene in 1992–1993 were a product of the broader regional political evolution occurring in the Horn of Africa at that time. These groups should also be seen within the context of the events that had shaped Islamist activity over the previous fifteen years.

Both Sudan and Iran became preoccupied by Somalia, partly through a sense of duty to their fellow Muslims and partly in response to the growing American military role there. Both Islamic states viewed the U.S. presence as quasi-imperialistic and as specifically intended to create a buffer against their own Islamic agendas. Iran sent $15,000 worth of relief food supplies—a pitiful amount compared with other aid suppliers—to Somali refugee camps in Kenya in early 1992, while emphasizing that the Somali struggle was an internal affair that had to be resolved by the Somalis themselves, though perhaps with some assistance from the Organization of the Islamic Conference.[27] Similarly, Sudan publicly stressed that it viewed the Somali conflict as primarily an internal dispute, though during 1992 the Sudanese sent 1,000 tons of food and medicine to Somalia.

Sudan, whose own civil war in the south of the country is characterized as a jihad by the Khartoum government, sought influence in Somalia. Baha al-Din Hanafi, director of the political department of the Sudanese president's office in the early 1990s, said:

We saw [the UN intervention in Somalia] as the imposition of the way the U.S. wanted things to be, and it has used the UN to do this. They see a dramatic change coming in the whole area, along Islamic lines. They see what happened in Sudan and what was about to happen in Algeria. So they want to be prepared for it if it happens. They want to be able to influence. They want to stop what they like to call Islamic fundamentalism spreading. Most of the friends of the U.S.—Egypt, Saudi Arabia, Tunisia—are in trouble. When you look closely at the senior foreign policy advisers in the U.S., they see this era as a clash of cultures. They are looking for another "ism."[28]

But Sudan found the potential for its involvement limited and its assertion of influence diminished in the face of the American-backed efforts at reconciliation conducted by the Ethiopian and later Egyptian governments.

In the chaos of late 1992, the identification of external support for the numerous groups preying on the Somali population relied upon the claims of the factional leaders themselves. Both main factions claimed that they had clashed with armed Islamic groups and that these groups were in possession of sophisticated weapons, which they believed had been received from external suppliers.

"The Islamic groups have come to the fore in the past two months. They are strong in the capital and in [the coastal town of] Merka, and were very important in Bossasso. In August they held a secret congress in Merka, which was attended by two Iranians," said General Ahmed Jili'ow, chief of police of the Somali faction led by Ali Mahdi Mohamed, in whose territory the *sharia* court would later be established. "Some Egyptian Muslims were captured in Bossasso earlier this year," he claimed. He also said that Ali Mahdi Mohamed's main rival, Mohamed Farah Aideed, was allied with these Islamic fighters and intended to use them as part of his army.[29]

Aideed himself denied this when I asked him about it, and he was not prepared to name the countries he believed had supplied the weapons to al-Itihad, the Islamist group with which he said his forces had clashed.[30] But after weapons had been found at the former American air base of Baledoglay, southwest of Mogadishu, in mid-1992, General Jili'ow and the faction led by Ali Mahdi claimed that Sudan was involved. They said that the arms had originally come from Iran, following a visit to Sudan earlier in the year by the Iranian president, Ali Akhbar Rafsanjani.

On 9 December 1992, the U.S. assistant secretary of state for African affairs, Herman Cohen, arrived in the Sudanese capital, Khartoum, ostensibly to warn the Islamist government of General Omar Hassan al-Bashir against interfering with the U.S. military operation in Somalia. That mission had been launched at 3:00 A.M. that day, when an advance party of bewildered American special forces troops emerged out of the Indian Ocean surf and landed on the beach at Mogadishu. Their initially discreet operation was recorded by as many as a hundred journalists, myself included, who illuminated their every move with bright television lights and followed their progress over the coming weeks and months. In all, some 19,000 foreign troops arrived to save Somalia from itself and to confront and coerce toward a settlement the leaders of its warring factions, whose conflict had brought famine and national disintegration.

The Arab Army Joins the Fray

"Allah Akbar. Allah Akbar. Allah Akbar." General Aideed raised his fist. The incantation filled the terrace of his Mogadishu house.

It was 11 June 1993. Startling pink bougainvillea gushed in a great cascade over a wall at one end of the first-floor terrace. The soft warm air, the sky as clear as the blue of the Somali flag, the soft sand that had choked Mogadishu's streets, all cushioned the sense of looming catastrophe, as a global army prepared to flee the ferocity of a culture at whose heart lay the determination to defend itself.

The trick was in the sense of calm that afternoon as Aideed, in his neatly pressed white shirt, sat at a table flanked by his allies, Colonel Omar Jess, Issa Mohamed Siad, and Mohamed Awali.[31] He read a prepared statement in which he denied that his supporters had been responsible for cornering, attacking, and mutilating twenty-three Pakistani UN troops four days earlier.

The killings had convinced the United Nations that it must take tough action to prevent Aideed and his followers derailing a $1.2 billion relief program for Somalia. The United States was preparing its military muscle. Four AC-130 Specter military aircraft with computer-guided missiles were on standby in Djibouti. A helicopter assault ship, the USS *Wasp*, awaited offshore, along with three troop carriers transporting 2,300 marines. United Nations staff were being briefed on evacuation plans inside their heavily guarded compound, surrounded by razor wire, watchtowers, and metal detectors.

Over the previous five days, UN troops had come under sniper fire every day. The silent streets oozed with suspicion. The chasm widened between the people of a devastated nation and the people who thought they had come to help, without realizing that they did not know how to. Mogadishu, where I lived for much of 1992–1993, became like nowhere else in the world, as if it were not in the world, such was the yawning depth of misunderstanding, misplaced determination, and vengefulness. Two civilizations faced each other amid the streets of an urban battlefield. One was equipped with a high-technology armory and the wish to create a "New World Order." The other brandished cannons, Kalashnikovs, rocket-propelled grenades—and a knowledge of the streets in which the battle would take place.

After gathering his papers, Aideed led his advisers back through the door of his first-floor apartment. He was calm and quiet, his small, sparkling eyes casting flickering glances over the gathered journalists as they prepared to leave. The midday heat cooled, and the afternoon slowly dimmed into the roseate light of evening. That night, I watched from a rooftop as the American AC-130 Specters began the battle in earnest, firing shells from their computer-controlled Howitzer cannons at compounds on the northern edge of the city, where the U.S. military said Aideed had hidden heavy weaponry. The skyline bloomed with the red flash of explosions until just before dawn. Ten thousand feet above the city, the aircraft firing the missiles hummed somewhere among the clouds. To the gunner, Mogadishu was just a grid on a computerized map.

Fred Halliday's view that "much of what passes for Islam and its associated codes and traditions is a particular, contemporary and arbitrarily formulated set of views, or local tradition dressed up as authoritatively 'Islamic,'" is particularly relevant to the reality of Somalia. Throughout 1993, the elements of a potential jihad gradually fell into place. Aideed's invocation of Allah's assistance, after years of famine and death caused by conflict and anarchy for which he was himself partly responsible, was an appeal to the last remnant of Somali culture available to him. He was about to launch the areas and populations under his control into the bloodiest battle the city had seen since the worst fighting of the civil war more than two years earlier. He was looking for a purpose and drew on the cultural fortitude of the Somalis time and time again. Islam is an essential part of an identity, which had been shattered by years of war. But in fact Aideed was not seeking to politicize Islam. To do so would perhaps have undermined his own position. He could not afford to opt for subservience to the ulama, the religious leaders, as this would have forced him to dilute the primacy of his clan in their struggle for dominance over the other clans. But then the Islamists came to him.

It was not until long after war had been declared on Aideed by the United Nations on 18 June 1993 and then abandoned three months later that Osama Bin Laden, the Saudi Arabian who had played such a vital role in organizing Arab recruitment to the Afghan Mujahideen, announced that some of his former Mujahideen had left their base in Sudan and arrived well-armed in Mogadishu to fight the American-led forces alongside the Somalis in mid-1993.

"The only non-Somali faction to fight the Americans was the Arab Mujahideen brothers who were in Afghanistan," Bin Laden said in 1996.[32] "The Americans knew perfectly well that we were fighting them, and announced that there were non-Somali extremist forces fighting— meaning us. There were successful battles in which we inflicted big losses on the Americans, and we preyed on them in Mogadishu. Aideed denied responsibility, and he was telling the truth about that."

Bin Laden's claim, which he has since repeated, is denied by senior American officials. His first public reference to the American defeat at the hands of Aideed's militiamen did not mention his own followers' direct involvement in the battles in Mogadishu. This first reference was made in August 1996, when he issued a statement declaring jihad against American forces in Saudi Arabia, in which he said:

> Your greatest scandal was in Somalia where, after huge media propaganda over many months regarding American power in the light of the fall of the Cold War, and American leadership in the "New World Order," you deployed tens of thousands of troops in an international force, amongst them being 28,000 American troops, to Somalia.
>
> Nevertheless, after a few small confrontations, where scores of your soldiers were killed and an American pilot was dragged through the streets of Mogadishu, you departed in defeat and humiliation with your dead and injured troops. . . . It became clear as to the extent of your in- abilities and weakness. In fact, the image of your defeat in the three Mus- lim cities of Beirut, Aden and Mogadishu brought joy to a Muslim's heart and delight to those who believe.[33]

Perhaps because they had no firm idea of Bin Laden's activities at that time, American officials did not publicly name him as the strategist behind whatever action his followers may have undertaken in Mogadishu. But as the conflict in the city intensified during the summer of 1993, accusations against Sudan and Iran were made public. The U.S. ambassador to the United Nations, Madeleine Albright, said that intelligence reports had indicated that a "tactical alliance" may have been formed between Aideed, "terrorists based in Sudan and the Iranian government," which had led to Iranian-supplied guns, mortars, and rocket-propelled grenades being smuggled into Somalia from Sudan and, possibly, Kenya.[34]

Bin Laden was based in Sudan in 1993. Only in 1996 did the Sudanese, under intense American pressure, ask him to leave. Neither Bin Laden's nor Albright's claims directly refute the other. Bin Laden does not claim that he sent weapons, only that his supporters were fighting in Somalia, though it may be assumed that his fighters arrived in Mogadishu armed. The United States does not claim that former Mujahideen were fighting their marines—even though Bin Laden claims that they knew this to be the case—but that external Islamist groups and states were providing weaponry.

Aideed was hardly in need of weaponry, having an arsenal—much of it captured from the departing army of Mohamed Siad Barre—that would last him for years, as it did until his death in 1996 and has continued to do for the son who succeeded him. What his troops may have lacked was the skill that the Afghan Mujahideen had gained in their conflict with the Soviet army. Somalia's interclan battles always made maximum use of firepower and had been deadly without being particularly skillful. Then the battle changed, at the very point the Arab Afghans were said to have stepped in. The war that followed culminated in a battle on 3 October 1993 that left at least 300 Somalis and 18 American soldiers dead, as well as hundreds more wounded. Two U.S. military helicopters were shot down. One plunged onto a road, the other into a sandy yard between huts. The following morning, children bounced up and down on the rotor blades of the crippled machine: "Americano," they yelled, as I walked among the debris. On the street nearby thousands of people ambled through the battlefield. A man dragged a piece of corrugated iron folded and tied, and stopped in front of me. He cut the rope. A white body flopped out onto the road. "Americano," the children yelled. The man retied the rope and dragged the body of the dead U.S. serviceman away. The tension rose. The battle was neither lost nor won. A week later, the United States announced plans for its withdrawal from Somalia. Strategies for the country's reconstruction were handed back to the United Nations. The UN itself left in 1995, and Somalia was left to find its own way.

A Land Set Adrift

"There were many systems which failed to solve the Somali situation. Now the UN is going without having solved the problem. And it's through *sharia* that there will be a solution," said Abdi Ali Alasow, the second chairman of the North Mogadishu Islamic court,[35] nodding anxiously as he explained the limited options available to his war-wracked community.

He had prepared the case against the thief Issa Mohamed Wahiby, collecting the evidence, calling the witnesses, and organizing the trial. "Of the fifteen districts of Mogadishu, the seven in the north and two of those in the south are practicing *sharia*," he explained.

> More people are found innocent than found guilty. The court doesn't have its own police, but the public volunteer to bring people. Before the introduction of *sharia* the public didn't know what to do. If somebody denies the charge against him, the procedure takes time. If somebody is caught red-handed it's straightforward. If somebody is caught with a knife and is harassing people on the road, he is brought to court and asked: Have you killed that man? They usually say: Yes. We haven't had anybody who has actually denied committing murder if they are accused of it. If a murderer is brought to court and is told to lift up the Holy Koran and is asked: Do you believe in this book and do you want us to pass judgment in accordance with the Holy Koran? They will say: Yes. We don't have people who say that they don't believe in the Koran. As a Muslim the criminal knows the Holy Koran. He knows the punishments for certain crimes. He knows already that he is guilty. So he comes here knowing he is guilty.

In the first six months after the introduction of the *sharia* in North Mogadishu in August 1994, eight people had their right hands and left feet amputated for robbery with violence, Alasow said. Five hands were amputated for robbery. Three people were executed, two by firing squad and one, a married man, by stoning, for rape. Another was given one hundred lashes for rape but was not executed because he was not married.

"The difference of opinion about *sharia* has been going on since the time of Mohammed. It's in human beings. But hopefully that will soon be overcome, because it is supported by the people. The people who are refusing the *sharia* are those who are leading their people into destruction and theft," Alasow said.

As the introduction of the *sharia* has spread to other parts of Somalia, these differences of opinion have become more complicated. In the southern town of Baidoa, a conflict emerged between the Islamists and secularists, the latter viewing the Islamists' plans as contravening the Somali constitution, to which they hoped to return once the country was rebuilt. For the clan chiefs, the introduction of the *sharia* in

Baidoa threw their traditional power further into doubt, beyond what they had already lost to the factional leaders, as it raised the prospect of two court systems vying for supremacy.[36]

Differences of opinion over the use to which the *sharia* could be put—as a wholly new and permanent legal system or as a temporary stick with which to beat those responsible for the criminalization of Somali society—have reflected the absence of coherence in any of the apparent solutions that have been offered to the Somali population. Among Islamists, the purpose is religious. Among the population, the need is purely social:

> Since the civil war started and property was destroyed, and after all the four years when there was not an organized body that could introduce law and order, and since the people in the country were divided into different factional supporters all with their own selfish ends and among themselves they couldn't agree on one issue for the betterment of the people and knowing that there had been all these problems in the past, it's been seen that *sharia* is the only solution.[37]

Sheikh Shariff Sheikh Muhyadin sat in his well-guarded villa in North Mogadishu, leaning against a wall decorated with paintings of Kalashnikov rifles, military aircraft, and parachutists dropping from the skies. The principal architect of the area's *sharia* legal code, he had received several death threats from the families of those who had been punished in accordance with the Holy Koran.

"After the fall of the government the mental hospital doors were opened. Mad people became free. Thousands of criminals were freed. All the crazy people and professional criminals are among the community. They are still being bad, while the good people have settled down. The good people are good, and the bad people are becoming fewer and fewer," Sheikh Muhyadin said. For him, the new system was there to stay:

> During the civil war we were hostage to the gunmen. Now everyone can move in the streets. Now there's no looting [in North Mogadishu]. That has come as a result of the introduction of *sharia*. And it's something that is going to be followed by the rest of the country. I not only feel that *sharia* has a sound legal basis. I believe that *sharia* can run the entire world. *Sharia* is a good way of solving problems in countries where there are problems. But in the end the whole world will see *sharia* because of the way it guards personal property and security and resolves disputes. That's what people want. There's no way that *sharia* is going to leave. It will stay even after the problems we now face are over.

But is this prescription for Somalia's ills adequate and well founded? In 1993 I was told during a visit to Sudan that such was the growing disarray under the democratic system that the military coup of 1989, which had brought the National Islamic Front (NIF) to power there in alliance with the army, had saved Sudan from becoming like Somalia. This view continued to prevail during subsequent visits I made to Sudan in 1995 and 1997. It was a view applied to the north of the country, which has been spared the devastation of the civil war that has raged in southern Sudan since 1983. The spectacle of Somalia, whose disintegration will take years to repair, had sent shivers through other countries on the Horn of Africa.[38]

The comparison with Sudan is relevant for several reasons. The most important is that it is made by those supporters of the NIF who wish to portray the Islamic elements of Sudan's political program[39] as having saved their country from national disintegration. All Islamists claim that the further the original teachings of the Prophet Mohammed are implemented, the greater the degree of social order.[40] The current practice of the Islamic *sharia* in some areas of Somalia has emerged from an intense cycle of crises, of a kind that few countries ever experience. The crises marked the culmination of a loss of national identity initially stemming from the brutality of Siad Barre's dictatorship and unprincipled flirtation with the ever-willing superpowers, in the interest of maintaining his own power. Later, this loss of identity was heightened by a loss of leadership, a loss of livelihood, and a loss of any form of personal security. Finally, the promise of foreign assistance to revive the country ended in catastrophe and betrayal, borne of misunderstanding and miscalculation on the part of the United Nations, and the failure of the factional leaders to place national needs above clan interests.

The NIF claim that its installation of an Islamic system saved Sudan from Somalia's fate[41] suggests that the Islamic system installed by the NIF in Sudan was itself sufficiently unifying to prevent that disintegration. In fact this is not the case. The Islamic element of the NIF's policy has been largely secondary to its political and security concerns, which are the real sources of its durability. It has suited Sudan's NIF government to legitimize itself on the basis of its Islamic credentials. In practice, it is difficult to distinguish which elements of its policy are born of Islam and which reflect its primary purpose, which is the retention of political power in the face of growing political and religious criticism of its policies by the country's Muslim population.

The convergence of Islamic belief and political power clearly lies at the heart of the Islamists' agenda. In theory it is incorrect to say that because Sudan's Islamist government relies heavily on the physical instruments of political power, and less obviously on the ability to attract support through its beliefs, it is therefore less Islamic and more political. For the Islamist, the two are indistinguishable.[42] But in reality, the ability to attract support to the Islamist cause requires a degree of political conviction that is detached from the question of pure religious faith. Most Muslims are not Islamists. In Somalia, the strict imposition of Islamic law has emerged for want of a better alternative, many of which have been tried and have failed on a grand scale. In Sudan, on the other hand, it was not stronger faith that saved the country from the Somali experience. Faced with political instability, the army staged a coup in 1989, dismembering the democratic system and centralizing power within an alliance of military officers and the NIF.

The credibility of the NIF's religious credentials, and therefore the claim that faith rescued Sudan and may yet have the power to rescue Somalia, will be examined in Chapter 7. But as Somalia remains wracked by political instability, the power of the faith to heal political wounds seems limited and the belief in a resurrection of the golden age of the Islamic past a delusion. The political resources available to the Islamists would seem to be much more potent than the religion they have attempted to co-opt. Political need overrides religious conviction, whether in Sudan or Somalia. So, how do these two elements of the Islamists' agenda relate? History lies at the heart of any explanation. This history opens with the arrival of European colonialists in the heart of the Islamic world. Today, this is nowhere more vividly illustrated than in the graffiti-daubed urban alleys, fear-wracked villages, and bomb-scarred towns of Algeria.

3

The Torn Heart

Algeria

"THE CRISIS THAT EXISTS is a crisis for everyone, because the Algerian personality was stolen. For years they uprooted that personality. It's that which has plunged us into this. The struggle is to find the Algerian personality." Bentounes Kelim Mourad, a member of the Sufi[1] Muslim community at the Zaouia Alaouia Sufi center, watched the sun sink at the end of the street at Mostaganem in western Algeria, where we stood talking.[2] The town was silent. The Sufi center was on a dusty backstreet. A heavy wooden door hid a cloistered courtyard where a fountain trickled. We had eaten sweet cakes and drunk hot tea in the cloister. For a few hours the hell of Algeria had seemed to recede.

Outside, silent people moved along the silent streets. In doorways, inside dark shops, leaning from windows, people watched and waited, without speaking. The battle for the heart of Algeria, the war launched to find the Algerian personality, which has left 70,000 people dead, was characterized more by silence than by the clamor of fighting. An all-pervasive fear had silenced the town. The years of bombs, ambushes, and slitting of throats interrupted the silence, a silence spent awaiting the violence.

"In the end we are all looking for that same thing. The Algerian personality," said Bentounes. The question hanging in the air was whether there had ever been such a personality. Was it not founded on conflict with all those who had disrupted the country's evolution—the armies that, since the consolidation of Arab power in the region in 710, had imposed their will, brought their religion, their culture, their class system, their own myths and rites? From within their cloister, the Sufis could see an entire country searching for itself. Their historical perspective was bound up in their understanding of their own role and that of their religious predecessors, who had in the past entwined Sufi religious practice with resistance to foreign domination.[3]

The crisis in Algeria has now, in 1998, reached a point where the history from which the conflict stems appears increasingly disconnected from the conflict itself. Whereas those with historical knowledge choose to believe that the Algerian personality can be found in the chapters of a history that has already been written, their opponents view the past as a compromise, history as a crime, and the future as an empty page that the past cannot be allowed to blemish. Although Algerians may be looking for their country's personality, the war has torn the past to shreds. Algeria's evolution, which in 1962 saw an end to 133 years of French colonial rule after a vicious 6-year civil war, followed by almost 30 years of one-party totalitarian rule and finally the creation of a democratic system in 1991, has ground to a halt.

The crisis in part stems from a determination to refight old battles. But to what end? The Islamists say that it is to free Algeria from the legacy of colonial domination, which they view as ongoing through the influence of a political and military elite that even now remains bound to French business and political interests. This elite, protected by the security forces that seized power in 1992, views the Islamist movement as a manifestation of the negative effects of past failures. The movement itself has brought together anti-French intellectuals, the unemployed, militant veterans of the Afghan war, and Islamic leaders determined to reverse the French colonial practice of co-opting religion to bolster the power of the secular political establishment. The war should be seen as being fought between the conflicting legacies of foreign domination, all of which have formed part of the country's modern identity. Algeria is fighting itself because it does not like what it is.

"Algeria Is My Country"

French colonialists viewed Algerian Islam as a scourge that had to be neutralized, diluted, co-opted, and allowed to wither. At a famous debate at the Sorbonne in 1883, the French writer Ernest Renan asserted that anybody with even a limited knowledge of current affairs could see that Islam was clearly an inferior religion that had produced decadent rule and a narrowness of vision that he claimed was caused by a "ring of iron about the head rendering Muslims absolutely closed to scientific advances, and incapable of either learning or opening themselves up to new ideas."[4] The Grand Mosque of Algiers was converted into the Cathedral of Saint-Philippe. A cross and a French flag replaced the crescent moon on its minaret.

The Islam with which the French colonialists in Algeria were to contend was at its heart a *popular* version of the religion, varying widely with Arab orthodoxy through its widespread veneration of Muslim saints[5] and the Sufi mystics whose living presence among Algerians had invested the religion with a strong local flavor. Just as important, the Sufi leaders had, through many generations, acted as mediators between the population and the succession of foreign rulers who had incorporated the Maghreb into their empires, particularly during the three hundred years of Ottoman rule, which drew to a close when the French arrived in 1830.

> This *popular Islam,* which did not explicitly dissent from orthodox Islam, ranged from the variety of Sufi brotherhoods and orders *(tariqas)* present in the Maghreb through to the more unorthodox marabouts[6] or "living saints." The Sufis, with their emphasis on the more mystic expressions and experiences of Islam, and maraboutism, which involved veneration of the lives and deeds of certain individual Muslims supposedly blessed with divine grace *(baraka),* together gave a less scripturalist and orthodox dimension and hue to Islam in the Maghreb.[7]

French attempts to co-opt the Muslim establishment in urban Algeria during the colonial period were partially successful. But this policy alienated many rural Algerians, swelling the membership of the Sufi sects, as the establishment came to be associated with the colonial power. Over time, however, the colonial administrators succeeded in neutralizing the political impact of even the rurally based Sufi sects. The medium- and long-term effect of this process was startling and was mirrored elsewhere in the Islamic world. As Muslims saw their religion confronted by the awesome power of the colonial occupiers, their response became increasingly inward looking. But far from attempting to strengthen the *popular* religion, they sought to clarify and reform it from within.

The unorthodoxy of the Sufi brotherhoods and the marabouts was addressed and ultimately condemned by the organization that emerged out of this period of introspection—the reformist Association of Algerian Ulama (AUMA),[8] founded in 1931 with the motto "Islam is my religion, Arabic is my language, Algeria is my country." The organization stressed its preoccupation with "moral education" and stayed out of politics. It turned on what it viewed as the unorthodox religious practices then prevalent in Algeria, arguing that maraboutism and the veneration of mystic saints denied the individual a direct relationship with God, which is a central pillar of Islam. The AUMA sought a return to Islamic orthodoxy as the centerpiece of its reformism. Although it avoided clashes with the French colonial power, its aim of reestablishing Arabic as the primary language of education had, by 1933, convinced the French that the group's demand for orthodoxy "hides a pernicious orientation."[9] The French took measures to stem its growing influence. Between 1937 and 1940, the group's leaders were arrested, its organization placed under close scrutiny, and its educational establishments subjected to closures. Consequently, the AUMA began coordinating its activities with other organizations, notably the Algerian Communist Party, and by the outbreak of World War II had shed its apolitical stance.

The effective coordination of Algerian anticolonial organizations, and the weakness of the colonial administration following the occupation of France by Germany in 1940, meant that by the end of World War II the ground had already been laid for the liberation struggle that would, in 1962, bring about Algerian independence. The alliance of politics and religion in colonial Algeria between 1940 and 1962—an alliance that had been anathema to the once rigidly apolitical AUMA—was a clear and vital sign of how the experience of colonialism had contributed to the politicization of the Islamic movement there. The collision between the cultural and educational agenda of the AUMA, and the "mission to civilize" that lay at the heart of French colonialism, was inevitable. Despite having advocated noninvolvement in politics, the AUMA's leader, Abd al-Hamid Ibn "Ben" Badis, who died in 1940 before the organization's political activities became overt, understood this when he wrote in the movement's newspaper, *Shihab*, in 1936:

> History has taught us that the Muslim people of Algeria . . . have their history, illustrated by noble deeds; they have their religious unity and their language; they have their culture, they have their customs. . . . The Muslim community is not France; it cannot be France; it does not want to be France. Its population is very far from France in its language, its life and its religion; it does not want to incorporate itself into France. It possesses its fatherland whose frontiers are fixed, and this is the Algerian fatherland.[10]

The article was written as a rebuttal to another article that had been written by a leading campaigner for Algerian assimilation into French culture, Ferhat Abbas, who had denied the existence of an Algerian identity and promoted the view that only the paternalistic protection of the French could facilitate the slow emergence of an Algerian identity.

The outbreak of the war of independence in 1954, and the establishment of the National Liberation Front (FLN) as the embodiment of Algerian anticolonial aspirations, led to the absorption of the Islamic reform movement by the political-military resistance movement. Consequently, the FLN, which was essentially a socialist movement, adopted a religious guise conferred upon it by the authority of the AUMA, depicting its fighters as Mujahideen and declaring as its aim "the restoration of the sovereign, democratic and social Algerian state within the framework of Islamic principles."[11] Younger members of the AUMA took the lead within the organization. In April 1956, Tewfik Madani declared the AUMA's formal support for the FLN in Cairo and disbanded it as a separate organization in 1957.

In view of colonialism's impact on all areas of Algerian life, it inevitably remains at the heart of the debate over the country's identity, which is today raging as virulently as it did during the war of independence. Algeria's history is a history of exposure to extremes: colonialism, war, totalitarianism, and more war. Its national characteristics have all emerged during periods of conflict, either political or military. The Islamic agenda has emerged out of this uncertainty as consistent with the reformist religious trend, which rooted itself in the disbanded AUMA and reintroduced religious orthodoxy as a way of strengthening Islam in the face of colonialism.

But the question remains as to whether Islam would ever have emerged onto the political scene at all had the colonialists not attempted to eradicate the indigenous culture of which it was so clearly a part. Although Islamists argue that political Islam has its roots in the religion itself, the Islamist movements of the twentieth century are the product of colonial history. Throughout the twentieth century, the consequence of colonial policy was the reform, refinement, and politicization of Islam. Far beyond Algeria, the imperialist West sought, to varying degrees during the nineteenth century, to rule the Islamic world, which had, according to Edward Said, "come to symbolize terror, devastation, the demonic, hordes of hated barbarians."[12]

Empires of the Orient

Algeria's war of independence (and the fury that has been unleashed since the early 1990s as a legacy of that failed liberation) brought together movements within the French colony whose separation the colonialists regarded as essential in order to guarantee European primacy. What was or was not "Algerian" came to be regarded as such because of the divisive presence of the colonialist. Islamists, nationalists, tribalists: the war of independence brought them together. By combining these movements, the advocates of independence shook a central pillar of colonial rule, which had always been the assumption that the subject population, through its disunity, through its weakness, through its general inferiority, could not unify and therefore had no credible aspiration to political power.

European colonial policy toward the Islamic world, the entirety of which came to fall within the imperial aspirations of one European power or another between the early nineteenth and early twentieth centuries, evolved as the nature of the contacts between the two worlds altered. European awareness of the Orient[13] had its historical roots in the myths, legends, and folk memories of the medieval Crusades, which characterized the Mohammedan[14] as a sly and fiery warrior determined to subject the peoples of Europe to military conquest. But during the European renaissance of the fifteenth and sixteenth centuries, Europeans celebrated the intellectual achievements of the Islamic world, in particular its science and architecture. Meanwhile, trade, travel, and political alliances across the Mediterranean brought familiarity that inevitably diluted earlier prejudices. By the eighteenth century, the English diarist Samuel Johnson was able to write: "There are two subjects of curiosity—the Christian world, and the Mahometan world. All the rest may be considered barbarous."[15] In 1700 the first accurate translation of the Koran was published in English, and English writers portrayed the Prophet Mohammed as highly intelligent, well-bred, and undoubtedly inspired by genuine piety.

Inevitably, variations developed within the European intellectual community as it sought to understand Islam. Albert Hourani portrays the academic world's study of Islam as varying along lines often dictated by the writers' attitudes toward Christianity: "There was a tendency to use the career and mission of Muhammad as an oblique way of criticizing Christianity, at least in the form in which the churches had taught it. Muhammad could be shown as an example of the excesses of enthusiasm and ambition, and his followers as examples too of human credulity; alternatively, he could be seen as preaching a religion which was more rational, or nearer to a purely natural faith, than Christianity."[16]

But Hourani also concludes that, over time, the European academic understanding of Islam, which Edward Said views as having in a largely cynical manner served to underpin the European colonial adventure, broadened. Hourani concludes that the academic study of Islam, which was subsumed in the broader discipline of orientalism, generally accepted "that Islam, as articulated in laws, rituals and institutions, has provided a norm which affects societies where it has been the dominant religion, but the nature of any particular society can only be explained in terms of the interaction between this norm and the specific traditions and situation of that society, and even the norm itself changes in different times and places."[17] Hourani broadly rejects the idea that in their pursuit of the academic discipline of orientalism, European scholars helped create the conditions within which politicians were then able to frame their colonial policies. He uses the examples of German and Austrian academics, whom he regards as having been the leaders in the orientalist field during the nineteenth century but whose countries had little or no imperial interest in the Islamic world.

However, the purpose of orientalism is not explained by a rebuttal of its alleged political role. Edward Said views the entire discipline as embodying the assumption that it is the study of a world that has ceased to evolve. By implication, such a world could be made at least to appear ripe for colonization:

> Of itself, in itself, as a set of beliefs, as a method of analysis, Orientalism cannot develop. Indeed, it is the doctrinal antithesis of development. Its central argument is the myth of the arrested development of the Semites. From this matrix other myths pour forth, each of them showing the Semite to be the opposite of the Westerner and irredeemably the victim of his own weaknesses. By a concatenation of events and circumstances the Semitic myth bifurcated in the Zionist movement; one Semite went the way of Orientalism, the other, the Arab, was forced to go the way of the Oriental. . . . Each time tent and tribe are solicited, the myth is being employed; each time the concept of the Arab national character is evoked, the myth is being employed. The hold these instruments have on the mind is increased by the institutions built around them. For every Orientalist, quite literally, there is a support system of staggering power, considering the ephemerality of the myths that Orientalism propagates. The system now culminates in the very institutions of the state. To write about the Arab Oriental world, therefore, is to write with the authority of a nation, and not with the affirmation of a strident ideology but with the unquestioning certainty of absolute truth backed by absolute force.[18]

Although individual scholars may not have delivered their conclusions to the various colonial governments of nineteenth-century Europe with the conviction that their work should be used to expand the borders of Christendom, the British empire, or the French-speaking world, Hourani responds to Said by portraying the orientalists more charitably, asserting that Said "makes the matter too simple when he implies that this [orientalist] style of thought is inextricably bound up with the fact of domination, and is indeed derived from it."[19] The study of religion and language was facilitated by the orientalists' examination of Islam, Hourani writes, allowing history to be pieced together into phases, in which the rise of Islam played a part.

The prejudice—racial, religious, and cultural—that Said sees at the heart of Western views of Islam evolved, over the course of several radical turning points, as the relationship between Europe and the Orient shifted. Fred Halliday does not believe that it is accurate to view early medieval "anti-Muslimism" as having been sustained from the time of the Crusades throughout the succeeding centuries.[20] Equally, orientalism "in Said's usage acquires an almost metaphysical power to pervade very different epochs and genres of expression; in so doing it loses analytic or explanatory purpose."[21] Halliday attributes greater strength to the Arab and Islamic worlds than Said, investing the region with its own dynamism that refuses to allow Western stereotypes to prevail. Historically, it is impossible for Western medieval prejudice to prevail in modern times: "The thesis of some enduring, transhistorical hostility to the Orient, Arabs, the Islamic world, is a myth, albeit one . . . which many in the region and in the West find it convenient to sustain."[22]

The myth has been sustained. Historical circumstances have ensured as much. Halliday himself provides sufficient evidence of this, citing examples from the postcolonial era that reveal the extent to which this prejudice has festered and found its voice in the nationalist wars that have characterized the conflicts of the post–Cold War era.[23] Equally, Said demonstrates that this prejudice—myth or not—is renewable, depending on circumstances, but that it has a common root across the centuries:

> One aspect of the electronic, postmodern world is that there has been a reinforcement of the stereotypes by which the Orient is viewed. Television, the films, and all the media's resources have forced information into more and more standardized moulds. So far as the Orient is concerned, standardization and cultural stereotyping have intensified the hold of the nineteenth-century academic and imaginative demonology of the "mysterious Orient." This is nowhere more true than in the ways by which the Near East is grasped. Three things have contributed to making even the simplest perceptions of the Arabs and Islam into a highly politicized, almost raucous matter: one, the history of popular anti-Arab and anti-Islamic prejudice in the West, which is immediately reflected in the history of Orientalism; two, the struggle between the Arabs and Israeli Zionism, and its effects upon American Jews as well as upon both the liberal culture and the population at large; three, the almost total absence of any cultural position making it possible to identify with or dispassionately discuss the Arabs or Islam.[24]

Beyond the academic study of Islam, honed by nineteenth-century European academics into the discipline of orientalism, the progress of history—perhaps, as Hourani sees it, placing the rise of Islamic civilization as the post-Roman, premodern European phase—timed the arrival of orientalism as an academic discipline to coincide with the de-

cline of Islam as a political force. The heyday of Islamic empires had
long disappeared by the time the Koran was translated into English. Islam, in the eyes of Europeans as much as in the eyes of those who
would reform it from within, was weak. "The degree of stagnation of
official Islam can be judged by the fatwa issued by the Mufti of Cairo's
Al-Azhar early in the nineteenth century," says Dilip Hiro, referring
to a demand by the leader of Egypt's Muslims to abide by the dictates
of the religious hierarchy. According to Hiro, the fatwa was as follows:

> The four orthodox schools are the best results, the finest extraction of all
> schools, because they count among their partisans many men dedicated
> to the search for truth and blessed with vast knowledge. Deviation from
> these four schools shows the desire to live in error. . . . No one denies the
> fact that the dignity of *ijtihad*[25] has long disappeared and that at the pres-
> ent time no man has attained this degree of learning. He who believes
> himself to be *mujtahid* would be under the influence of his hallucina-
> tions and of the devil.[26]

The Mufti was asserting the primacy of the status quo at a time
when Islamic societies had rarely been weaker. Hiro regards the infil-
tration of Western "secular ideas and practices" and political models
into the political makeup of the Islamic world as responsible for its
"dilution and corruption."[27] His view echoes that of the most influential Islamist thinkers who emerged during the rise of European colonialism, who sought to reform and strengthen Islam in the face of imperial expansion.[28]

The politicization of Islamic reformism, as experienced in Algeria,
is widely regarded as having its source in specific colonial policies.
Secular government, as practiced by the colonial powers, was regarded
by Muslims as a tool of repression rather than as a guarantee of rights:
"[Secularism] more than anything else served to guarantee the rights
of outsiders brought in [by the colonialists], or those non-Muslim mi-
norities, Christians or Jews, upon whom the foreigners leaned to establish their domination," writes Burgat.[29] Even where the Algerian
assimilationists sought to benefit from the French education they had
enthusiastically received, the colonial power denied them the fruits of
their effort, discrediting the indigenous secular movement by refusing
to make any greater concessions to them than to the Islamists.[30] The
French policy of appropriating large tracts of land, and the centraliza-
tion of the administration in towns, heightened the importance of urban centers, in which the reformist trend of the AUMA became
strongest, thereby greatly expanding popular exposure to the Islamic
reformers at the expense of the rurally based *popular Islam*. "There
can be no doubt that, however profound the Islamic identity of the in-

dividual and community level remained, it was the disruptive nature of French colonial policy that ultimately provoked the aggressive re-assertion of an indigenous Algerian identity with strong ties to native Islamic culture."[31]

As Islam reformed from within and colonialism reached the peak of its power, the Islamic world regarded the arrest of its own decline as an essential turn of events with which to seize the political initiative. The first stage was the reversion to Islamic orthodoxy. The second stage, which I shall look at more closely in Chapter 4, saw Muslims who favored assimilation with European culture overshadowed by those who realized that such accommodation was impossible while the political reality of colonialism prevailed in all its inequality. The third stage saw Islamists take the political path—in defense of culture, in defiance of assimilation—along which they have been traveling ever since.

The Road to Catastrophe

The airport police were suspicious. They had not known of my arrival in advance. They expected to know everything in advance, to plan, to control, to observe, to influence. All for my own safety, they would tell me later. Embassy officials in Rabat, the city where I lived in 1995 and 1996, had said that I should give them my flight number before I left Morocco for Algiers, so the authorities could be ready for me when I arrived at the airport. Instead, I made my own way, keen to avoid falling into anybody's hands for at least the first few hours after my arrival. The police yelled into their radios, angry at this lapse in their organization. I waited for half an hour. The other passengers from the Royal Air Maroc flight passed into the sun outside the airport terminal. I told the police I would find my own way to Algiers, but they told me to wait. In a gloomy office filled with cigarette smoke a telephone rang on a desk littered with empty tea glasses. Still nobody from the foreign ministry was available to meet me. I said I was leaving for the city. There was nothing they could do but instruct me that I must stay at the Hotel Aurassi. I walked out into the morning sun and found a taxi parked beyond the giant concrete blocks intended to deter car bombers from approaching the building, which had been bombed in August 1992.

"You should sit in the front of the car," the cabdriver told me. "Because when the French were here they would always sit in the back. So, if you sit in the front, from a distance it will look as though you may be Algerian. That'll look better if there's a terrorist checkpoint."

With this advice heeded, I asked him to take me to the Hotel Saint Georges.

"The freedom fighters will not allow there to be an election."[32] The words of the Islamic Salvation Front resonated as I drove out onto the motorway that morning in early November 1995, three weeks before the presidential election. I could only wonder if this threat would be carried out, reconciling it with the reality of the tortured nation unfolding beyond the window of the Peugeot as it sped beneath pedestrian walkways daubed with the fading letters: FIS.[33]

Three months earlier, the military government had begun preparations for the election, scheduled for 16 November, by which it hoped to legitimize the coup that had brought it to power. More than five years earlier, on 12 June 1990, the first stage of Algeria's move away from one-party rule under the FLN had revealed the extent of Islamist influence. The FIS had seized control of 853 of Algeria's 1,539 communal councils as well as 31 of the 48 *wilayas,* or district councils, in the first multiparty local elections to have been held since protests had forced the government to lift a 30-year ban on multiparty politics.[34] Eighteen months later, on 26 December 1991, in the first ballot of elections for the national legislature, the FIS confounded the expectations of the army, the government, and the other opposition parties by capturing 47 percent of the vote, giving it outright victory in 188 of the 231 seats in which there would be no second ballot.[35] This compared with 16 seats for the ruling FLN. The remaining seats, in which no candidate had achieved 50 percent of the vote, were to be subject to a second ballot between the two leading candidates in each constituency.

As the results of the first ballot emerged,[36] it became clear that the FIS was within 5 percent of an overall majority in many of the seats that would be contested in the second ballot, scheduled for 16 January 1992.[37] The intervening three weeks saw Algeria's senior military officers come to the realization that they could soon be at the behest of an FIS-led government. It was a prospect they were determined to avert. Using a selective understanding of the constitution as their weapon, the officers convinced President Chadli Benjeddid—who had made it clear that he was prepared to work with the FIS if they won control of the parliament—that he should resign. The officers, led by the defense minister, General Khaled Nazzar, secured Chadli's resignation on 10 January 1992, only after Chadli had also been convinced that he should dissolve the national assembly. The army's aim was to prevent its Islamist-leaning president, Abdelaziz Belkhadem, from becoming interim president after Chadli's resignation, as the constitution allowed.

The military had intended that a politician less tolerant of the FIS— the president of the constitutional council, Abdelmalek Benhabyles—

would become interim president. They had understood this to be constitutionally correct in the event of the president's resignation if, as they planned, the national assembly were suspended. Benhabyles refused the post, however, on the grounds that he could only assume it if the president died. Such was the military's confusion that Chadli eventually handed power to the High Council for Security[38] (HCS), also a constitutional body, but one limited to providing the president with advice on security issues and certainly not invested with the power to run the country.

The HCS gave itself the power to appoint a president, and on 11 January President Chadli publicly announced his resignation made the previous day. On 12 January tanks rolled out onto the streets of Algiers. The HCS canceled the second ballot for the legislative elections on the grounds of the "impossibility of continuing the electoral process until necessary conditions were achieved for the normal functioning of institutions."[39] A five-man collective leadership was appointed as the public front of the military regime, under the name of the High Committee of State (HCE). This group was headed by a former hero of the war of independence, Mohamed Boudiaf,[40] who had long been in exile and could perhaps project an image not tainted by the corruption of the former one-party regime. By the end of January, the FIS's key leaders had been arrested. The army began replacing the imams of the 8,000 FIS-controlled mosques in the country, and on 8 February the interior minister began moves to have the FIS dissolved on the grounds that it had attempted "insurrection against the state."[41] On 17 February the regime established five detention centers in the Sahara desert, housing up to 30,000 FIS activists (according to the FIS);[42] the group was formally dissolved as an organization on 4 March.

The rise of the FIS had begun four years earlier, in 1988. Social unrest had been building up as far back as 1985. In 1986, as many as 75 percent of all Algerians between the ages of sixteen and twenty-five were reckoned to be out of work.[43] Several factors contributed to this. The high birth rate had led to the population increasing from 18.3 million to 21.6 million between 1980 and 1984.[44] By the end of the decade, 70 percent of the population was under thirty,[45] a vital factor in turning deprivation into militancy. Although President Chadli had attempted to introduce economic liberalization during the 1980s, his aim of using oil and gas revenues to cushion the blow of rising unemployment failed when a price slump caused energy revenues to fall in 1985–1986, leaving national income $5 billion below projections.

The FIS drew its ethical inspiration from the Koran, but its real role during the late 1980s was as a social movement able to articulate the discontent among the rapidly growing section of the population that was bearing the brunt of the worsening economic hardship. "The FIS is not a religious movement, strictly speaking. Rooted in the social discontent that has been expressed in urban violence since 1985, the FIS gives political form to an emergent social movement."[46] The FIS, as the local election results of 1990 and the first legislative ballot showed, enjoyed massive support. Its role as a social movement contributed to this. However, its ability to provide welfare depended, before 1990, on the financial support provided to it by individuals. Until it took control of local councils, it did not have a state budget to spend on social projects. Nevertheless, it was able to assist thousands of deprived people by dispensing funds raised through donations.

Just as important, in particular to the thousands of people of the older generation who provided the FIS with its financial backing, was the role it played as a source of credibility for the Algerian state. "The state is perceived as a political entity that confiscated independence by reappropriating for itself the historic role of the 'real people' to establish its power. Placed in the position of a contestant, the state cannot function as the regulator of social conflicts," Meriem Verges writes. The FLN, which by the late 1980s had become a corrupt mutation of the liberation movement that had, largely voluntarily, subsumed all other interests—including the Islamist movement in the form of the AUMA—in the pursuit of independence during the 1954–1962 war, simply became an elite, incapable of forging genuine social cohesion. "Support for the FLN in the 1950s and the FIS in the 1980s rests on similar foundations: an identity defined by religious belief, an organic representation of society, and demand for social justice. . . . The FIS, by inserting itself into this troubled structure, was able to represent a large group of atomized individuals."[47] Meanwhile, Algerian lay civil society never met the challenge that the crisis required of it, as the FIS emerged in the late 1980s. The Union Générale des Travailleurs Algérien, once the sole trade union in Algeria, was barely able to mobilize people on the scale it had managed during the early 1980s, when it had claimed 3 million members. The military wanted to mount a broad campaign against the Islamists, but in fact tightly controlled the means by which lay society could do so, by controlling the press. The Algerian intellectual class used the French press to communicate: "There it was, the entire problem: the opportunity for that class to see that the degree to which they could communicate with their own society was close to nil."[48] Meanwhile, the social role pursued by the FIS formed only part of its agenda, as its power increased and the ambitions of its supporters grew.

"Between 1988 and 1992, around a thousand Algerians returned home from Afghanistan, even before the crisis started," said Karim

Omar, the Syrian ex-Mujahideen who established close ties with the Algerian Islamist movement after the 1992 coup.[49] These returnees accounted for around half the Algerians who had originally gone to Afghanistan during the 1980s. The return of the Arab Afghans injected several elements into the Algerian Islamist political scene. Despite the FIS having secured the largest share of votes in all the elections it had contested, the possibility that it would have to seek support from other parties to secure a majority of parliamentary seats still remained. "The FIS would have to share leadership with other, non-Islamic parties, which would work together to destroy the Islamic element in the FIS program, and then there would be another election," said Karim. "This fear led to a new strategy among the militants. The militant leaders took several thousand people from the FIS, and took them to the desert," where they underwent military training.

Even before the January coup, armed Islamist groups had begun forming outside the auspices of the FIS, which had retained its commitment to the democratic process that had brought it to power. After the coup, the disparate groups that emerged drew on several Islamist strands. First were the remnants of the Takfir wa Hijra, literally "Expiation and Rejection," a movement that had been active in Algeria during the mid-1980s and evolved into what became known as the Mouvement Islamique Armée or MIA.[50] Second were the remnants of the FIS who had remained at large following the arrests of January and February 1992. Third were the Arab Afghans, several of whom were already to be found within the FIS in early 1992. By 1993, the Islamist organizations that had retained a commitment to the democratic process curtailed by the military coup saw their influence increasingly overshadowed by the appearance of a new organization that from the outset rejected the democratic path followed by the FIS and sought power purely through armed struggle. This was the Jaamat Islamiyya Mousalaha, the Armed Islamic Group or GIA.[51]

Battle for the Soul of a Nation

Narrow streets wound up the hill upon which Algiers rose out of the Mediterranean Sea. Even during the bright mornings the sun failed to breach the cool gloom thrown by the shadows of the tall, elegant townhouses with their intricate iron balcony railings. The city swept dramatically around its bay, a mass of roofs evoking the clutter of Paris, though the gentle swaying of palm trees was a constant reminder that one was far from Europe. The roads twisted and turned through the city, past government buildings draped with barbed wire, surrounded by meter-high concrete blocks to prevent car bombers parking their wired vehicles unnoticed. Spirals of razor wire were slung over the jagged spikes of fences encircling the ministries, their entrances staked out by meter-high clusters of metal spikes along the roads, the entries turned into chicanes patrolled by security men with masked faces, their fingers on the triggers of their Kalashnikovs. Past them, people went to work, accompanied their children to school, carried their heavy shopping bags, even chatted in the street. Shop entrances were open, people came and went, there were traffic jams and buses picking up passengers who waited in queues on the pavement. War and peace existed alongside each other among the cool streets. The calm was broken by the sound of sirens, and a convoy sped past. Three unmarked cars, all Renault 20s painted a green-blue color, forced a path through the traffic. Men in dark suits hung out of the car windows with pistols in their hands, yelling and gesticulating at other drivers for the street to be cleared so that the convoy could pass. The sirens' wail echoed among the townhouses until it faded into the distance.

"The politics followed up until now, and throughout the period from 1992, has been the politics of force," Abdelhamid Mehri, the secretary general of the FLN, the defeated former ruling party, had told me.[52] Following the resignation of President Chadli and the 1992 coup, the FLN had become alienated from power and its leadership had sought dialogue with the FIS. Six months later, on 29 June, Mohamed Boudiaf was assassinated. His death is generally believed to have been planned by senior establishment figures worried that the head of state they had chosen to legitimize the coup was going too far in exposing official corruption as part of his effort at regaining popular confidence in government.[53] Boudiaf was replaced as president of the HCE by Ali Kafi, who was replaced in January 1994 by General Liamine Zeroual. In November 1994 and January 1995, the FLN and other parties, including the FIS, met in Rome and issued a joint communiqué outlining plans for a solution to the crisis.[54] Their efforts came to nothing, owing largely to the government's refusal to participate in the talks. "There's no willingness to change that politics. It's failed to bring a solution because the regime has always presented a dialogue that is one removed from the real power. They simply want to use the opposition to apply their politics, while not wanting to discuss the politics itself," Mehri said.

Both the FLN and the FFS boycotted the 1995 presidential election, while the FIS remained banned. "Only the candidates who don't really stand a chance of winning a full election have put their candidates forward," Mahiou Mebarak, a member of the FFS executive, told me. "The conflict in Algeria is more complex than just a battle between the government and the Islamists. That's why it's necessary to have a national conference which will oversee the running of an election. Then an election would be held which would see all the different political currents represented. All the currents—including the Islamists," he said.[55]

Meanwhile, the FIS itself was operating in different forms, as an armed group in the form of the Islamic Army of Salvation (AIS), while facing increasing factionalism. In Germany, the official responsible for political affairs, Rabeh Kebir, vied with the Washington-based spokesman of the exiled FIS parliamentarians, Anwar Haddam. Both claimed to speak for their leaders imprisoned in Algiers, Ali Belhadj and Abassi Madani. The war against the security forces was by 1995 being conducted by several Islamist groups. The blurring of identities, despite real differences, intensified as the government abandoned hope of a negotiated solution[56] and increasingly followed the hard line of those officials known in Algeria as the *eradicateurs*, the eradicators,[57] owing to their wish to eradicate the Islamist movement altogether.

The taxi driver pulled up at the entrance of the Hotel Saint Georges, which had officially changed its name long ago—to the Hotel Algérie. So why did everybody call it the Saint Georges? "That's what it was always called," he said. Who called it that? "The French." But the name was changed thirty years ago. "Well, it takes a long time for these traditions to change." He asked me if I wanted to hire his taxi to go around the city. I looked at him. Where could he take me? "All over the city, and outside it if you want to go." We agreed on a price, and an hour later we left the hotel. He lulled me into a sense of security. Forty Algerian journalists had been assassinated during the previous three years of conflict.[58] They had been targeted by the GIA beginning soon after that organization's foundation. Sid Ahmed Mourad, known as Djaffar Afghani, had taken over the leadership of the GIA in July 1993 and had issued a statement that said: "The journalists who fight against Islamism through the pen will perish by the sword."[59] For the GIA, most journalists were legitimate targets, while foreigners in general—Muslims and non-Muslims alike—were targets due to the assumption that they did not share the GIA's perspective.

"The GIA moved from the idea that democracy is *kufr*, or against Islam, to the point where they believed that anybody who believed in democracy is *kufr*," Karim Omar explained to me in London. From 1993 he had seen his own influence within the GIA grow. His message, drawing on his experience elsewhere, had spread widely throughout Algeria among the activists, whose main source of organizational cohesion was the internal publication *al-Ansar*. This evolution of opinion within the GIA was, despite growing tension between

the two Islamic groups, reflected within some areas of the FIS, as it became clear that the government's basic negotiating position would
never allow an Islamist party to take power in Algeria. "There are people within the government who are opposed to any political solution,
and we are trying our best to undermine their efforts," Anwar Haddam, who though an FIS spokesman had established close ties with
the GIA in 1993–1995, had said.[60] For the GIA, democracy was *kufr*;
for the *eradicateurs* there was only one way of dealing with the Islamists: "The best way of relaunching the crisis is to talk more to
those responsible for it," the former prime minister and hard-line anti-
Islamist Redha Malek[61] told me. "What has dialogue achieved? Nothing. These militant groups have refused to involve themselves in the
process of power. Instead they use terrorism like a business, and it is
necessary to confront them."[62]

The taxi driver drove quickly to the Foreign Ministry. We wove
through the maze of barriers. On an upper floor, an official in a quiet
rage couldn't contain his anger at the fact that I had not announced my
arrival in Algiers in advance and that I had, according to him, ignored
the airport police when they had said they would drive me into the
city. There was no question that this offer had not actually been made.
The official told me I would have to move from the Saint Georges to
the Hotel Aurassi for my own protection. I nodded, then left.

At 5:00 A.M. the next day I left on a small plane from the Algiers airport on the campaign trail. We flew west to Oran and then drove in a
convoy to Mostaganem. Fading graffiti sprayed in red paint on a wall
was a reminder of a previous period in Algeria's crisis: "FIS: Grève Nationale,"[63] it said. FIS posters flapped, torn in the slight breeze. Said
Sadi, one of the four presidential candidates, waved and smiled as he
walked through the town. Nobody waved back. "In the streets nobody
wants to show who they might favor, so they keep quiet and just
watch," the spokesman for Sadi's Rally for Culture and Democracy
(RCD) party told me.[64] Sadi made his way to the town's cemetery.

"I can tell you nothing. Just bring us peace," said the mother of Ayachi Chaoudi. The woman, in her mid-fifties, was sitting among the
graves as Sadi arrived with his entourage. She was staring at a photograph of her seven-year-old son. His grave was one of seven, with the
large photograph standing at its head. At the center of the graves was a
memorial. In handwritten script it commemorated the deaths of seven
boy scouts—among them the son of Ayachi Chaoudi—a year earlier.
"He was standing near the memorial in the cemetery at Sidi Ali, our
village. Somebody had put a bomb in an empty grave just beside the
boy scouts, as they were marking the First of November, the start of
the liberation war."

Mrs. Chaoudi wrung her hands. Said Sadi touched the memorial. His party moved on. The bomb had appalled the people of Mostaganem and the surrounding villages. Among those arrested for the crime was the imam of the local mosque. The marking of liberation day with a bomb had a resonance that Algeria's Islamists had made the central thrust of their message. "In 1991 the Islamists started to say that the Algerian war [of liberation[65]] needed to be refought, that it had not brought liberation, because the people who took over the running of Algeria after independence were a French-speaking cultural minority of Algerians," said Yves Lacoste,[66] a leading French writer on North Africa.

The Islamists in Algeria are essentially the adversaries of the Algerian Francophones, and the current conflict within Algeria is between the Islamists and those they consider to be bad Muslims, who are viewed as supported by France. Equally, the Islam of the armed groups expresses its anti-Western sentiment by attacking its most obvious target—France, and by fighting the *agent* of France, which [for them] are the Algerian army, the intelligentsia and the professionals.

Said Sadi represented the anti-Islamist groups as overtly as President Zeroual, even more among the professional class. His political career began falteringly when it was discovered that his spoken Arabic was poor, as he practiced his profession as a psychiatrist using French or the Berber language of his native Kabylie region. He took Arabic lessons but remained the candidate most closely identified with what the Islamists call the Hizba Fransa, the Party of France. "The Islamists are young, and they are essentially an economic problem," Sadi told me.[67] "It's necessary to respond to their demands. But as armed groups they are finished and their terrorist campaign has been a failure in terms of winning support," he claimed, as we drove then walked to the Zaouia Alaouia Sufi religious center.

In 1958 the former French president Charles de Gaulle visited Mostaganem and asked to meet with the Sufi leader in the town. The Sufis refused on the grounds that it would have compromised their image in the light of the war of independence that was then being fought. Thirty-seven years later, France, its war with Algeria, and the legacy of colonialism were still able to pierce the skin of the presidential election and the regime's efforts to present the contest as a self-confident reassessment of the country's independent identity. President Zeroual appeared to seek official and public French support for his candidacy when he timed a meeting with the French president Jacques Chirac to effectively mark the launch of his presidential campaign.[68] Algerian responses to the planned meeting, which was later canceled by Zeroual after Chirac refused to allow it to take place in the presence of television cameras, revealed the lurking influence of France.[69] "We regard this [French support for Zeroual] as a mistake," said Abdelhamid Mehri of the FLN. "It is an attempt to justify a democracy of formalities and an appeal to the Algerians to accept a second-class democracy. We demand nothing, either from the French government, or from the French president. We demand nothing from France. It knows the situation in Algeria."[70]

France still lingered as an influence, as the embodiment of Algeria's past, as the only model of secularism to which the country could refer. The Sufis had refused De Gaulle an audience while Algeria was still a colony. But President Zeroual had sought the backing of the former colonialists in the form of Chirac, the leader of France's Gaullist Party. What had independence really brought, if such gestures, laden with symbolism, could be engineered by key figures in the Algerian political scene in their search for lost legitimacy, at a time when the process of building the future depended so strongly upon exhibiting proof of ones' *Algerianness?*

De Gaulle was refused, but the most Francophile of Algeria's election candidates, Said Sadi, was welcomed. The Sufis, themselves viewed by the Islamists as having strayed from religious orthodoxy, suited Sadi's secularist politics. Though involved emotionally, the Sufis did not seek political power. "It's fifteen centuries since Islam came to Algeria, and the people who support me do so because they don't want the FIS to come to power," Sadi said. "It's necessary to protect religion from political Islam, and I am the only one who says this."[71]

From Mostaganem we flew south toward the Saharan Atlas mountains surrounding the military base at Djelfa. Handguns and Kalashnikovs were loaded into a sports bag by the security officers provided to each candidate at state expense, in addition to the 13 million Algerian dinars each candidate had received for election expenses. We set off in a convoy of twenty cars along a desert road that looped through rocky hills and across plateaus. For two hours we drove, eventually arriving in the midafternoon at Laghouat. Sadi addressed a rally in a conference hall near a large mosque. The oppressiveness of Algiers, even of Mostaganem, diminished as the open space of the Sahara loomed on the edge of the town.

"Religion is a belief. It's a principle. A conviction," Imam Mesaudi Yaya told us over tea and cakes in his small house near the mosque, where he entertained Said Sadi and his entire entourage, who sat at low tables arranged on four sides of the room. "Religion is like the palm of the hand. We feel its fingers, through different tendencies. But people have to return to the palm of the hand to be in control of the fingers."[72] To know the core belief—religious, political, personal—was the issue, but the process of discovery was what had brought chaos.

"People are rediscovering their nationality. But this has been coupled with the rediscovery of religious extremism," said Sadi, as we talked while night fell and the aircraft bore us north toward Algiers. "Now, a minimum of legitimacy is required by the government. To bring that it's necessary to change the regime. For the Islamists, they are young. It's necessary to respond to their demands. But if people vote for me, it will be because they don't want the FIS to come to power," he said, knowing that even though the FIS was banned and not participating, the election would still reveal much about its continued support. The Islamic identity remained at the heart of the election.

Travels with a Sheikh

"The Algerian people are Muslim, and their origins are Arab." The voice of Sheikh Mahfoud Nahnah boomed out across the neat square of Ain Temouchent. The rallying cry of Abd al-Hamid Ibn "Ben" Badis, the leader of the AUMA, raised a few cheers among the thousand people who were there to hear him. But mostly they remained silent and attentive. Nahnah was a curiosity. A former schoolteacher and leader of the Hamas party, he had led the creation of an Islamic group during the early 1960s that was closely modeled on the Egyptian Muslim Brotherhood, with whom he has close ties. He promoted a pan-Islamic strategy that was in marked contrast to the nationalism prevailing in Algeria following independence. During the 1980s, when differences within the Algerian Islamist movement first developed over the question of an armed struggle, Nahnah was among those opposed to violence, as were Islamists such as Abassi Madani, the future leader of the FIS. In December 1990, when the ban on multiparty politics was lifted in Algeria, Nahnah turned his association into the al-Irchad wal'Islah, known by its Arabic acronym Hamas, the Movement of the Islamic Society, which was officially launched as a political party on 29 May 1991. In 1995, in response to its moderation and the army's assumption that Sheikh Nahnah could not win the election, Hamas was allowed to contest the presidential election as the legal Islamic party.

Nahnah sought to represent himself as the inheritor of Algeria's Islamic past: "Islam is the religion of all Algerians, and it alone can reunite the country, and November 16 is the hour of total change," he told a crowd of supporters as we sat in the art deco cinema in Ain Temouchent.[73] In a long convoy guarded by well-armed state security

officials, we drove for four days through the rolling hills of western Algeria. In the town square of Mascara, Nahnah held up a newly printed
1,000-dinar banknote, recently introduced by the government. Until
1995, the 1,000-dinar note had depicted the religious leader of Algeria's early anticolonial resistance movement, Emir Abd al-Qadir, who
had led the opposition to the French between 1832 and 1847. The military government had decided to replace the head of Abd al-Qadir with
the head of a buffalo, Nahnah told the crowd, who booed the decision.
Mascara had been Abd al-Qadir's home.

As with Zeroual's attempts to secure overt French backing for his
campaign, the ambiguous attitude toward the past, from which the Islamists drew so much of their program, again seemed to be falling into
the hands of those seeking a new beginning. Nahnah, the apparently
acceptable face of Islamism, seemed to represent the failure to find
that new beginning: "I'm not a danger," he told a thousand people at
Tlemcen. "I have come to destroy the Mafia which controls the country's finances. This clan must disappear. Algeria is for everybody, not
just for certain groups. And they say I am a danger. Am I a danger?"

He was not a danger, because the movement he leads lacks the credibility of the FIS. Hamas, with its historic links to the relatively moderate Muslim Brotherhood,[74] represented a religious movement with a
strong intellectual base but lacking the social credibility born of the
attitude of defiance toward the past encapsulated by the FIS. But in the
absence of the FIS:

> The most noteworthy candidature of all was that of Mahfoud Nahnah.
> The participation in the regime's plans by one of the leading figures of the
> Algerian Islamist movement since the 1960s was seen by most Algerians
> as marking a final stage in the transition of the Sheikh[75] from subversive
> opponent of the regime in the 1960s and 1970s to reliable ally. . . . Nah-
> nah saw himself as a "middle way" between the discredited regime and
> the excesses of the armed groups.[76]

The radical Islamists accused Hamas of opportunism, even though
the party's program included the introduction of the Islamic *sharia* as
the basis of the legal system and other elements that barely distinguished it from the FIS's program. But these Islamist parties differed in
more profound ways. The FIS had organized a social network that,
during the 1980s, and particularly after the 1990 municipal elections
when its control of local councils accorded it a state budget in many
towns, made a difference in peoples' lives. The FIS stood for action,
power, and mobilization. Hamas was a well-oiled party machine that
intoned religion as the national identity in a way that did not mobilize
people as the FIS had done, because at heart the Islamic identity did

not have the power to mobilize in the way that political grievance and social deprivation did. The FIS party organization, coupled with its defiant articulation of grievances, lay at the heart of its power. Nahnah relied only upon rhetoric.

"In meeting these young [FIS] people, one *is* struck by their great discipline and by the organization of their local cells," writes Rabia Bekkar, who studied the rise of the FIS in Tlemcen during the 1980s. She continues:

> At the same time, as a woman, as a democrat, I find it terrifying that an institution this well organized can do so much. In the [1990 and 1991] electoral campaign[s], we saw this same efficiency and mobilization. They were everywhere. Islamists came into a completely empty field. You had a society that was morose, mired in a kind of lassitude, where people were completely burned-out, in despair—and [the FIS] suggested something. In the electoral campaign, the FIS brought up questions of honesty, of justice. The FLN had a program: housing, work, education. But the FIS said: we won't promise you anything. We'll have a state where we apply Islam, where honesty and justice will reign. . . . It's a moral contract, not an electoral program.[77]

The FIS had grasped the march of history by confronting outright the authority that had dragged Algeria into disillusionment. Hamas, meanwhile, had played the regime's game and could not represent the same attitude of defiance toward the past as that of the FIS, even though a large proportion of FIS supporters eventually voted for Hamas in 1995 and the subsequent parliamentary election in 1997.

Signs of the crisis did not litter the red-brown earth and olive tree orchards of the countryside. The signs were in peoples' minds. "The election has brought people out of themselves,"[78] said the local correspondent for one of the Algerian national newspapers as we stood on one of Tlemcen's elegant streets watching Nahnah and his entourage walk through the town along a tree-lined boulevard toward the imposing walls of the al-Mechouar castle. "It means that they can go out on the street and scream and yell, and nobody will tell them they cannot. And they can make a choice, and the choices are quite real ones. Even so, it's premature. The people have spent thirty-three years in the dark. They need time to be politicized. Perhaps three years would do it. The police are always summoning journalists, not because of what they write, but because they just want us to say that everything is fine," he said, as a rally in a sports hall convened, Nahnah delivered his message, and we drove out of the fine town.

We drove quickly through villages, across wide plains ending at rolling hills. At Ain Tellout somebody had painted words on a wall:

"je vote donc je suis," I vote therefore I am, an appeal to be allowed to have significance. In four days we traveled a thousand kilometers, through deserted land punctuated by towns, villages, and rural military checkpoints where armored cars and heavily armed troops peered at the passing spectacle of democracy. At Saida, a windswept hilltop village, I asked a man whether he would vote for Nahnah. "Well, I don't know," he replied. So, why had he come to listen? "Well, it's something to do on a Friday after prayers."

For miles the roads were deserted, except for the occasional bus packed with passengers who stared ahead out of the windows, watching for the *faux barrages*, checkpoints resembling those of the army but in fact thrown up by the Islamists, who would order people onto the roadside and murder them there and then before fleeing into the hills. Danger was palpable in the emptiness. As we drove from Tlemcen along a tree-lined road, the convoy became disjointed until the slow car in which I was driving fell behind the rest of the pack. Then the car juddered to a halt with an engine problem, slowing until it stopped. A car coming up from behind, the driver having failed to see that we had slowed, crashed into the back of us. We were alone, surrounded by hills and trees, in an area where hundreds of people had been killed in the previous months. The damage to the cars was not too serious. Birds whistled in the trees. The fields, mostly orchards, were empty. Ahead of us the convoy had disappeared. We waited as the long minutes passed, watching the empty fields, the empty road. The drivers, both in a state of panic, fumbled with the engines of their damaged cars, until they started and we could set off, straining to get up to speed. We chased the lost convoy, catching it at the roadside village of Oued al-Djamaa. Troops armed with bayonets pushed back a crowd of curious onlookers as Nahnah led Friday prayers on the main road while one of the national television journalists, his mouth full of figs and *mechoui*, exhausted by the travel, quietly told me: "It's true that we are being told to be biased. We're forced to do it, because the people that are running the television station are not professionals. They are worried about what will happen to them if President Zeroual does not win."[79]

After a rally in Oran, Nahnah flew to Jijel, a small seaside town east of Algiers. We arrived at the airport, to be told that a bomb had been defused beneath a bridge our convoy was to pass over. The silence of the Islamists, who had threatened to prevent the election from taking place but who had stopped the killing throughout the election campaign, had become inexplicable. Had they come to a deal with the government, which throughout the conflict had been accused of infiltrating the organizations and even conducting some of the Islamists' worst atrocities in an effort to besmirch their name? On the way to the town we crossed the bridge under which the bomb had been placed and then defused. Jijel was sinister. It was in the grip of the Islamists' campaign, having been the scene of numerous acts of violence. After soft drinks at the town hall, Nahnah insisted on walking to a rally at the cinema. The streets were almost deserted. Men peered suspiciously at Nahnah and his entourage. The bomb scare had raised the level of anxiety. The security officials were on hyperalert. Nobody waved, nobody responded to Nahnah's gestures. In the cinema, a few hundred people cheered the Hamas leader. The tension was intolerable. The cold welcome in the town, the bomb, the fact that this was Nahnah's last rally, all these elements meant that it was the militants' last chance to carry out their threat. The rally was cut short, after about ten minutes. Nahnah was rushed to a car; I was thrust into another. We left for the airport at great speed. Nobody said why. Nobody explained anything. And we returned to Algiers.

"The Hour of Total Change"

"We had our revolution in 1954 to liberate our country from the French. But now our country is again in danger, and we're making war again to save it."[80] Omar Sadi stood with thirty other armed men at the village crossroads in Ammouche, seventy miles east of Algiers, high in the hills of the Grand Kabylie, the heartland of Algeria's Berber region. In 1994 the government had begun arming civilian militias to provide security in rural areas. In Ammouche the group had been formed after an attack by Islamists had left two villagers dead. "My father was one of those killed," said Ahmed Diwani. "Now there's nothing on offer except the election, as a way of finding a solution to the crisis. And I have taken up arms to make sure there is an election," he said, a new Kalashnikov slung over his shoulder.

The village administrator, who refused to give his name, pointed to the hills from where this village and others had been attacked. He even knew which villages the attackers had come from. All the villages had banded together to provide mutual security, creating a force of 250 people under arms. "Algerians have a tendency to watch and observe," he said, as we drank tea and ate fried meat in the village cafeteria. "But now the time for waiting has finished, and it has become the time to react."

Next day, election day,[81] people queued early at the polling stations in Tizi-Ouzou, the capital of the Kabylie region. "We can't live like this forever. We can't live in fear," said a woman waiting outside the

Ecole Dali, one of several polling stations in the town. "We hope there will be change," said another. "We women simply can't go out anymore. This morning I told my mother that I was going to vote, and she asked me if I didn't have fear of doing so. She stayed at home, but for me I hope that very soon after the election there will be a great effort to change things for women," she said, adding that she and her husband were voting for different candidates, a sign perhaps of an unquenchable wish for change.

The road from Tizi-Ouzou to Algiers was once tree-lined, but the stately eucalyptus had been chopped down to prevent their being used as cover for ambushes. By midday Algiers had not experienced even a murmur of violence. Deep in the heart of Bab el-Oued, the city stronghold of the GIA, people lived up to the instruction to "watch and observe." Graffiti on the wall of a narrow alley proclaimed: "VIVA GIA." The claws of a mangy cat tore at rubbish thrown on a tip as gendarmes, their faces covered by balaclavas, drove by slowly, staring through the windows of their bulletproof Toyota Land Cruisers.

"I don't think it's going to change anything, this election. We really need a miracle to bring change," said a twenty-year-old woman standing in the shadow of Sekardji prison, where the government has held many FIS prisoners since 1992. "This district where I live is dangerous. There are people here checking out everybody who goes to vote, because they want people to boycott the poll. The armed groups are surveilling everybody. I am sure they are watching me, but I voted anyway," she told me.[82] At a mosque nearby, men bowed to pray.

"A lot of the threats are rumors," said a man on his way home from shopping. "Personally, I voted for President Zeroual, because he is the man of the FLN, the old ruling party." He was apparently unaware that the incumbent president was no longer part of the FLN, which, along with the FIS, had called for a boycott of the poll. "My father was FLN, and so am I, even if I live in an area where there's supposed to be only fundamentalists," he said, disappearing into the gloomy hallway of a once-elegant tenement building.

Few were surprised when Zeroual was elected.[83] But the "hour of change" never came. A demand by election observers[84] that the government explain why the electoral register had grown in size by 4 million names since the FIS's victory in the parliamentary contest of 1991 was ignored. Several months after the election, a leaked French intelligence report suggested that Nahnah had been only 6 percentage points behind Zeroual, not the 36 percent the government had reported.[85] Nahnah claimed massive electoral rigging but also called upon the government to use its victory to good purpose: "The authorities should now open themselves up to all political forces within Algeria, without exception and including the armed groups, and should initiate true dialogue to set the conditions for a truly pluralist democracy."[86] The Islamists also took the opportunity to push Zeroual toward forging a turning point in the crisis. Rabeh Kebir, the FIS's leader in exile, wrote to Zeroual acknowledging his victory. The strategy of Kebir, as well as that of the FLN and the FFS, was directed more by the obvious failure of their boycott call than by the mathematics of the victory. In view of this, Kebir told Zeroual: "We confirm our permanent willingness to engage in dialogue, consultation, and cooperation with the ruling power and the opposition."[87] By contrast, Anwar Haddam, the spokesman for the exiled FIS parliamentarians, issued a statement that reflected the deep divisions within the organization:

> Algeria is definitely sending a painful message to Muslim people around the world. If any credibility is given to such Algerian presidential elections, Muslims all over the world will question their leaders' willingness in the future to participate in the electoral process. . . . The FIS calls on the sincere members of the Algerian army and security forces to get rid of those among the military-security establishment who are responsible for the suffering of the Algerian people.[88]

This overthrow of the central government did not happen. Instead, the Islamist organizations found themselves in chaos. The lull in violence during the election period stemmed from differences between the FIS's armed wing, the AIS, which advocated a cessation of violence during the poll; and the GIA, which wanted to step up the slaughter. Both groups needed to know which way public opinion had really evolved since 1992. The election turnout had been high. Rabeh Kebir responded on behalf of the FIS's jailed leaders by offering an olive branch, while Anwar Haddam condemned the election. Meanwhile, the GIA became wracked by division. One of its military commanders, Abou Abderrahmane Amine, issued a statement declaring war on the FIS because it had opted for "democracy, elections, and the ballot boxes . . . It is a duty to fight them."[89]

Feuding within the GIA reached a climax soon after the election when a faction led by Djamel Zitouni executed two leaders of the Jazara Islamic group,[90] Mohammed Said and Abderazak Redjam, and twenty of their supporters following their growing criticism of the random nature of GIA violence. Said and Redjam had joined the GIA in 1994 in an effort to moderate it from within. In August 1994 Said had been appointed supreme leader of the GIA, and his appointment had been announced in a statement signed by Zitouni, who had been second in command to Said's predecessor, Gousmi Cherif. But Zitouni's suspicions of the moderates did not take long to surface. Their murders began the process of clarifying the differences between the groups that have subsequently determined the course of Algeria's search for a solution. Said and Redjam were accused by Zitouni (correctly, as it turned out) of infiltrating the GIA in order to soften it. Meanwhile, the FIS began to reorganize its military wing in response to the growing threat from the increasingly extremist GIA. Anwar Haddam, who had retained contacts with the GIA while operating as a spokesman for the FIS, broke off links with the GIA after the killings of Said and Redjam. But he also accused the FIS political leadership, particularly Kebir, of seeking compromise with the government. Haddam hoped that a new Islamist military organization would emerge, capable of pursuing the war against the government while attempting to win popular support by avoiding terrorism against civilians.

The divisions within the Islamist movement have contributed as much to the spiraling violence that continues to plague Algeria as the determination of the government to crush the Islamist movement. On 21 September 1997 the AIS, the armed wing of the FIS, declared a unilateral truce and committed itself to exposing the excesses of the GIA. The divisions within the Islamist armies are deeply rooted, in terms of both strategy and philosophy. The severity of Algeria's crisis stems from the virulence of belief in aspects of its cultural, religious, and political identity, which have all, at various points along the road, been stunted by the emergence of alternative trends. Islamism, republicanism, and democracy have been subsumed by colonialism, dictatorship, and conflict. A solution to the internal battle would revitalize Algeria's Islamist movement and perhaps move it away from the atrocities with which it is now associated. Such a solution would have a marked impact throughout the Islamic world, as this battle dawned many years before Algerians even saw their independence on the horizon. Like Algeria's identity crisis, the battle was spawned by colonialism and its legacy, and has its origins in the foundation and effects of the first party of political Islam, the Muslim Brotherhood, which appeared in Cairo in the 1920s.

4

The Community
of Muslims

Egypt

FROM THE STREET, 20 Sharia Malek Salah appeared derelict. A narrow offshoot of the Nile slid by on the other side of a low wall before rejoining the river past the island of Roda. Rubble had been dumped at the end of the street, where the gates of a small college had rusted closed. The low-rise block, number 20, faced the river; a few steps rose to a shabby hallway, the only light in the narrow stairwell coming from the sunlight that filtered in from the ground floor. The light receded as it rose to the upper floors. A bell rang behind a glossy wooden door, which was opened by a young man who led the way along a carpeted corridor past carpeted rooms to where chairs had been set around the bare walls. Tea was served, then there was silence. The tranquillity was broken by the murmur of prayer in a nearby room. The lead, then the response, gave the impression of a large gathering. For ten or fifteen minutes the hum of the ritual filled the apartment, then broke up into quiet conversation.

Mamoun al-Hodeibi paced into the waiting room in his socks. An assistant brought his shoes from the prayer room. His welcome was warm. He tied his shoelaces while talking animatedly, defying the signs of his advanced age with a reservoir of youthful energy and the dignity unique to those who have survived a lifetime of struggle into old age, offering the chance for reflection after the heat of the apparently endless battles. For the spokesman of the Ikhwan al-Muslimin, the Muslim Brotherhood, the battle had straddled the latter half of the twentieth century. For the movement, it had been punctuated by violence, assassination, prison sentences, and torture. The old men, and some younger ones in the room next door, who walked past us as we

73

talked were the intellectual guardians of a rich history, the keepers of an Islamist tradition, the descendants of a distinguished line of religious thinkers whose claim to represent the will of the people has left them condemned to a rubble-strewn Cairo backstreet beside the river.

"People believe in Islam. But the government has not become more Islamic. Even so, what people want will be achieved,"[1] al-Hodeibi said. In 1928, Hassan al-Banna, the founder of the Muslim Brotherhood, rallied his followers with a call to create an "Islamic homeland." Seventy years later, aspects of al-Banna's program, and that of the important nineteenth- and early-twentieth-century scholars who influenced or followed him, have filtered occasionally into the political programs of the ruling regimes of the Islamic world, though usually as a mild concession to the Islamists rather than out of conviction. Al-Banna's vision is in fact far from being realized. In 1946 the Muslim Brotherhood claimed to have 500,000 active members and 500,000 sympathizers organized in 5,000 branches throughout the country.[2] Now it is banned in Egypt. Many of its followers are in jail and its leaders are silenced and barred from organizing their undoubtedly still significant constituency in any meaningful way.

The cultural and religious elements of the Arab identity, which for a century the Islamists have sought to bring to the fore in their bid to confront the formidable influence of Europe, have been channeled into the strategies of the modernizing regimes that have led Egypt since independence in 1952. The Egyptian Islamists have alternately been courted, ridiculed, tortured, and finally silenced by the passing regimes. But at no point has a more credible political philosophy succeeded in supplanting the Islamists' influence, despite their lack of a party political machine through which to apply their program. A certain resilience has ensured the continuity of influence. This continuity has been built upon a cultural identity itself formed by centuries of contact with other cultures. The question remains as to what constitutes an *Egyptian*, after the arrival and departure of foreign armies, governors, and bureaucrats. As in Algeria, the Islamist movement was born out of the anticolonial struggle. But the cultural identity it harnessed in Egypt had much deeper roots than nationalism. "In short, Islam is to all intents and purposes the essence of Arab history and Arab civilization, and anyone who calls himself an Arab nationalist is bound to take pride in Islam and its achievements."[3]

Even before Arab nationalism had mobilized populations against colonial rule, the reform of Islam in Egypt, as was to be instigated in Algeria by the AUMA of Ben Badis, sought to clarify religious identity by refinement. But, unlike the original AUMA members, Egyptian Islamists sought to harness growing anticolonialism into a formidable political movement from the beginning. The "Arab civilization" that was the Islamists' raw material was both exalted for its qualities and recognized as having been diminished during many centuries of decline. This decline, both in terms of the internal decay of the religion and its weakness in the face of colonialism, was obvious. But, as with the ambiguity over the Arab-European relationship, there had traditionally been differences over whether Arabism or Islam was the essential element of that identity. "We are Arabs before being Muslims, and Muhammad is an Arab before being a prophet,"[4] said Faisal, son of Sharif Hussain of Mecca, the ruler of Hejaz.[5] Five decades later, at his trial for sedition in 1966, the Egyptian writer Sayyid Qutb appeared to refute the call to ethnicity and nation when he told the Egyptian court that was later to sentence him to death: "The bonds of ideology and belief are sturdier than those of patriotism based upon region, and this false distinction among Muslims on a regional basis is but one expression of crusading and Zionist imperialism, which must be eradicated."[6]

While some argued that Arabism should be viewed as an essential part of the Muslim identity by virtue of the Arabs' role as the guarantors of Islam's survival over the centuries, Qutb and the line of Islamist scholars of which he was a key part argued that the religion was itself the core of the Muslim identity. In Egypt, the weakness of the Arabs in the face of Muslim Ottoman rule and the British occupation of 1882 was accompanied by the decay of the religion, for which Cairo had been a major center of scholarship for eleven centuries. "Prayer is called *salah*. Five times in the course of every day is its performance required of the Muslim; but there are comparatively few persons in Egypt who do not sometimes, or often, neglect this duty, and many who scarcely ever pray,"[7] one English traveler to Egypt, Edward Lane, noted in the 1830s. While the rituals of religious observance were well known, they were not necessarily widely practiced in nineteenth-century Cairo. In his discussion of the mosque as a male preserve, Lane even claimed: "Very few women even pray at home,"[8] though he offers no firsthand evidence of this. Similarly, without presenting evidence, Lane states with regard to each Muslim's duty to perform the pilgrimage to Mecca: "Many, however, neglect the duty of pilgrimage who cannot plead a lawful excuse; and they are not reproached for doing so."[9]

Lane's lack of evidence does not necessarily exclude him as a source. The failure of Muslims to practice their religion as was required of them emerged as a central tenet of the Islamists' own agenda. Strict observance and the return to orthodoxy have been the hallmark of the Islamists' message in the twentieth century. Such demands emerged from the lax practices that, as loaded with European pomposity as the orientalist Lane is, the Islamists themselves generally recognized as having infected the religion even before European cultural and political imperialism stirred the Islamic reformers into action.

The Scholars of the Islamic Revival

The modern Islamist tradition was born out of a long period of dynamic personal reflection, *ijtihad*, which has in the late twentieth century faced a highly conservative backlash that advocates strict orthodoxy in which *ijtihad* is often regarded as unislamic. The intellectual progress of the early Islamists drew heavily upon the political reality within which they found themselves.

> The main problem [for the Islamist scholars] was still what it had been for the Ottoman writers of the seventeenth and eighteenth centuries—internal decline, how to explain and how to arrest it. The political ideas and practical ideas of Europe were necessary for the one and the other alike, and Europe therefore was first of all a teacher and political ally for those who wished to reform the life of the Ottoman community.[10]

Albert Hourani stresses the imperatives of the early Islamists as having been threefold: arresting the decline of Islam, confronting the political threat posed by European imperialism, and attempting to exploit the exposure to European civilization and systems of thought and social morality as a model for the reassertion of Islam as a civilization rather than just a religion. Chief among the early scholars to give this view wide credibility in the Islamic world was Sayyid Jamal al-Din al-Afghani (1839–1897), a Persian whose most productive years were spent in Cairo between 1871 and 1879. In order to broaden his influence among Islam's Sunni majority, he adopted the name "al-Afghani" to dispel suggestions that he was from the Shia branch of Islam, which predominated in his native Persia (and which remains the principal branch of Islam in modern Iran).[11] Al-Afghani was strongly influenced by what were essentially European humanist and utilitarian ideas, which held that human beings had the power to change the condition in which they lived. Politically, this was essential to Muslims, most of whom lived in a state of submission to colonial powers when al-Afghani began publishing an influential periodical, *al-Urwa al-wuthqa*.[12] The publication first appeared in Paris in 1884 and was soon widely read in many parts of the Muslim world. Al-Afghani traveled widely and sought the support of Muslim political leaders in his attempts to bring cohesion among sects, factions, and rivals in order to forge an Islamic civilization within the Ottoman empire.

Most obvious to al-Afghani was the need for the Islamic world's internal reform. His encouragement of the internal cohesion of the *umma*, the global community of Muslims, was confounded less by a lack of popular faith than by the inadequacies of the Ottoman and other political leaders to whom by necessity he had to present his ideas in the hope of achieving such reform.

> He was not a constitutionalist on principle; his ideal of government was rather that of the Islamic theorists—the just king recognizing the sovereignty of a fundamental law. . . . Each time he was disappointed. The ruler turned out neither to be innately just nor to recognize the authority of the law standing above him. . . . For their part, the rulers who had hoped [al-Afghani] would rally Muslim sentiment behind their thrones found that his real intention was to use their power in the service of Islam.[13]

For al-Afghani, the logic of the internal cohesion of the *umma* was drawn from the concept of civilization based on justice, which he saw as central to the strength of the imperial European powers. Justice had brought the solidarity that had strengthened European states politically. The challenge was to apply the concept of civilization not to the political entity of states but to the religious entity of the *umma*. Within the framework of civilization, al-Afghani projected the view that "true religions . . . taught three truths above all: that man was monarch of the earth and the noblest of created things, that his religious community was the best of all, and that he had been sent into the world to perfect himself in preparation for another life. From acceptance of these truths sprang the three virtues which were the bases of society: modesty, trust and truthfulness."[14]

Al-Afghani identified reason and the individual's ability and desire to reason as the central feature of civilization in general, as well as the central feature of Islam in particular: "The first pillar upon which the religion of Islam is built is that the idea of divine unity should burnish the human mind and cleanse it from the weakness of illusion."[15] He asserted that individuals could establish a just civilization by their own reason, but that the individual's wish to do so stemmed entirely from belief in God, the eternal life, and the Day of Judgment. The appeal of al-Afghani among Muslims lay, and lies today, in his assertion of individual reason, *ijtihad*, which applied as much to individuals' understanding of the Koran as to their understanding of the mechanics of creating a just civilization.

Al-Afghani's thesis was revolutionary. It defied the views of the Islamic religious establishment, the ulama, that the established schools of Islamic thought required no modification.[16] It opened up the door to the renewal of Islam through reasoned personal reflection and group discussion by Muslims. Drawing on the thirteenth sura of the Koran, which deals essentially with punishment, al-Afghani based much of his assertion of the Koranic justification for individual reason on the line: "Verily, God does not change men's condition unless they change their inner selves."[17] The verse goes on: "And when God wills people to suffer evil [in consequence of their own evil deeds], there is none who could avert it: for they have none who could protect them from Him." For al-Afghani, it was clear that people's ability to "change their inner selves" was inherent in the Koran and that individual will existed within the context of the religion. "In its wider sense, this is an illustration of the divine law of cause and effect which dominates the life of both individuals and communities, and makes the rise and fall of civilizations dependent on people's moral qualities and the changes in 'their inner selves,'" writes Muhammad Asad in his commentary on the Koran.[18] For al-Afghani, the decline of Islam represented the decline of a civilization. "Becoming indifferent to God, [Muslims] also became indifferent to each other; solidarity grew weak and with it strength decayed," Hourani writes in his analysis of al-Afghani.[19]

By the time of his death, al-Afghani had witnessed only minimal signs that his debates and writings were moving toward arresting this weakness and decline. His direct political impact was limited, dependent as it had been upon the whims of the Ottoman rulers, whose priority was to cling to their crumbling power. But al-Afghani was compensated for his political impotence by his steadily expanding influence among a new generation of Muslim scholars, whose political outlook would take his concept of Islamic civilization further. Muhammad Abduh (1849–1905) had collaborated with al-Afghani in Paris on the publication of *al-Urwa al-wuthqa*. He had been strongly influenced by al-Afghani during the latter's stays in Cairo during the 1870s, when foreign—particularly British—influence was growing in Egypt, with a consequent growth of national consciousness.

Abduh became directly involved in nationalist politics, leading to his imprisonment and torture by the British. During periods in exile he wrote and lectured, basing himself mainly in Beirut but also traveling to France and England. His openness to European thought and writing, his readiness to debate with European orientalists, and his acceptance of change—which in his lifetime implied Europeanization—exemplified the intellectual vitality of the Islamist school during its early years. Abduh's central aim was to bridge the gulf between the acceptance of change along essentially secular lines and the need for morality derived from Koranic law. "It could only be done by accepting the need for change, and by linking that change to the principles of

Islam: by showing that the changes which were taking place were not only permitted by Islam, but were indeed its necessary implications if it was rightly understood, and that Islam could serve both as a principle of change and a salutary control over it."[20] In seeking to bridge this gap, Abduh injected into the debate over Islam's revival the possibility of diluting with European ideas a religion that he and other Muslims recognized as having weakened through stagnation.

The logic of Abduh's position depended ultimately upon an acceptance of Islam as a code of beliefs intended to explain human existence and provide guidance for social life. Reason lay at the heart of this code; reason dictated that Mohammed was a prophet, and that acceptance of him as such over centuries by educated people was one of several *reasons* for accepting his status as a prophet. Humanity had heightened Mohammed's validity. For Abduh, Mohammed made his appearance when humanity, having witnessed the arrival of Moses and Christ, was ready for the last Prophet, who would correct the waywardness into which it had fallen. Humanity's intelligence and reason lay at the heart of acceptance of Mohammed as a prophet. The assumption is that the work inspired by the Prophet—the Koran, in the form of the hadith, and the *sunna* or practice of the Prophet as recorded in the Koran—should be accepted in its entirety. But at points the Koran and the hadith are unclear. Abduh advocated the use of individual reason to establish how this lack of clarity should be overcome. For him, *ijtihad*, based upon experience, knowledge, and education, was essential as a means of untangling the complexity of the Koran. By using their reason, Muslims could establish the truth of the Koran and, living in accordance with these revealed principles, rebuild the lost Islamic civilization.

Islam's decline had also been caused by the failure to distinguish between central principles and everyday religious observance as practiced by the early Muslims. While for Abduh the elders of early Islam, the *salaf* who refined the religion during the two centuries after the death of Mohammed in 632, were valuable as interpreters of the sacred text, their own acts were not to be viewed as holy. These *salaf* had used their personal reasoning, *ijtihad*, just as the Muslims of the nineteenth and twentieth centuries should use theirs. The *salaf* had made good use of Islam's golden age by applying it to the needs of eighth- and ninth-century society. The religion's subsequent decline had been precipitated by the eclipse of reason, which led to Islam's stagnating, then losing ground to the dynamism of European thought.

Abduh, unlike al-Afghani, was able to practice much of what he believed. In 1899 he was appointed Mufti of Egypt, the highest official authority on matters of religious law in the country. He introduced the practice of allowing judges faced with conflicting directives in the Koran to pass judgments based on what they viewed as that most likely to improve human welfare. Schools of law, of which four exist within the Islamic world, were opened to all jurists, who could follow the directives of any of the four schools. Until Abduh's arrival, jurists had remained confined within the school to which they had become accustomed. This reform allowed for much broader interpretations and more reasoned judgments, precipitating the evolution of a unified system of Islamic law.

Unlike al-Afghani, Abduh secured a tangible legacy, the intellectual movement he founded that came to be identified as the Salafiyya. But equally important for him was the continued evolution of his ideas by his followers. As Abduh had been to al-Afghani, so the Syrian Rashid Rida (1865–1935) was to Abduh. Rida's evolution is of symbolic importance for the process of religious refinement, which reformers saw as essential to strengthening their faith. He was virulently opposed to the rituals of Sufism,[21] which he regarded as a major diversion from the true faith. Like al-Afghani and Abduh, Rida's obsession was with the task of reversing the decline of Islam, as religion and civilization, by reasserting the practices of the *salaf*, the early practitioners of the religion, while practicing individual interpretation, *ijtihad*, to apply unchangeable religious *principles* to current religious *practice*. His numerous writings, which were published in many journals but mostly in *al-Manar*,[22] the periodical he published in Cairo from 1898 to 1935, express uncompromisingly his view that bad political rulers had caused the decline of Islam by failing to refer to their faith when making decisions of policy.[23] Rida, like his two mentors, was in awe of the strength of Europe, and he sought to balance what he saw as the European strength derived from the replacement of religion by nationality, with the claim that Muslims could derive similar strength from unity and loyalty to their religion:

> It is impossible to exaggerate the importance of unity for these writers, and the scandal of disunity. . . . Islamic unity meant for them, in essence, the agreement of hearts of those who accepted each other as believers and dwelt together in mutual tolerance, and the active co-operation of all in carrying out the commandments of religion. The community which was so constituted held authority from God: this was witnessed in the *hadith*: "My community will not agree upon an error."[24]

Rida used his formidable knowledge and intellectual power to further clarify the distinction between what was unalterable in Islam and what was subject to human judgment. As with the juridical innovations of Abduh, Rida asserted that religious judgments could be made on the basis of what was of greatest benefit to the community. The general approval of a judgment, the process of 'ijma, was accepted as a derivation from Islam, though such approvals were subordinated to the *sharia* if there was a conflict of interpretation. Decisions that resulted in such judgments, to reflect their contemporary relevance, were to be arrived at by consultation before they became law. This required political evolution, with decisionmaking based on a representative legislature, not upon the authority of those who had traditionally controlled the religion and had been responsible for its decline.

The need for a new, unified system of Islamic law was given added urgency, for Rida, by European opposition to Islamic civilization and European economic penetration of the Islamic world. "Necessity makes legal what would otherwise be forbidden," is how Hourani encapsulates Rida's approach. Rida's pragmatism was balanced by his attachment to the *salaf*, whose model of individual reflection upon religious matters he sought to follow. On this basis, a new Islamic state could be created, not based upon the apparently successful European concept of national identity that had exalted individuals to positions of power—a process that in the Islamic world had led to weak political institutions—but upon loyalty to religion. For this revival to take place, he equated Muslim needs with Arab needs, which, after the ousting of the Ottoman sultan by the secularist Young Turks in 1908, he increasingly saw as dependent on an end to colonial rule, particularly that of the British in Egypt and the French in his native Syria. "The British government has taken upon itself to destroy the religion of Islam in the East after destroying its temporal rule,"[25] he wrote.

The weakness of the Ottoman empire, within which al-Afghani had envisaged a revival of the *umma* centered upon a revitalized pan-Islamic caliphate but which Rida saw as the quintessential example of Islam's decline, spurred Rida's nationalist activity. Circumstances played a key role, as Rida had anticipated that the imminent collapse of the Ottoman empire would invite greater European interference in the Arab countries of the Islamic world. But "the suppression of the [Ottoman] caliphate [by Kemal Ataturk] in 1924 forced the *salafiyya* to abandon the myth"[26] that a unified *umma* could be revived within this preexisting political structure of the Ottoman empire. Consequently, Arabs sought their own course, whereas modern Turkey followed a secular path.

The Muslim Brotherhood

The Islamist path in Egypt, where the most influential Islamist thinkers continued to gather and emerge, was led by Hassan al-Banna

(1906–1949), a schoolteacher from the Nile delta. Al-Banna sought to shift the Islamist agenda away from the ambiguous love-hate relationship with the West that had been prevalent in the outlook of his intellectual predecessors and assert a distinction between Westernization and modernization. He also sought the reassertion of Islam through a highly eclectic incorporation of the religion's own intellectual and social history. In Cairo, he associated with the most influential Islamic thinkers, notably Rida, and immersed himself in the intense religious-intellectual life to which the city was host.[27] In 1928, having qualified as an Arabic teacher, al-Banna was appointed to a state primary school in Isma'iliyya. There, he was as active in promoting discussions about Islam, politics, and the condition of the Arab world as he had been in Cairo. That year he founded the Society of the Muslim Brothers, also known as the Muslim Brotherhood, apparently in response to a demand by a group of British-employed laborers for the creation of an organization that would ameliorate their sense of servitude and that would allow them to follow al-Banna's leadership. In 1932, al-Banna transferred to another teaching job in Cairo, establishing a branch of the organization in the city and setting up its headquarters there.

It was in Cairo that the founding principles of the Muslim Brotherhood, formulated in the prevailing atmosphere of political ferment and religious debate, were set forth. The brotherhood would have at its core "a Salafiyya message, a Sunni way, a Sufi truth, a political organization, an athletic group, a cultural-educational union, an economic company, and a social idea."[28] It established a clear link between the Arab world and Islam, citing examples of the leadership of the religion by non-Arabs—Umayyads, Abbasids, Turks—as a cause of the religion's decline, owing in part to these nationalities' inability to fully understand the language of Islam, which was Arabic. But it also particularly targeted Cairo's Al-Azhar Islamic University and the religious authority of the Grand Sheikh Al-Azhar, the supreme authority in Sunni Islam on matters of jurisprudence. The brotherhood condemned this revered thousand-year-old institution and its head for what it regarded as its failure to stem Islam's decay and to resist encroachment by foreign ideas. In 1914 the Al-Azhar ulama had issued a statement urging Egyptians not to object to the state of martial law imposed by the British colonialists, on the grounds that to protest against such a law—derived from British military concerns rather than indigenous Egyptian interests—was sedition, or *fitan*. The statement said: "Praise be to God who cautioned the believers to avoid all *fitan*. . . . Thus it is our duty to remain tranquil and silent and to advise others to do so, to avoid interfering in things which do not concern you." According to al-Banna, the Al-Azhar authorities "had failed to represent Islam to Muslims—ruler and ruled alike—as a vital, living code of life; it had failed 'to lead' and 'to teach,' and with the abdication of these duties came the corruption of Islam."[29]

The influence of Abduh and Rida was clear in al-Banna's reference to Islam's early practitioners, the *salaf*. He also retained a lifelong relationship with the Sufi movements, which Rida had condemned but which for al-Banna remained an essential element of Egypt's religious identity. While he viewed specific Sufi sects as having strayed radically from the path of pure Islam, he also viewed pure Sufism, through which Muslims could worship, assert their asceticism, and glean insights into what he recognized as the mystical elements of God's purpose, as close to the heart of Islam. Such spiritual searching embodied the process of personal reflection—*ijtihad*—that was an essential and orthodox part of the religion. Where he differed was on the issue of the hermetic, withdrawn life of the Sufi sects, which was at odds with the social activism of the brotherhood members, who viewed such activism as an essential force for political change. The brotherhood also viewed Sufi sectarianism as it viewed factionalism in Western-style multiparty politics, both of which undermined the unity of the Arab purpose. "In the social order imperialism was seen as the fountain head of corruption. When the armies of Europe came to Egypt, they brought with them their laws, schools, languages, and sciences; but also their wine, women, and sin. The introduction of the traditions and values of the West has corrupted society, bred immorality, and destroyed the inherited and traditional values of Muslim society."[30]

In confronting the decline of the religion, al-Banna criticized the institutions whose historical task had been to keep it together. The potential political impact of unity was clearly at the forefront of his thinking. But this unity had its source in the Koran: "We believe the provisions of Islam and its teachings are all-inclusive, encompassing the affairs of the people in this world and the hereafter. And those who think that these teachings are concerned only with the spiritual and ritualistic aspects are mistaken in this belief because Islam is a faith and a ritual, a nation and a nationality, a religion and a state, spirit and deed, holy text and sword."[31]

The organization evolved at a time when other religious groups were also active. Throughout the 1930s it developed its ideas as its presence in the mosques, coffeehouses, and homes of Cairo continued to widen. Richard Mitchell, whose work on the Muslim Brotherhood remains the most authoritative if incomplete account of its genesis and evolution, argues that the organization took eleven years to clarify its political agenda. In 1939 al-Banna projected his vision of the organization's future role, when it would be fully prepared to immerse itself in the process of leading a social transformation. He told the participants of the fifth conference of the brotherhood:

> At the time that there will be ready, oh ye Muslim Brothers, three hundred battalions, each one equipped spiritually with faith and belief, intellectually with science and learning, and physically with training and athletics, at that time you can demand of me to plunge with you through the turbulent oceans and to rend the skies with you and to conquer with you every obstinate tyrant. God willing, I will do it.[32]

World War II allowed the brotherhood to expand its political role, in the face of increasingly authoritarian demands by the British intended to thwart the activities of anticolonialist and antimonarchist Egyptians who had established channels of communication with Nazi Germany.[33] Al-Banna established close ties with politically active nationalist elements within the Egyptian army, from whose ranks a virulent stirring of anticolonial feeling was then emerging; the army's liaison with the brotherhood was conducted by Anwar al-Sadat, later president of Egypt.

The end of the war saw the stature and credentials of the principal Egyptian nationalist party, the Wafd, undermined by its corruption, elitism, and affirmation of loyalty to the British against Germany during the war. By 1945 the Muslim Brotherhood was the most formidable opponent to the Wafd on the Egyptian political scene and had positioned itself as the most important rightist political organization, sharing common cause with other movements opposed to communism and accepting the monarchist system despite King Farouq's playboy image and pro-British views.[34]

Al-Banna's links with the royal palace during the late 1940s, facilitated by al-Sadat, allowed the Muslim Brotherhood the greatest period of political freedom it had known since its foundation. The organization was allowed access to cheap publishing facilities, cheap land upon which to build mosques, and army camps in which to train the uniformed activist *jawalla* or "rovers," who after 1937 made up what became known as the brotherhood's *kata'ib* or "battalions." Their role was the propagation of the organization's message and the defense of its structure.

The brotherhood was viewed by the elite surrounding King Farouq as a weapon against the Wafd party, which quickly identified itself after the war as the mouthpiece of Egyptian nationalism. Post-1945 maneuvering in Egyptian politics revolved around the progress of negotiations for Egyptian independence from Great Britain and the growing likelihood that the United Nations would seek to solve the growing violence in the British colony of Palestine by partition and the foundation of a Jewish state there.

Activism, mobilization, and the ability to organize firmly established the brotherhood and the Wafd as the only credible political forces in Egypt. The brotherhood sought to use its growing political weight "to return—ourselves and whoever will follow—to the [true] path."[35] For Mitchell this does not imply a return to the seventh century but a return to the values of the early Muslims—a return to an "Islamic order," the *al-nizam al-islami*, not necessarily to a "Muslim state." For the brotherhood, the application of the Islamic order, in which the *sharia* was the heart of the legal system as well as the embodiment of principles governing all aspects of social and cultural life, was the challenge for Muslims in the twentieth century. But the aim was to apply it to modern life rather than to simply turn back the clock. These principles could be applied without overthrowing the political order,[36] as long as the Islamic *sharia* was applied by the existing order. "The immediate concern of the Muslim Brothers was not the organization of a 'Muslim state' . . . but rather the more profound issue of the nature and destiny of Muslim society in the twentieth century—'the Islamic order,' the most important elements of which were: (1) the *sharia* and its validity for modern times; and (2) the related question of 'the separation of church and state.'"[37]

As a further accession to modernity, the brotherhood declared that Muslims should be able even to break with Islamic traditions if such traditions hindered the modern reinterpretation of the Koran's true meaning. "The Traditions . . . were felt to need serious re-study. . . . A common belief among Brothers was that no more than a handful of Traditions would survive such a study,"[38] Mitchell writes. Islam's renewal, *tajdid*, would be ensured by allowing individuals to exercise their own personal interpretation, *ijtihad*, which had been central to the views of the Islamic scholars, of whose tradition the brotherhood became the key part.

As its importance grew, the brotherhood became increasingly fractious. Al-Banna's use of arbitrary power, as well as his use of a "secret apparatus" of informers, loyalists, and the *jawalla*, which also had the support of an armed element, had resulted in a powerful militant core within the broader organization. Senior members vied for power and fell by the wayside as al-Banna affirmed his supremacy during the 1945–1948 period. In 1947 al-Banna decreed that the Muslim Brotherhood's branches should prepare for jihad to "save" Palestine from partition. In doing so he launched what has since become the key rallying call of Middle Eastern Muslims, identifying Zionism as the enemy of the Arabs, identifying the West as having betrayed the Arab world by supporting Israel, and driving a wedge between Western "modernity" and Islamic reformism. The Arab League organized arms supplies and training for volunteers, and when Arab forces began fighting the army of the new state of Israel in May 1948, the Muslim Brotherhood dispatched both combatants and auxiliaries to ferry supplies to the various front lines.

The war in Palestine, coupled with an increasingly violent struggle between the Muslim Brotherhood and the Wafd, unleashed turmoil in Egypt, which only came to an end in 1952 when the nationalist element of the army seized power. The amassing of arms to fight the war in Palestine had essentially legitimized the creation of an armed Muslim Brotherhood, trained and equipped on Egyptian soil, at a time when those militants brandishing weapons could not be relied upon to use them solely for the defense of Palestine. They could just as easily turn their weapons upon their domestic opponents. The Egyptian government became aware of the brotherhood's "secret apparatus" and in November 1948 carried out a series of arrests after discovering documentary evidence linking the brotherhood to bomb attacks against political opponents and British interests, as well as against Jewish businesses in Cairo following the outbreak of the war with Israel.

On 8 December 1948, the brotherhood was dissolved by a governmental decree, accused of terrorism and of planning an armed insurrection aimed at seizing power. How that power might have been exercised is obviously a matter of conjecture. The brotherhood's program did not envisage the creation of a "religious dictatorship," a theocracy, in Egypt. The prevailing view within the brotherhood was that it should insist upon the reform of the current system along Islamic lines—within a modified "consultative" parliamentary system; within the monarchical system; within the labor unions; within business, banking, and education. Despite its wide support and organizational as well as military structure, the brotherhood did not envision an armed seizure of power as part of its agenda.

Upon the dissolution of the brotherhood, the "secret apparatus" fell apart. The government ceased to maintain contact with Hassan al-Banna, who sought meetings with King Farouq and Prime Minister Mahmud Fahmi al-Nuqrashi Pasha in an effort to resolve the crisis. On 28 December al-Nuqrashi, who was at the forefront of the efforts to destroy the brotherhood, was assassinated by a brotherhood member. Seven weeks later, on 12 February 1949, Hassan al-Banna was assassinated by the Egyptian political police[39] on a Cairo street; the act is thought to have been in revenge for the killing of al-Nuqrashi.

Death, Defiance, and the Call to Jihad

A year after al-Banna's death, thirty-two brotherhood members went on trial. The court found the evidence intended to prove their insurrectionist aims so flimsy that, although they were found guilty of violent acts, their violence was all but excused by the judge as having been caused by the charged atmosphere inspired by the war in Palestine.[40] Despite this lenient verdict, the brotherhood was in disarray, hounded by the government, deprived of its leader, and confronted by the failure of the Arab states to defend the Palestinians. Divergence within the organization developed into pronounced factionalism, resulting in the emergence of vastly different strategies. Political activism had brought conflict with the Egyptian authorities, who imprisoned, tortured, and, in some cases, executed those they considered enemies of the state.

At the same time, the consolidation of Israeli power in the midst of the Arab world convinced millions of Muslims of the treachery of the West and undermined the call by some Islamic modernists for the reform of the religion to follow a process of adapting to Western institutions along Islamic lines. In the 1950s and 1960s, following the nationalist revolution of 1952, the overthrow of King Farouq, and the rise to power of Gamal Abdel Nasser, the brotherhood's real influence over Egypt's political direction weakened. While the group's moderates urged social work as a means of retaining its relevance and profile, the radicals forged a new agenda of resistance to increasing state repression. Activism, originally rooted in the theory of religious revival, evolved in response to repression. Torture and imprisonment created a new momentum. The religious debate of the 1940s was halted. Jihad was declared as the only means by which the Islamic civilization and way of life, the *din*, could be revitalized. Leading this call was Sayyid Qutb (1906–1966):

> This *din* is a universal declaration of the freedom of man from slavery to other men and to his own desires, which is also a form of human servitude. . . . This declaration means the usurped authority of Allah be returned to Him and the usurpers thrown out—those who by themselves devise laws for others, elevating themselves to the status of lords and reducing others to the status of slaves. . . . [The Koran] makes it clear that obedience to human laws and judgments is a sort of worship, and anyone who does this is out of the *din*, because he or she is taking some men as lords over others, whereas the *din* seeks to annihilate such practices, declaring that all men and women should be free of servitude to anyone other than Allah.
>
> When they have no such freedom, then it becomes incumbent upon Muslims to launch a struggle through individual preaching as well as by initiating an activist movement to restore their freedom, and to strike hard at all those political powers that force people to bow to their will and authority. . . . After annihilating the tyrannical force, whether political or a racial tyranny, or domination of one class over the other within the same race, Islam establishes a new social, economic and political system, in which all men and women enjoy real freedom.[41]

Born in the Egyptian town of Asyut, Qutb joined the Muslim Brotherhood in 1951, following two years studying education in the United States, where he had been appalled by the extent of racial prejudice leveled against Arabs.[42] Free will, individual reason, and the absence of compulsion,[43] all integral to the "universal system" of Islam, are the key doctrinal elements to which Qutb refers time and again in his major works. His clarity contrasts sharply with the ambiguity of al-Banna. Moreover, his profound knowledge of the Koran, the entirety of which he had memorized as a child, injected a dynamism into the Islamist lexicon that encapsulated the position of humanity within the complicated political-religious web within which the Islamists found themselves in the Egypt of the 1950s and 1960s:

> The Qur'an mentions some aspects of reality that man has not been given the power to understand, because either they are not within the limits of his finite nature or else their knowledge is not needed in the performance of his assigned task. . . . [But w]ith the exception of these elements or aspects of the Islamic concept, which man can never fully comprehend, human thought, or human perception, in its comprehensive meaning, is called upon to ponder upon all the signs of Allah both in the Qur'an and in the created universe, to see and learn, to understand and then to apply the implications of the Islamic concept in the world of conscience and in the world of events. This all-inclusive concept opens up before every individual numerous vistas of positive action.
>
> No religion other than Islam shows so much concern for awakening the human faculty of perception.[44]

Freedom, discipline, variety, and the pursuit of learning are pillars upon which the thriving, evolving, renewed *(tajdid)* religion would rest. The social pressures to which the Muslim Brotherhood found themselves subjected played a major part in Qutb's interpretation of the Koran. The relationship between the ruler and the ruled, between the ruler and God, and the equality of races—these are the key issues to which Qutb says Muslims, in their struggle to achieve the *din*, must address themselves: "But when the above-mentioned obstacles and practical difficulties are put in [the way of the *din*], [the Muslim] has no recourse but to remove them by force so when it is addressed to peoples' hearts and minds, they are free to accept or reject it with open minds."[45]

Qutb discusses, with compelling force, the highly complex questions of individual freedom within the confines of an all-embracing system; the absence of compulsion within a system in which, in his own words, "there is no room for people to follow their divergent beliefs";[46] and the impact of a climate of political repression on the radicalization of Koranic interpretation. The condition of the world required jihad as an act of purification, whether or not the religion itself was threatened. "In order to propagate the oneness of God on earth and to put an end to the power of those who, by word or deed, challenge His omnipotence, Islam allows Muslims to fight. Such is the only war allowed in Islam,"[47] Qutb declared; while in *Milestones* he states: "The eternal struggle for the freedom of man will continue until all religion is for Allah, and man is free to worship and obey his Sustainer."[48]

Qutb identifies "the overall conditions prevalent in society"[49] as the obstacle to the free expression of religious belief. By implication, society for him was entirely devoid of Islamic characteristics, whereas belief in the Islamic system, the *din*, is the ultimate freedom for which humanity as a whole is striving. No compulsion is therefore necessary, conflict in the form of jihad constituting a form of resistance to obstacles confronting all humanity in its divinely inspired path toward the *din*. Force, in the form of jihad, is a consequence of a particular situation in which freedom has not been achieved:

> One should always keep in mind, however, that there is no compulsion in religion; that is, once the people are free from the lordship of men, the law governing civil affairs will be purely that of Allah, while no one will be forced to change his beliefs and accept Islam.
>
> The purpose of jihad in Islam is to secure complete freedom for every man throughout the world by releasing him from servitude to other human beings so that he may serve Allah, who is One and who has no associates.[50]

It is necessary that prevailing conditions in a particular country be viewed as having no impact on the practice of jihad, the understanding of which Qutb believed had been corrupted by the writings of orientalist scholars.[51] Jihad is itself the process of purification of the world in pursuit of the *din*; it was not meant as a defensive measure in the face of aggression from those opposed to Islam but as a vital process in which Muslims should take the initiative as a "Divinely-given right to step forward and establish political authority, so that [they] may establish the Divine system on earth, while leaving the matter of belief to individual conscience."[52] The struggle, which has emerged in the politics of the twentieth century, is a process that has adopted its own rules. Its success will lead to the freedom from which peace will emerge, and the harsh practice of jihad will then be replaced by the cohesion and justice that lie at the heart of the *sharia*. But first the world must be cleansed by struggle.

The State of Islam

For Qutb, as for his predecessors among the scholars of the twentieth-century Islamic revival, the relationship of the individual to political power lay at the heart of the religiously inspired strategy for political action. As the century has progressed, strategies have become increasingly radical, violent, and divisive. The place occupied by Islamism in the Egyptian political scene of the 1990s reflects the victory of repression over idealism. The regime of President Hosni Mubarak (1981–), though more open than its predecessors, remains reliant upon the military and security apparatus, has no substantial ideological credibility, has no proven popular appeal, and has stunted the intellectual advances that began with al-Afghani a hundred years ago.

In July 1954, Sayyid Qutb was arrested along with an estimated 50,000 other members of the Muslim Brotherhood.[53] A year later Qutb was sentenced to fifteen years in prison with hard labor, accused of planning the overthrow of the government. He was released a decade later, but rearrested within a year. In 1966 he was tried and found guilty by a military court of planning the assassination of President Nasser. On 29 August 1966, he was hanged. Qutb's legacy has been profound. He projected jihad to center stage and unequivocally grasped the mechanics of the reformist trend, eschewing al-Banna's tendency to ignore or diminish the significance of questions that were difficult to answer. Qutb's doubts about the relevance of the traditions of Islam—essentially the practices passed down through time in the words of Islamic jurists, whose rulings had developed into the body of the four schools of Islamic jurisprudence, the *fiqh*—stemmed from his assertion of the Koran as the sole source of law: "All codes of law, ancient or modern, are deficient while the Islamic legislation alone is complete,"[54] he wrote, insisting that man-made law was innately partisan and lacked the pure justice of the Islamic *sharia*.[55]

The introduction of the *sharia* as the sole source of law remains the goal of all Islamist movements, necessitating their control of political power. Olivier Roy defines these movements in such a way on the grounds that they have identified modern society as the target of their Islamization, which they aim to achieve through political action outside the mosques.[56] The Islamists are not interested in reworking interpretations of the past; rather, they seek to Islamize all the contemporary institutions that are associated with the wielding of political power. They are essentially modern, though variations exist as to whether the political power they are seeking should be held by authoritarian theocrats, influential imams making firm but diplomatic suggestions to open-minded secularists, or Muslim democrats relying on a parliamentary system to Islamize society.

"Islamic principles can be introduced slowly,"[57] the Brotherhood's spokesman, Mamoun al-Hodeibi, told me. "It's not accepted in our religion to smash everything and then introduce everything in one go

... to destroy everything. If an Islamic party comes to power, it will need to be in power for many years, more than twenty years, and go on step by step, to apply the Islamic principles." His view reveals much in its subtext and contrasts sharply with Qutb's call for purity achieved through the process of jihad. Al-Hodeibi, a former senior judge, argues that the normal term of office for a democratically elected government would not allow sufficient time for the *din* to be established.

At heart, the brotherhood, which now stands in the shadows of Egyptian politics—more of a dinosaur than the dynamic force its intellectual, social, and historical significance warrants—draws its continued sense of purpose from the depth of popular religious faith. This strength is coupled with the failure of successive regimes to adequately address or ameliorate pitiful social and economic conditions. But, seventy years after its foundation, the brotherhood is no closer to achieving direct political influence—in Egypt or elsewhere—than managed by al-Afghani in his attempts to convince the sultans of the Ottoman court that they should revive the *umma*. This denial of influence, perpetuated by regimes fearful of ideology per se, has left this potent intellectual trend in religious thought stillborn. The society of which it is an integral part now lies in a state of intellectual repression; Egyptian political life is moribund and its leaders more concerned about halting political evolution than risking a looser power structure in the search for a valid national identity. Within this void, the Muslim Brotherhood has proved durable, extending its role as a provider of welfare and as a social movement with broader roots than any other Egyptian political organization. Al-Hodeibi says:

> Until now, no other real political body has operated, so we are the stronger. We continue to work and go to prison, while others remain silent. The other [opposition political] groups don't want to struggle and go to jail. Egypt is an Islamic nation. People have put it in power by their own will. But there are some things that can't be achieved except by being in government—introducing laws, taking measures on media and films. Ordinary people can't do anything about these things. The people in power are afraid of all groups. They know they are not supported. Everybody is against them, and the government has to portray us as being the main threat. That's what the West understands. It's done for the West.[58]

Nasser, Sadat, and Mubarak, the successive leaders of independent Egypt, view the faith of the Islamists as "a mere security problem and not a political question," said Adel Hussein, secretary general of the Labour Party,[59] the least conservative of Egypt's Islamist political organizations. Emerging out of the secular radicalism of the 1960s, Hussein shifted allegiance from nationalism and was ultimately drawn to Islam, remaining outside the Muslim Brotherhood, which he viewed as conservative and reluctant to act decisively:

> I started to apply a radical nationalist line. Through this I came to the conclusion that Islam is the decisive component of our national identity, and is the real basis of what we fight for as national Arab unity. Ultimately I was fully convinced that Islam isn't only useful in a pragmatic way, that is as a way of communicating to ordinary people. I was convinced that it is useful in the sense that it can build a modern civilization.

Hussein, whose political party remains small but nevertheless representative of a shift within the generally inert Egyptian political field, has taken the debate in Egypt back to where it began, to al-Afghani's concept of "civilization." Where the different strands of the Islamic movement stand apart most starkly is in their methods: "There are real ideological and theoretical differences between different Islamic directions. But the balance of forces between them is affected by the general political situation. Their radicalism also makes them more influential," Hussein said.

Relative influence has now, in the twilight of the twentieth century, exposed political strength and weakness without allowing political Islam—*Islamism*—to enjoy its new golden age. "Islamism was a moment, a fragile synthesis between Islam and political modernity, which ultimately never took root," writes Roy.[60] "The revolutionary project of ideologically transforming the society is being replaced by a plan to implement the *sharia* and to purify mores. . . . The right to individual interpretation *(ijtihad)* has been surrendered. . . . Today's Islamism, from which both political reflection and ascetic elitism have disappeared . . . replaces a discourse on the state with a discourse on society."[61] Islamism, according to Roy, has largely been replaced by neofundamentalism. Far from striving to realize the political aims of the Koran as the all-embracing concept promoted and envisaged by Qutb and his predecessors, Roy claims that the Islamic movements of the late 1990s lack an intellectual vision and instead promote a form of "popular Islam," which involves ensuring the right to practice Islam in areas where Muslims are present. This goal marks a profound departure from the quest to restore the *umma*.

Roy's broad assertion encompasses hundreds of organizations and thousands of activists. Their variety, internal conflicts, and troubled relations with the states in which they operate are the major political issues facing an Islamic world out of which a plethora of radical movements has emerged. One hundred years after al-Afghani, the simplicity of the colonial foe has been replaced by the complexity of Islam's internal conflicts. The Islamists have found their opponents among monarchists, nationalists, communists, and capitalists. The relatively straightforward opposition to colonial occupation has been replaced with the far more profound issue of whether Muslims should be permitted to declare jihad against fellow Muslims.

The profusion of Islamist organizations has created the shadow in which the Muslim world's entire political agenda now operates. The relative simplicity of independence from colonialism, with all the promises of liberation that such a significant and rare historical turning point was supposed to bring, has been followed by political experiments whose consequences have been the social and economic conditions out of which mass support for the late-twentieth-century Islamist movements emerged. But with the regimes they are confronting apparently too weak to thwart them, and the Islamists themselves too weak to seize political power, stalemate has ensured the Muslim world of instability for some time to come. In this climate, the movements have now opted to play a waiting game.

5

The Myth of
the Golden Age
The Maghreb and Arabia

"WE ARE NOT UTOPIAN. Nor are we idealists. There wasn't perfection during the time of the Prophet. In fact there were many imperfections. But even with them there can be a workable society, with all its imperfections."[1] Nadia Yassine sat demurely on a carved and cushioned armchair in a corner of the sitting room of the small ground-floor apartment where she lives with her husband and children in a district of the Moroccan town of Salé.[2] She continued:

> The world is becoming foolish. It's going too fast, and if it's not slowed down there will be fewer and fewer people who can keep up with it. Economic inequality is monstrous. At the same time, we want to return to our spirituality. The Islamic movement is essentially spiritual. And the great chaos we are living in is essentially spiritual. We don't know who we are. Are we Arab, African, or members of a deprived economic group? There are social causes. Poverty is a determinant. But the social situation doesn't explain the Islamist influence, because the middle classes are in the movement. It is because religion alone can give people a new life.

Nadia Yassine lives in the twilight world of the Moroccan Islamist movement. It is uncertain whether there really *is* a Moroccan Islamist "movement." Her father, Sheikh Abdesalam Yassine, has been under house arrest—in a house a few muddy streets away from his daughter's—since 1990. The illegal movement he leads, al-Adl wa'l Ihsane, "Justice and Charity," operates clandestinely, mainly among university students.

Late one evening in December 1995, outside a newspaper shop on a nearly deserted street off African Unity Square in central Rabat, an aging Mercedes Benz stopped beside the postbox agreed as our meeting place. Through the car's open window the middle-aged driver asked me for my name, opened the door, then beckoned me into the car. We drove through the elegant Moroccan city, out past the great medieval walls, and south toward the new suburbs that line the road to Casablanca. In a modern apartment, al-Adl wa'l Ihsane's official spokesman, Fathallah Arsalan, waited in a brightly lit room lined on three sides by a modest *salon Marocain*, the embroidered settee that serves as seating for guests and bedding for children and that has symbolic importance as the first item of furniture bought for a new home.

"Our current strategy is bound up in safeguarding our existence. Ensuring our existence is our man preoccupation, to ensure our position in the political life of the country," Arsalan began.[3]

> We are not authorized to play our role in social life. We are waiting for the day when we will be able to play our role. We are now preparing for that period, by educating people, and propagating our vision secretly, by publishing books and secretly circulating them, and videos of Abdesalam Yassine, at meetings in peoples' houses. We cover the entire country, and we're present in all social groups. The loss of confidence among people with regard to the political life, means that people are spontaneously coming to us.

The organization is closely watched by the Moroccan security services. Its leaders have their telephones tapped and are denied passports to travel, even to participate in the Muslim pilgrimage to Mecca, the haj.

"We constitute a threat, not because we advocate violence. We are against violence," Fathallah Arsalan told me. "But we constitute a threat because we are popular. The state of siege we face, and the trials [of our supporters], have given us publicity. We think that the situation will become truly explosive, and everybody will become desperate for change." Dominating the strategy of al-Adl wa'l Ihsane is the need to forge a new, religiously inspired identity without directly confronting the claim by the Moroccan monarch, King Hassan II, that he is the rightful leader of the country's Muslims as a direct descendent of the Prophet Mohammed, who carries the title not only of king but also of "Commander of the Faithful." "If he was only head of state, that would be fine," said Fathallah. "But as Commander of the Faithful there are many contradictions. He doesn't apply true Islam because he doesn't apply the *sharia*, and he doesn't give an example of the Islamic way of life. His hypocrisy is visible. He maintains non-Islamic traditions."

Contradictions are the essence of Moroccan political life. Nadia Yassine is able to visit her father, Abdesalam Yassine, in his home, despite his house arrest. "Morocco is a great waiting room. The politics of the *makhzan*[4] is always to do what is unplanned. The most successful repressive regime is here, because it's very intelligent repression. It's very original and successful," she said. For the Islamists the ultimate goals of the regime, as well as the goals of reform, remain unclear, confused, and ill defined in the Moroccan context. From the 1960s King Hassan has used torture and long-term imprisonment as the primary weapons in his arsenal to suppress political opponents. Such measures have now been largely replaced by a lurking, ever-present sense of fear. Political reform, signs of economic liberalization, and the freedom of human rights organizations to function in Morocco have not signaled any decline in the absolute power, derived from fear, that the monarchy continues to wield. Indeed, the monarchy's willingness to use terror in the past is what prevents would-be opponents from overstepping the very clearly defined limits of political debate that prevail today.

"The Islamists don't have a significant role in Morocco because we are not free. If the state allowed us to operate, then that would change," said Mustapha Ramid,[5] an Islamist lawyer who has defended Islamic activists charged with organizing activities on behalf of al-Adl wa'l Ihsane. He continued:

> The state controls religion. The authorities have left the Islamists between the earth and the sky. And the situation for the Islamists is worse than that of the political opposition parties.[6] The Islamists are marginalized, so we are not influential in society in a way that is [practically] effective. Even so, the Islamists are present in all areas, whereas the left-wing parties have a very limited presence, and the right-wing parties have no presence at all among the population. The government has no solutions regarding the political and economic crisis, and we Islamists can arrive at our goals, because of the force of Islam. Islam will find its origins.

It is the apparent reluctance of Morocco's Islamic movement to stir up their politically stagnant country that has *allowed* the ruling elite to treat them with caution and a degree of restraint. "We are the only [real] opposition in Morocco. And we are silent," Nadia Yassine said. "We can't do much else. [King] Hassan II doesn't want my father to be a martyr. He had the intelligence to understand that a martyr would be much more influential." So, Morocco remains what she aptly described as a "waiting room." The question then arises: What is being awaited? Explanations of what may happen in the future are more pertinent among Islamists within the country, even those not associated with al-Adl wa'l Ihsane, than among any of the secular parties, whose role is essentially to provide a pluralist gloss to monarchical absolutism.

"Public opinion isn't politicized. So the political parties don't repre-sent public opinion. They represent the political elites of Casablanca, Fès, and Rabat,"[7] said Mohammed Yatim, president of the moderate Is-lamist organization the Mouvement de la Renaissance et de Renou-veau,[8] which functions mainly as an editorial body for the newspaper *al-Arraya* (The Flag). "The [secular political] parties don't have ideol-ogy. They have only regional and personal allegiances. These lie at the heart of the political crisis in Morocco. These parties haven't brought the masses on board. And the process has excluded the Islamists. There's no stability without mass participation in politics, and mean-while there is general discontent. We will see how it develops. Tomor-row, or the day after."

Politics in the Wilderness

Morocco's political stagnation is less of a problem for the Islamic movement than it may at first appear. The absence of immediate change, the apparent reluctance of al-Adl wa'l Ihsane to force a change in its own status, and the readiness with which its leaders are prepared to await that change until some point in the future are all elements of a strategy that is decidedly long-term, derived from the basic assump-tion that change is inevitable. "Those who are opposed to change are simply afraid to lose their privileges. That is why they tend to equate change with heresy. . . . The Prophet Muhammad always looked to the future and very rarely looked back on the past. It is even said that, when he walked, he always looked ahead and never turned his head," wrote Mahdi Elmandjra, a professor of social science at Rabat's Mo-hammed V University and one of the Muslim world's leading writers on the future of Islam and its relations with the non-Muslim world.[9] "When young Muslims return to their cultural sources, it is because they are seeking guidance from their endogenous values. The future that the Arab-Islamic world is looking for depends on the revival of Is-lam in its innovative acceptation, not on Islam of blind imitation which led to the fall of a once brilliant civilization," he said.

Harnessing popular disillusionment to achieve effective political ac-tion has not been an entirely successful strategy for Islamist move-ments in Morocco and elsewhere in the late 1990s. But much of this strategy's success has been of a secondary nature. Incumbent regimes have been forced to adopt a variety of Islamic measures—in the law, in education, in the assertion of their public image—to pacify the Is-lamists and draw popular support to themselves in an effort to under-mine that of the Islamist movements. Nevertheless, the legitimacy of

the Muslim world's various regimes—socialist, monarchical, techno-
cratic, or military—has yet to be established in the eyes of large
swaths of their subject populations, which have never had the opportunity to participate in fair elections. Elmandjra continues:

> One of the greatest handicaps of the Islamic world nowadays lies in the
> fact that the ruling elite has no clear vision of the future and its require-
> ments. For it is unaware of the currents of thought that shape today's re-
> ality and insensitive to the major preoccupations of the population.
> . . . Our rulers' attention is focused on the slightest move by the opposi-
> tion, convinced as they are that it is intent on toppling them and remov-
> ing them from power. So much so that, when it comes to tackling the ills
> of society, they can only improvise patchwork solutions and soothing
> measures with no lasting effect.[10]

Expectations of the era of independence from colonial rule were
enormous. "We live in an age which can be defined as one in which
freedom and independence are not an end to which peoples and nations strive, but a means to ends higher, more permanent, and more
comprehensive in their benefits," the Egyptian writer Taha Husayn
wrote in the 1930s.[11] In Morocco the transition from colonial rule, a
process that began with the formation of political parties in the 1950s,
generated lively debate about the future of the country. But this subject was quickly excised from the political agenda as soon as Hassan II
consolidated his power following the death of his father, Mohammed
V, in 1961, five years after independence from France. That year,
Mehdi Ben Barka, who had founded the Union Nationale des Forces
Populaire (UNFP) political party in 1959, wrote to King Hassan: "Our
task is to pursue the work started by our sovereign [Mohammed V] toward the creation of a free, democratic, and prosperous Morocco, con-
forming with His Majesty's ideals and popular aspirations."[12] Five
years later Hassan silenced the last of the voices of independence
when his interior minister, General Mohammed Oufkir, was dispatched to Paris, where Ben Barka was in exile. On 29 October 1965
Oufkir tortured Ben Barka to death in a Paris "safe-house," and Morocco's monarchical despotism was firmly established, with King Hassan as its figurehead and Oufkir its policeman. Institutionally, Morocco remains in the late 1990s what it has been since independence.
Fear remains the key weapon in the regime's armory. The population
knows what the regime—the makhzan—has done in the past. The
same people are still controlling the country, and nothing has occurred
to suggest that there has been a definitive break with past practices.

The aspirations on independence in neighboring Algeria in 1962 were
intensified not only by the prospect of what the future might bring but

by the immense sense of deliverance that marked the end of the vicious war of independence from France, in which a million Algerians had died. Unlike Morocco, where the real power of royalty has engendered the stagnation that characterizes political life, republican Algeria institutionalized revolution in the form of an alliance, what John Esposito calls the "ruling bargain,"[13] in which the population rescinded their right to free political organization in return for the state providing adequate social welfare and job security.

Esposito, like many other writers, ascribes the rise of Islamism to the dire social and economic conditions of many Muslim societies coupled with the ability of the Islamist organizations—in Algeria, the Front Islamique de Salut (FIS)—to organize welfare provision and, in the areas in which it later took control of local councils, to prove itself more efficient in meeting social needs than the central government, run (in Algeria) since 1962 by an alliance of the army, the bureaucracy, and the National Liberation Front (FLN). "Algeria's Arab socialist state was legitimated constitutionally by a thin veneer of Islam," Esposito writes. "In fact the FLN, in the guise of Islamic socialism, pursued an essentially secular path of political and economic development implemented by a western-oriented elite."[14]

Despite the important role the Islamist movement had played in the evolution of Algerian responses to colonialism, as detailed in Chapter 3, the resurgence of political Islam as a response to the social and economic failures of the independent states of the Islamic world—in Algeria as elsewhere—should be seen as rooted in both its immediate popularity as well as in its appeal to deeper cultural values. Poor educational standards, which in some Muslim countries have resulted in illiteracy rates of 80 percent,[15] have heightened the sense of disconnection from cultural values. For the Islamists, this is most acute in the understanding of religion. Illiteracy denies the individual Muslim the fundamental Islamic right of being able to have direct communion with God. Islam has no clergy, and the individual has no go-between with Allah. An ability to read and understand the Koran is a vital element in the essential freedom of the religion itself. Growing illiteracy, chronic unemployment particularly among university graduates, and poor educational standards, coupled with state control of mosques and a stagnant political environment, have hardly constituted auspicious beginnings for populations that risked much to loosen the shackles of colonialism.

In Algeria, the FIS did for a time succeed in stepping into the void that had engulfed the old regime. Now, seven years later, the violence perpetrated by the armed groups and the security forces has generated its own momentum, throwing into doubt whether the conflict has anything left to do with religion. More and more, it appears to have become a grotesquely violent war of attrition between individuals inspired by personal revenge and acting on behalf of larger interests that lack the ability to find a solution. On 13 May 1994 the FIS's main Islamist rival, the Armed Islamic Group (GIA), issued a statement entitled the "bayane al-wihda," the "declaration of union," in which it announced that it was the "only legal group now fighting jihad." The statement was signed by Abu Abdallah Ahmed, the emir or leader of the GIA at that time; Abderazak Redjam, apparently on behalf of the FIS; and Said Mekhloufi, representing the Harakat al-Dawla Islamiyya, the Movement for an Islamic State.[16] The statement appeared to indicate that the entire Islamist movement had been subsumed by the GIA, with FIS leaders—most of whom were either in prison or in exile abroad—and representatives of other Islamist organizations having become members of the GIA consultative council. Doubt has been cast on the authenticity of the declaration. What it did reveal, however, was the kind of vision of the ideal scenario that the most radical of Algeria's groups at one time had had: they sought a unity of purpose among the variety of Islamist groups and they sought a single political structure with other Islamist groups, with the single declared aim of fighting jihad, understanding that political unity was essential in the face of the concerted efforts of Algeria's *eradicateurs* to annihilate the Islamist trend altogether.

"When Abu Abdallah Ahmed was leading the GIA, the organization grew to around 100,000,[17] though only 3 percent of them were former Arab Afghans," Karim Omar, the London-based former Afghan Mujahideen fighter, told me. He continued:

> It was the golden period, which went on well into 1995. Then extremists took over the group. The GIA was spread out over 1,400 kilometers. It was so spread, and it became difficult to organize them. But all of the troubles are connected to areas close to Algiers. Abdallah was killed, and he had named Abou Khalil Mahfoud as his successor. But he was sidelined within a few weeks. The situation now in Algeria, for the GIA, is that from the east of Algiers to the Tunisian border, the area is working already according to the rules of jihad. In the western area, to the Moroccan border, the GIA is very well organized and strong. The chaos is in the center, around Algiers, where different people have criticized what has been going on. Which is what led to them killing Zitouni.[18] The powerful GIA leaders are close to the Moroccan groups, and two of the GIA cells are talking to the Moroccan Islamists.[19] Now there are effectively three groups, all of which have had associations with the GIA. When they split, they reverted to what they had been before uniting, and they each have an area: Said Mekhloufi in the west, the former AIS[20] in the east, with some of the Arab Afghans and a mix of original GIA around Algiers.

Algeria's conflict has now claimed at least 65,000 lives. A key feature of the conflict has been, despite allegations of Moroccan support—allegations which are unlikely, despite the relish felt by many Moroccans at the predicament now facing their long-time regional rival—that it has shown the essentially national character of the conflict. It has not spread across borders and engulfed neighboring countries, despite the presence of Islamist movements in both Morocco and Tunisia. This fact reveals a great deal about the condition of the umma, the community of Muslims. "In Algeria, the conflict is a settling of scores. It's got nothing to do with Islam,"[21] said Nadia Yassine, daughter of the Moroccan Islamist leader. Other Moroccans have little sympathy for their regional rivals across the Atlas mountains, whom they view as having opted for violence too early—merely as a form of proof that they still have the same courage and determination that saw their country through the war of independence.

On its eastern frontier, Algeria also finds that its experience has isolated it from its neighbor. In the eyes of many governments in the Muslim world, Tunisia has provided the model strategy for dealing with the Islamist resurgence. The Tunisian government's ruthless policies vis-à-vis the Islamist movement has allowed it to pursue policies of Westernization that no other government in the region has been able to do in such brazen defiance of the Islamic resurgence, which has planted considerable roots and which has broad support.

The character of the Tunisian Islamist movement, which in 1981 had adopted the name Mouvement du Tendence Islamique or Islamic Tendency Movement (MTI), but which came to be known as the Ennahda (Renaissance) Party, was forged as much by the circumstances of its position in Tunisian politics as by the intellectual background of its leader, Rached Ghannouchi.[22] His imprisonment during the 1980s and later exile in Great Britain stemmed as much from the virulently anti-Islamist policies of Tunisia's founding president, Habib Bourguiba, as from any radicalism within Ennahda itself.

"More often than not it is the state that has led the way into violence. . . . A close examination of the chronology of mounting 'Islamic' violence shows that the regimes with their shaky support have often exploited the need to rid themselves of the Islamist bogeyman,"[23] writes François Burgat, in a general reference to the governments of the Islamic world. Seen historically, his view is in some cases flawed. The original Islamist movements did not propagate violence. However, their successors, smarting from the failure of the nonviolent groups to achieve their aims, have from the beginning openly adopted the violence of jihad as a central principle. Violence has thus spiraled, often in response to government policies—a view shared by Esposito.[24]

The Tunisian movement did not evolve in this way, however. Although it evolved from being a highly public organization, which hid few of its aims, to being more secretive about its structure, it did so without entailing the creation of wholly separate splinter groups formed with the avowed purpose of using violence. But perhaps the absence of this element of the organization's evolution is explained by the government's destruction of Ennahda. In November 1987 the increasingly irrational and aging Bourguiba was removed from power in a palace coup that brought the interior minister, Zein al-Abdin Ben Ali, to power. In an effort to win popular support, Ben Ali promised democracy and proclaimed that the Islamists would be allowed to operate publicly at least to the extent of being able to publish a newspaper. Within two years, Ben Ali's promises had been withdrawn. The intervening period had seen Ennahda candidates score well at an election in 1989, and the FIS rise to great influence in neighboring Algeria (a process that would culminate in the Algerian Islamists winning 54 percent of the votes in the local elections of 12 June 1990). The genuine popularity of the Islamist movements across the Arab world was becoming quickly and plainly evident. In light of these events, Ben Ali refused to register Ennahda as a legal political party. In May 1991, the group's "military wing" was accused of a plot to overthrow the government. Its leaders, as well as many alleged activists from within the armed forces, were arrested, rapid justice was meted out, heavy prison sentences were imposed, and Ghannouchi fled into exile.

"Now, we have no reason to think that the Tunisian people that elected our government in 1989 has changed its mind,"[25] said Rached Ghannouchi. He continued:

> Just as I don't think the Algerian people changed their minds in November 1995 [when the Islamists' call for a poll boycott failed and President Zeroual was elected]. But they gave a chance to Zeroual to return peace and to release the people who are in the prisons. We can't judge that the Algerians have changed their minds. The Tunisian people are the same as the Algerian people. The secular minority has very limited popularity. Once the people have gained their freedom, they will elect the Islamists. We believe that people cannot be governed forever by violence, and we have enough patience to wait, because we believe that the tendency towards democracy is universal.

Ghannouchi, like many exiled and imprisoned Islamist leaders, is viewed by many of his own supporters as having lost much of his value, being no longer able to conduct operations on the ground. Because one of the key elements of Ghannouchi's outlook was to promote "Tunisianness" in the context of Islamization (which contrasts sharply with the all-embracing, pan-Islamic approach of the Muslim Brotherhood and the scholars seeking the unity of the *umma*), his disappearance from Tunisia was a severe blow.

"We believe that we are in a transition period. And we have enough patience to deal with this transition period," Ghannouchi said. He insisted:

> We think that living [in exile] in the West gives us the opportunity to know this great [Western] civilization. To know the positive and negative factors. We can learn many things and can explain our views. Our country is influenced by the West more than by Iran or Sudan. Our country is very far from Iran or Sudan. The establishment of *sharia* isn't part of our agenda now. Our situation is different from Iran and Sudan. We believe in the *sharia* and an Islamic state, but we don't believe these are the current problems for the Tunisian people. The problem in Tunisia isn't: which law should we apply, *sharia* or secular? The problem in Tunisia is the absence of law. Even the laws which are recognized in Tunisia aren't implemented. And I can't see how the police state will develop from dictatorship to democracy. The only way left now is strikes and demonstrations, or using violence. And we are against violence.

Ghannouchi vowed to fill the political vacuum that Ennahda remains convinced it alone can occupy when the government is ultimately exposed as having no conviction other than assuring its own survival.

The Building of a Nation

The context of political Islam's rise to influence is, from the mainstream Western viewpoint, regarded as the key to comprehending its true purpose. The politicization of the Association of Algerian Ulama (AUMA) and the Egyptian Muslim Brotherhood was a response to colonialism, intended to exert pressure to end foreign domination. However, the prevalence of two other influences on the Islamist trend should be viewed as being equally significant, as forming a triad of pressures that have done much to forge the character of the Islamist movements. The first is the call to faith itself, which lies closest to the heart of all Muslims, whether they are Islamists or not. Religion in itself has a great hold on the life of Muslims, and the Islamist movement is essentially a call to abide by religious principles that are already deeply embedded in the consciousness of the great majority.

The other element is the interaction between the Islamist movements and secularist politics. Drawing upon the arguments of orien-

talists such as Gustave von Grunebaum,[26] the tendency in the West—
which has attempted to use its media power as well as its overwhelming political and other resources to forge a global *image* of Islam for
Muslims and non-Muslims alike—has been to assert that proof of the
Islamists' regressiveness lies in the fact that, after decades of exposure
to other cultures (according to von Grunebaum, *Western* cultures), Islam per se has attempted to retain its alleged "medieval" purity by rejecting modernity, which for him and many others is equated with
Westernization. This view is entirely wrong.

For the orientalist scholars, in particular von Grunebaum, the tortu-
ous and unresolved coexistence of Islamists and their opponents
within the secular regimes of the Muslim world flies in the face of his
and others' assertion that the Islamists ignore cultural coexistence.
Von Grunebaum writes essentially about the centuries that had passed
since Islam's golden age several hundred years ago rather than about
the twentieth century, in which the difference between Islamist and
secularist Muslims is perhaps clearer.[27] But the debate *within* Islam has
been intense throughout the twentieth century (during which time von
Grunebaum has been writing), beginning with the days of Sayyid Jamal
al-Din al-Afghani. The West's role in influencing scholars such as al-
Afghani, Muhammad Abduh, and Sayyid Qutb has been extremely significant. Viewed historically, it was the West that politicized the entire
debate, by providing a target for the Islamists—as the colonial oppres-
sor—into whose superior way of life the orientalists find it difficult to
comprehend Muslims not wishing to assimilate themselves.

Because it is opposed by the centuries-old cultural values of Islam, it
is no surprise that this assimilation was largely rejected. But, having
spearheaded the rejection of one Westernizing influence, the Islamist
movements have subsequently found themselves confronted by its
legacy, in the form of postindependence autocratic systems of government whose bodies of law, security apparatuses, and methods of political manipulation have been inherited from their colonial predecessors.
Experiments with monarchism, nationalism, and socialism have characterized the leadership of most countries of the Islamic world since the
independence movements achieved their aims. The secularization of
politics is the central element of Western modernism, and this trend became a central element of the postindependence political movements in
the Islamic world. Although the new political elites formed a secular
national character that was detached from the larger social classes who
were not part of that elite, the masses religiously guarded their traditions.

Cross-class adherence to the Islamist cause is the most significant
testimony to the failure of the various secular ideological forms of

government that have dominated the Islamic world from the dawn of independence to the current Islamic resurgence.[28] But the confidence with which *modernizing*, secular nationalism dealt with the Islamists evaporated when its internal political strength was put to the test.

"The defeat of 1967 was a declaration of the end of the Arab nationalist project. The Arab nationalists were in power, and their project very clearly failed."[29] So said Hosam Issa, formerly a strategist for Egypt's Arab Democratic Nasserite Party and now professor of law at Cairo's Ain Shams University. The nationalism of Gamal Abdel Nasser, which had drawn Egypt toward independence and led to the creation of an economic system heavily reliant upon export barter agreements with the communist countries of eastern Europe and the creation of sprawling and barely habitable urban developments around Cairo, was put to the test when Israel launched the Six-Day War on 5 June 1967. Issa continued:

> After the defeat, people would say: we tried liberalism before the revolution in 1952, then we tried Arab nationalism, and then we had to find another form of identity. Then the Islamists came and said: before we are Arabs we are Muslims. And this approach, after 1967, can explain part of the [Islamist] phenomenon. It can explain why Algeria, Egypt, Tunisia, Sudan, Syria, all went that way, all at the same time. It's a change of identity. Now the Muslim intellectuals are coming to say: we are Arab Muslims. Meanwhile, the Arab nationalists are coming closer to the Islamists, whereas the Islamists are becoming more Arab.

But Nasser's legacy is perhaps more profound than a simple association with an ideology. "He still forms the political horizon," said Issa. "Everyone has to still define themselves in terms of him. He said that everybody has the right to dignity." The same view is to be found elsewhere, in analyses of the Six-Day War and its impact upon the standing of nationalists. Nationalism, writes Edward Mortimer, "was not abandoned. . . . Indeed, it was precisely the conviction that there was indeed an Arab nation with a collective destiny which made the disaster so deeply felt. . . . But even among the nationalists . . . there was a widespread feeling that nationalism by itself was not enough."[30]

The fundamental issue raised by nationalism with regard to the evolving identity of the Islamists, in Egypt as elsewhere in the Islamic world, was the question of *nation* itself. The concept of the pan-Islamic *umma* appeared to contradict the spirit of nationhood espoused by nationalism. Moreover, the nationalists harnessed *modernism* to their cause in a manner that isolated the Islamists, who also sought the modernization of society but who found the process much more complicated than the nationalists did during their heyday. The latter could superimpose Western modernity—a process that took less than a generation to falter and collapse. The Islamists, meanwhile, had first to finalize their manifesto in order to marry modernity and *ijtihad* with their vision of the Islamic way of life as they felt it should be applied in the current circumstances. "The idea of an Egyptian nation, entitled to a separate political existence, involved not only the denial of a single Islamic political community, but also the assertion that there could be a virtuous community based on something other than a common religion and a revealed law. . . . [It] was the British occupation which fused Islamic modernism with Egyptian nationalism,"[31] writes Albert Hourani, referring to the issue as it arose after 1882, when the British took over Egypt. The absence of a clear leader of the *umma* during the latter years of the Ottoman empire, owing largely to the decay of that empire, had fostered an intense nationalism among Arabs—as one section of the Muslim community—that sought "a reform of the law, the creation of a modern and unified system of law by the use of *ijtihad* . . . [and] a shift in the balance of power inside the *umma*, from the Turks back to the Arabs."[32]

Trends within nationalism varied widely. From Syria to Egypt, the different strains of thought were influenced by history, cultural life, and the evolving relationship with the colonial powers. However, Islam is a fact of Arab history, and consequently the conundrum that the secularists of the Arab world had to resolve was how to emulate the model of the *secular* nation-states—that is, the European colonial powers—in building nations that were clearly the inheritors of a strongly *religious* culture. The failure of the Ottoman empire to lead the *umma* had estranged the Arab world from the would-be caliphate. This heightened Arab nationalist resolve to form a wholly separate Arab identity rooted in Islam. This can be seen in the evolution of Egyptian Islamic thought, particularly in the increasingly political outlook of writers like Rashid Rida.

Central to the growing sense of Arab nationalism before World War II was the common thread of the Arabic language. After the war, the intellectual architects of Egyptian nationalism who had been prominent earlier, notably Taha Husayn, seemed less important. An important aspect of the nationalism promoted by Husayn was its relationship to colonialism and the intense belief that intrinsic to national assertion was the belief that Egyptians were not inferior to Europeans. After the war the world was divided, and it mattered less what Europeans thought of Arabs. The Cold War provided new choices, and Nasser took Egypt into the communist orbit beginning in the mid-1950s, which isolated him from the more conservative Arab states. Simultaneously, Nasser "saw Islam in general and Al-Azhar[33] in particular . . . as potential instruments not only for internal security but also for a 'revolutionary' foreign policy."[34] This policy centered on turning the annual haj into a "political power" at which a congress of the leaders of the Islamic world would be held to formulate policies. The idea was dropped after a few years, as Nasser's close ties with the Soviet Union drove a wedge between him and the Saudi Arabian leadership, upon whom the success of the congress relied. Nasser's control of religion, the execution in 1966 of Muslim Brotherhood member Sayyid Qutb, and the blatant use of the Al-Azhar establishment as a weapon of control and propaganda had, by 1967, entrenched the mainstream Egyptian nationalist view of political Islam, in particular its relationship with the by-then largely imprisoned Muslim Brotherhood.

The 1967 war, which engaged several Arab armies, resulted in Israel's seizure of the Golan Heights from Syria, the Sinai desert from Egypt, the West Bank from Jordan, and, most important of all, East Jerusalem, wherein lay the third holiest shrine in Islam, the al-Aqsa mosque. But it was Egypt that suffered the most serious political fallout. The defeat compounded a growing sense of disillusionment that had emerged over the previous years. "The vast majority of people had come to the conclusion that there was something seriously wrong in our previous experiments with development, and that we had to find something else. In the search for a new hope people came to Islam, and it was the defeat of 1967 which really raised this issue,"[35] said Adel Hussein of the Islamist-leaning Egyptian Labour Party.

Even at the opposite end of the political spectrum, a similar analysis is to be found: "Secular ideologies aren't working, and the vacuum has been filled by the Islamists,"[36] said Mohamed Sid Ahmed, Egypt's leading leftist and avowedly secular political commentator, of the situation thirty years after the Arabs' humiliation in 1967. "The Islamist leaders are poor, perhaps, but certainly intelligent. They are not thugs. But unlike the original liberation movements of the developing world, they are movements out of despair rather than hope."

Out of that despair emerged the Islamist organizations. The secular elite's realization of its own lack of legitimacy since the Six-Day War, in Egypt as elsewhere, has been a key influence on its response to the challenge from the Islamists. The political evolution of the past thirty years has centered upon the determination of that elite to prevent this lack of legitimacy from resulting in its own loss of power. Political survival has become paramount, at the expense of social needs, economic logic, and political freedom. It has been in this highly pressured environment that the dynamics of mass support for the Islamists has been generated into the Islamic resurgence and the calls for stricter adherence to religious practice as laid down in the Koran. The combina-

tion of social deprivation in newly urbanized areas, political illegitimacy, and national humiliation on a pan-Islamic scale[37] served to
unite Muslims in a quest for a new identity. Consequently, the *context* of the Islamist movements' evolution should be seen for what it
is: not an innately regressive political phenomenon,

> not rebellious because they are opposed to development (or even, to an
> extent, to modernization), but rather because they desired it so strongly
> and yet could not get it. Theirs is the proverbial case of "sour grapes":
> they hate modernity because they cannot get it! The Islamists are not an-
> gry because the airplane has replaced the camel; they are angry because
> they could not get on the airplane. . . . [Had] Nasserism (and other simi-
> lar development projects) "delivered" in the sixties, we would not be wit-
> nessing the same political revival of Islam that we see today.[38]

The appeal of the Islamists for the victims of disillusionment, unemployment, and frustration has now strengthened considerably. "Re-
siding in the same neighborhoods, speaking the same language, and familiar with the same deprivations as the audience to whom they
appeal, Islamist activists leading some of Egypt's major professional
associations have to a large extent managed to bridge the gap between
elite and mass culture."[39] Meanwhile, the growing gulf between the
ruling elites and these same masses was starkly exposed by events
that positioned the Muslim world on the global agenda as never before. Egypt's demonstration of its ability to confront Israeli military
power by recapturing stretches of the Israeli-occupied Sinai in 1973
was portrayed as a victory for the Islamic call made by Nasser's successor, Anwar al-Sadat. The Arab oil embargo the same year showed
the world that the states of the Middle East could no longer be taken
for granted, as they had the economic clout to significantly affect the
global economy. But these events, ultimately, did not help the leaders
of the Arab world establish any greater legitimacy among their own
populations. Al-Sadat's victory in 1973 was, for the Islamists, wasted.
Furthermore, his invocation of Islam was exposed as an opportunistic
ploy when Egypt and Israel signed the 1979 Camp David accords,
leading to a formal peace treaty in 1981, an act that contributed to al-
Sadat's assassination by Islamists on 6 October that year. The oil price
hike—a message to the world—subsequently allowed the sheikhs of
the Gulf to wallow in undreamed-of wealth, whereas the vast majority
of Arabs lived in poverty. The disappointments have mounted, and no
ruling ideology has since, except perhaps by default, addressed the al-
leviation of poverty and backwardness.

Behind a grand desk in the dim evening light of the seventh floor of
an Adli Street office block in the buzzing heart of downtown Cairo,

the turmoil of the century's history seemed to be borne by the heavily hunched shoulders of Seif al-Islam al-Banna. The son of the founder of the Muslim Brotherhood speaks slowly and carefully, just as Hassan al-Banna was said to have done as he forged history in similarly wood-paneled rooms, when downtown Cairo looked much the same but for the cars that jam the road outside.

> Now, we feel that our problem is not religious. There have always been religious differences. No, our problem now is the political and economic one. We have lost ourselves. Our problem now is how to protect our independence, in the name of Islam, not nationalism. Because we believe that justice . . . that what is just, we must do. The majority of Egyptian people believe in our theory. We have succeeded in convincing people of it, and in a true election it would show. In union elections we got 80 percent of the vote,[40] until the state began to appoint commissions to control them.[41] Our problem here isn't a religious one. It's a political struggle. The question is: what ideology do you present to the people? We think we have to draw our ideology from the *sharia*, and to modify it to make it relevant to these days. It's our choice, to take from the Koran what is suitable for these times.[42]

Islam's renewal, *tajdid*, has been forged by necessity as much as by a belief in the intrinsic evolution and renewal of the faith. Seif al-Banna says of his father: "Hassan al-Banna was a very flexible man." As with any political organization, the reality of the moment has influenced the Muslim Brotherhood. During the 1970s the organization renounced the use of violence. The military element allied to the defunct *jawalla* has long been disbanded, and the organization's leaders have increasingly played the role of elder statesmen of the *umma*, though with an ongoing appeal to the young. "In the political Islamic movements, the conservatives have the majority. This is because of tradition,"[43] said Adel Hussein of the Egyptian Labour Party. "From the ideological and religious point of view both the Muslim Brotherhood and the al-Gama'a al-Islamiyya[44] are conservative in their interpretation of what an Islamic state would mean. They are attached to early books. Both are really antiquated. These books answer all the questions which are very different from the questions we face today." The pursuit of relevance, both political and ideological, dominates the strategies of the various Islamic movements in Egypt, all of which not only have to vie with each other for influence but also must tolerate constant repression by the state. The Muslim Brotherhood has seen much desertion among its supporters over the last quarter century, beginning with the establishment of the radical wing within its own organization led by Sayyid Qutb in the 1960s.

The complexion of the Islamist movement in Egypt as a whole reads like a family tree, with different groups splitting, rejoining, and adopting different guises and names. In 1996, younger members of the Muslim Brotherhood sought to join the Islamist-oriented Labour Party but were instead encouraged by the Labour Party to establish a new Islamist party, al-Wasat, drawing on the support of the brotherhood's younger members. This strategy quickly ran into opposition from the authorities, which refused to register the party owing to its Islamist leanings. The radicalism of the Jihad group, which was responsible for the 1981 assassination of Anwar al-Sadat, and the Gama'a al-Islamiyya "always makes them more influential."[45] But now, six years after the two groups launched their strategy of armed attacks on Coptic Christians, foreign tourists, and the security forces, they are increasingly recognizing that they have become alienated from the masses, whose support is vital to their credibility.

"The situation now, among the militant groups, is one of reshuffling the cards,"[46] said Yasser al-Sirri, a London-based exiled Egyptian Islamist with close links to both militant groups. He continued:

Many of those who were militarily active have now left [Egypt], and the order now is how to break the barrier that has come to exist between the movement and the masses. There was a strong link during the 1970s and 1980s, but now the [groups'] activities are quite limited. Gama'a al-Islamiyya have committed blunders, in their choice of targets. For example, killing conscript soldiers alienated ordinary people—those soldiers' families. Also, killing the Copts: there was no reason for this. This muddled their image, both internationally, and more importantly domestically. The common people became alienated. The common man has become the fuel of the fire, instead of the people at the head of the regime.

Consequently, the two organizations declared an unconditional and unilateral cease-fire in their low-level insurgency on 5 June 1997 to allow themselves time to review their strategy. Al-Sirri went on:

It will be a corrective move. There will be a review of how the ideology of jihad was carried out. The internal organization of the movement rather than the ideology will be reviewed. The jihad point of view itself won't be discussed, though the question of jihad against your own government may be discussed. The policy of unlimited confrontation established by the Gama'a was wrong. Most of their activity has not been productive, even though the Egyptian situation has the ingredients for success. Even so, the organizations are weak, because the connection with the masses has been weakened, by some [activists] being forced to leave the country, and because of the state control of the mosques. Also there wasn't enough use of the one-to-one contact between the Islamists and the people who needed education.[47] Some of the groups are possibly still calling for military activities[48] against military targets. But most want to concentrate on the popular level, and this needs leadership. The leadership is lacking, because the Islamists have failed to take it up. This must be corrected.

However, division within the ranks of the Gama'a al-Islamiyya emerged rapidly, in response to the cease-fire call. The military leaders inside Egypt—Rifaat Zeydan, Mahmoud Farshouty, Hamed Abbas, and Farid Qudwany—followed the directives of the exiled leadership, in particular Mustapha Hamza. This division emerged starkly on 17 November 1997, when six gunmen attacked sightseers at a pharaonic temple in the southern city of Luxor. A total of sixty-two people were killed, fifty-eight of them foreign tourists. Hamza and his close adviser Ahmed Taha have both operated from Afghanistan since the mid-1990s. Their role in the attack was claimed by Muntassir al-Zayat, a Cairo lawyer who had defended scores of Islamist militants at military trials. "Hamza and Taha would be entirely responsible for the planning of this [attack]. These two only. There is a direct link between Mustapha Hamza and the military wing of the Gama'a in Egypt," al-Zayat said.[49] The exiled leadership's ability, or even desire, to communicate with the imprisoned leadership held in Egypt's high-security Tora prison is thought to be nonexistent.

A day after the attack, a statement issued by the Gama'a al-Islamiyya claimed that organization's responsibility for the killings. The statement said that the attack had been launched in order to take foreign hostages, who would be freed in return for the liberation of Sheikh Omar Abdel Rahman, the spiritual leader of the Gama'a al-Islamiyya jailed in the United States for his involvement in the bombing of the World Trade Center in 1993. "The Gama'a al-Islamiyya will resume its military actions as long as the regime does not respond to our demands, the most important of which are the application of God's law, severing relations with the Zionist entity,[50] noncompliance with the American will, returning our emir to Cairo,[51] setting free our women, leadership, and members, and ceasing all oppressive policies."[52] Two days later, the organization issued a further statement saying that it would consider halting its military operations if the demands already made were met.[53] However, a third statement issued on 7 December 1997 reversed the two previous declarations and revealed a major difference of opinion within the organization. The statement specified that the Luxor attack had not been approved by Mustapha Hamza and that the cell of the organization responsible for the killings "was from the movement's young and new recruits, and that they were not entitled to carry out an operation of this sort, and that they did it entirely on their own."[54]

A month after the Luxor attack, Yasser al-Sirri, the London-based Egyptian exile, was approached by a mediator seeking dialogue between the Egyptian government and the Gama'a al-Islamiyya. Al-Sirri said that an Egyptian journalist, Adil Lutfi, had approached him on behalf of Sami Talat Suleyman, an official at the Egyptian embassy in London. Al-Sirri said that the mediator had hinted that in return for a cease-fire, the government would be prepared to release some Islamist prisoners and introduce a moratorium on the execution of Islamists sentenced to death. The government, for whom the mediation would have marked a major policy shift, abruptly terminated contact, under pressure from anti-Islamists within the regime. It denied that there had ever been any tentative steps toward mediation, despite a detailed and convincing account by al-Sirri of what had taken place.[55] With mediation blocked, the jailed leaders of the Gama'a reverted to exerting pressure for their cease-fire call to be heeded, while the government continued with its security-centered approach and refused calls for dialogue.

Men of Deeds, Men of Words

The Islamist wave of the past thirty years has been marked by political failure. Even so, although governments have resisted Islamism, they have been forced to adopt some elements of the Islamists' agenda for reasons of political expediency, as will be outlined in Chapter 6. But the movements have largely failed in their attempts to compete successfully with rival ideologies in a democratic debate. And they have not succeeded in sweeping to power on a broad front by use of force. Meanwhile, the intellectual evolution of the Islamist movement has undergone modification, while its credibility has been subjected to close scrutiny, particularly by its practitioners.

"We are waiting for a catalyst, because events can escalate. At the moment there's not enough dry wood in Saudi Arabia capable of turning the situation into a fire."[56] From exile in London, Mohamed al-Massari, the leader of the Saudi Arabian Islamist pressure group, the Committee for the Defence of Legitimate Rights (CDLR), is reliant upon the existence of a steadily expanding groundswell of discontent directed against the Saudi monarchy as the rationale of his campaign for its overthrow. "The most potent question is that of the [royal family's] legitimacy as religious leaders. They are accepted [or not] on the basis of their religious leadership. People accepted the [al-Saud family] because of Islam, but the Islamic nature of the state has now become a mockery. In fact the government is trying to soften peoples' commitment to Islam, and to detach its own credibility from its religious purpose."

Al-Massari's ability to nurture the discontent from afar is limited, and his admission that in fact Saudi Arabia is not yet on the verge of an upheaval has both political and ideological implications. The duty of Muslims to overthrow corrupt, iniquitous, decadent, or otherwise non-Islamic regimes appears to have been accepted as unrealistic by not only al-Massari but other of Saudi Arabia's Islamist dissidents. The complexity of the Saudi Arabian monarchy's position within the Islamic world has influenced the character of the movements that have drawn upon Islam as a source of inspiration for their opposition to it.

"They hate the religion,"[57] said Khaled al-Fauwaz, the London representative of the Advice and Reformation Committee or ARC (the Hayat Annaseyha Wa'ahisla), speaking of the Saudi royal family, which numbers around ten thousand individuals and beyond them another half a million people with royal connections. Al-Fauwaz continued:

> We no longer have any hope of reforming the regime and the leaders. Now our policy is to reform the people, not the regime. But we know it will take a long time to bring reform, so we decided that the majority should work in secret, and that we can even work from outside the kingdom. The ones outside would have to accept that they are in danger, that they would expose themselves as known members of our organization. But the majority would work in Arabia, working in secret.

Both Mohamed al-Massari's CDLR and Khaled al-Fauwaz of the ARC fit into what Olivier Roy has called the phenomenon of neofundamentalism.[58] Both organizations have moved away from direct political action—which is the heart of Islamism—toward social action, centering around religious observance and the pursuit of the *sharia*. Both activists admit that success is a very long way off. Such a point of view must be seen in context. Saudi Arabia has not been associated with the kind of intellectual debate that has clearly dominated academic life in Egypt for over a hundred years. Equally, the association of the establishment with religion has been strong, in both the political and spiritual spheres. The financial backing of Saudi Arabia ensured the continued existence of the Afghan Mujahideen and demonstrated official Saudi commitment to the cause of jihad. But the credibility the government had succeeded in perpetuating was shattered when its weaknesses were exposed. As al-Fauwaz put it:

> When the Gulf War came, it was the first time that people saw the Americans really present in the country. People had accepted that there had been a few [military] instructors. But before the war the American presence wasn't that big. But the Gulf War made the American influence in the country much clearer, and it exposed the shortcomings of the Saudi

forces. And the people in the army decided that they should start to release the information which showed the extent to which the *sharia* was not being followed.[59]

Covert operations coupled with a deluge of propaganda sent by fax or via the Internet from havens abroad are central to the strategy of the exiled Islamist opponents of the Saudi monarchy. In September 1997 Osama Bin Laden, a founding member of the ARC, signed a five-year deal along with Ayman al-Zawhari, the exiled leader of the Egyptian Jihad group, with a Dutch company to rent a satellite television channel that will broadcast to Europe and the Arab world for ten hours a day. Despite such moves, the structure of the ARC, both in and outside Saudi Arabia, is a closely guarded secret. The composition of its ruling consultative council is not disclosed, and the identity of its supreme leader is not known. Only the fact of the organization's existence, announced in April 1994, has been made public. After announcing its presence, the organization immediately began publishing communiqués, concentrating on the question of the Saudi rulers' legitimacy:

> What we have in Saudi Arabia is a number of people in power who change the system according to their own needs, not the needs or religion of the people. And this is strongly influenced by international needs, mostly that of the Americans. The leaders must be under the authority of the law. That is our main interest. But we realize we need a lot of time. Now is not even the time for a peaceful act. Our strategy is to clear out wrong knowledge, and to reestablish understanding. We have a lot of money, and we worked very hard to put everything in place from the start. Even so, our influence is limited when compared to the nation as a whole. So we have to concentrate on certain categories of people: people in power. The most important shield of the regime has been the committee of scholars. We decided to destroy that shield. It was already damaged, and in a number of communiqués we attacked that shield.[60]

Conflict with the Saudi regime emerged vociferously in September 1994. The Islamic scholars, the ulama, at that time themselves attempted to assert a degree of independence from the regime and demand greater influence over religious matters. Mohamed al-Massari's CDLR encouraged public support for the scholars, whereas the ARC urged the scholars to simply leave the country and agitate from outside. However, they remained in Saudi Arabia, and many were imprisoned. Subsequently, the distribution of communiqués sent from abroad became more difficult, and then ceased altogether. The CDLR suffered an acrimonious internal split. Al-Massari faced the increasing determination of the British government, under intense Saudi pressure, to expel him to a third country. Plans to expel him to the Do-minican Republic were abandoned when a British court deemed the move illegal, as this would have amounted to al-Massari's expulsion to a country where his security could not be ensured. The ARC, mean-while, began facing problems of its own, with the London-based ele-ment being questioned about its activities by the British immigration authorities. Osama Bin Laden, at that time based in the Sudanese cap-ital, Khartoum, experienced mounting problems communicating with the organization's supporters in Saudi Arabia and was also under in-creasing pressure from the Sudanese government to curtail his activi-ties. It was decided that al-Fauwaz would become the public face of the organization. But at that same time Bin Laden's profile was on the rise, as he became identified by U.S. authorities as a leading activist apparently under the protection of the Sudanese.

Criticism of the Saudi regime's scholarly foundations has been ac-companied by the identification of a more tangible enemy. Al-Fauwaz explains:

> We had to choose an enemy. So the Americans were the number one en-emy. Particularly as the Americans became more and more involved. They didn't want to leave us alone. The U.S. were using this area as their own piece of land. If people were going to be angry with anybody, then they should be angry with the Americans. We have to get rid of them. But we don't want the scholars to be used to protect the Americans. Then we will go ahead with our plans against the Americans. Our strategy is to have an internal, political campaign against their presence.[61]

The ARC has not declared the aim of launching a violent campaign against the U.S. presence, and the organization disassociated itself from Osama Bin Laden's declaration of jihad, issued in 1996 against all foreign troops in Saudi Arabia, deeming it an individual initiative. But the declaration nevertheless damaged the ARC's reputation, as the group was accused of advocating an economic boycott of American products and a political campaign against the U.S. military presence. Bin Laden's declaration of jihad also came as a shock to other mem-bers of the ARC, as until that time he had shared their view that vio-lent action within Saudi Arabia was inadvisable. His change of course stemmed from his growing belief that it was necessary to be more di-rect in criticism; otherwise the ultimate purpose of the campaign—to overthrow the Saudi regime—would be obscured. Bin Laden's strategy also differed from that of the ARC with regard to its position within the broader Islamic world: "We believe the crisis in Arabia isn't to be dealt with by Saudis alone," said Khaled al-Fauwaz. "Because we are the keepers of the two sacred places.[62] Our aim is to break the international support for the al-Saud. But I am not very optimistic. And the Americans can only leave after bloodshed."

His conclusions are of a kind that have set the tone for the relations between the Islamist movements and the governments of the Muslim world. The failure of the movements to take power has forced many to all but abandon this goal and instead to promote grassroots social change. Whereas the movements are undertaking a profound reevaluation of their strategy and organization, the national governments have learned from each others' techniques. Despite rare examples of Islamists being co-opted by ruling regimes—for example in Jordan, where the Muslim Brotherhood was invited to accept government posts in 1996—most governments aspire to the eradication of Islamism, through direct confrontation, military trials, harassment and discrimination, exile, or detention without trial. But the states of the Islamic world have also been forced to incorporate various aspects of Islamism, to assert their own religious credentials and display greater sensitivity and understanding of the dire social, economic, and political conditions that have hardened attitudes and driven a wedge between the rulers and the ruled. Although the struggle is far from over, the Islamists face an uncertain future, whereas the ruling regimes are attempting to consolidate the advantageous positions they believe they have achieved.

6

The Iron Hand of the State

North Africa and the Middle East

"THE ACTS OF THE GOVERNMENT and politicians have been victorious over the currents in society,"[1] Hammadi Benjaballah, professor of history and the philosophy of science at Tunis University, assured me, as if drawing strength from the tension prevailing between the ruler and the ruled. Also an adviser to Tunisia's minister of higher education, Benjaballah articulates without reserve the political philosophy of repression with which Islamism has been confronted across the Islamic world. "Does this mean constant conflict with the people? No. The people are seduced. People are taught about what it is that is best for them. Tunisia has never been populist. That is to say that the peoples' will isn't followed."

Benjaballah's portrayal of the policy of confrontation with Islamism is startling. The same political attitudes that had fostered the rise of Islamism were to be used to confront that rise. The arrogance of one-party rule, the corruption of government stemming from political stagnation, the gulf between power and those upon whom power was imposed, all appeared unaffected by the challenge presented by the Islamists. Tunisia's Ennahda (Renaissance) Party emerged as the most direct political challenge ever faced by the ruling regime. Even so, the government—led for thirty years by Habib Bourguiba and since 1987 led by Zein al-Abdin Ben Ali—has forged its own path. The popular appeal of the Islamist movement is barely countenanced by the ruling regime. Bourguiba brutally condemned Islamism in theory and its manifestations in practice. Ben Ali opened a dialogue with Ennahda but quickly slammed the door, though for practical reasons that he clarified in 1989 following his refusal to legalize the party on the grounds of "our firm belief in the need not to mix religion and politics, as experience has shown that anarchy emerges and the rule of law and institutions is undermined when such a mixing takes place."[2]

Ben Ali's motives were purely political. To have legalized Ennahda, in particular at a time when the Islamic Salvation Front was rising uncontrollably in neighboring Algeria, would have marked a spectacular diversion from the prevailing philosophy of "modernization" that had dominated Tunisian political life from even before independence. In his influential work *The Clash of Civilizations and the Remaking of World Order*,[3] Samuel Huntington highlights the stark choice facing the modernizers of the Islamic world by emphasizing what he regards as the mutual exclusivity of Muslim and "Western" society—an exclusivity for which, of course, Islam is blamed—when he says: "The general failure of liberal democracy to take hold in Muslim societies is a continuing and repeated phenomenon for an entire century beginning in the late 1800s. This failure has its source at least in part in the inhospitable nature of Islamic culture and society to Western liberal concepts."[4] Modernization in Tunisia was, and has remained, essentially Westernization or, more specifically, Europeanization. Also, educational standards in Tunisia are exceptionally high relative to those in neighboring countries, and illiteracy rates are low. Boys and girls attend school and university, both of which are state financed. The government has bound the Tunisian economy to Europe and aspires to meet European industrial standards of production and efficiency. Three million mainly European tourists are greeted every year by modernity in the form of luxury hotels, which vie with resorts in Florida and Spain for tourist dollars.

"It's not the state security measures which have stopped the Islamists coming to power," said Professor Benjaballah. "We are in a situation where their ideology is against all the modern history of Tunisia, which has seen the majority benefit. In Tunisia, the [modernizing] reforms have created the Tunisian character. The *integriste*[5] is the opposite of the movement towards Tunisian modernization." Ben Ali's political approach to the Islamist movement is consistent with his broader attitude toward political opposition. Despite the existence of nongovernment political parties, Tunisia remains a state whose political direction is determined by the interests of the ruling elite, protected by an extensive security service that uses the methods of the police state to intimidate critical voices. The government insists that such methods, when used against the Islamists, have popular support. But the use of these same measures against human rights activists and left-wing political parties has undermined the government's credibility as a "modernizing" regime. The organized Islamist "threat," at least in

the form of Ennahda, has been silenced, but tight controls over all political life remain firmly in place. These ongoing practices have hardened the shell within which the ever-anxious government operates, attempting to lead the people without necessarily feeling an obligation to
explain why the direction they are taking is in the public interest.

"I am first a Tunisian. After that I am of the Arab-Islamic culture."
Professor Benjaballah's view echoes other claimants to simple identities, stretching as far back into history as Islam itself. Debate over
Tunisia's identity does not figure in any profound way in the government's agenda, and the more vibrant political arena of the 1980s is not
viewed as having raised and then settled the debate. Nevertheless, education has been a key weapon in the government's armory against Islamism, utilized as a way of asserting its worldview without engaging
in direct debate with the Islamists, whom it portrays as essentially
treacherous. In 1978, Benjaballah was "accused" by Ennahda leader
Rached Ghannouchi of promoting secularism in education. During
the same period, the universities became strongly influenced by Islamist politics, which rose to the peak of its influence in the late
1980s. Throughout, the government sought to assert "Tunisianness"
as the alternative to Islamism.

"The reform program introduced [at Ben Ali's accession] on 7 November 1987 is a total project. The clarity of that vision embraced all
aspects of Tunisian society: the economy, politics, social and cultural
affairs, and education."[6] So said Jelloul Jeribi, president of Zaitouna
University, Tunis's world-famous, 1,300-year-old university and center
of religious study. Bourguiba had closed the university as part of his attempt to rid the country of all facets of its religious identity beyond the
mosques. Just as Benjaballah's attitude toward the relationship between the ruler and the ruled is startling for its advocation of autocracy, so Jeribi's choice of words evokes the vocabulary of the Islamists
themselves. For the Islamists, Islam is a "total project" incorporating
all aspects of society. For Jeribi, appointed to his post as president of
Zaitouna—wherein Rached Ghannouchi had received his religious education—by the Ben Ali government with a brief to "modernize" the
university once it was reopened, a global "vision" appears as appropriate as it does for the Islamists. The Islamists at heart, despite the religion's process of internal renewal, *tajdid,* and despite the individual's
right to *ijtihad,* remain entrenched in the "total project" of the Holy
Koran. The secularists installed by Ben Ali have a similarly all-embracing vision. Both systems seek to control and are mutually exclusive.
The conflict is starkly illustrated in the field of education, as Jeribi
shows: "The rehabilitation of Zaitouna was intended to permit it to re-
discover its historic role on the national and international level, by pro-

moting the teaching of philosophy, the humanities, and nine foreign languages. The university reflects a real demand, by its role of propagating the values of tolerance, interreligious dialogue, peaceful coexistence between different nationalities and ideological adherents." Claiming that Tunisia is a unique model in the Arab Muslim world, Jeribi asserted that other countries would follow its example. What is unclear is whether there is an example to follow beyond the example of repression. Tunisia's influence on the anti-Islamist policies of neighboring governments has been more pronounced than that of many other countries. Ben Ali banned Ennahda, forced its leaders into exile, jailed many of those who stayed behind, and then launched a campaign of intimidation against those who remained at liberty—in particular the families of the jailed Islamists—in order to keep the pressure on. He did not allow the genie out of the bottle, as the Algerian government did by initially legalizing the Islamic Liberation Front (FIS). Egypt was strongly influenced by Ben Ali's decisive action, while Morocco effectively compelled the Islamist movement led by Abdesalam Yassine to operate underground.

"But we can't say whether the influence of the *integristes* is finished," Hammadi Benjaballah acknowledged, in spite of all the measures taken in Tunisia to that end. "It can hide itself, and can revive." Unleashing the Islamist "bogeyman" is a nightmare scenario that the repressive regimes of the Islamic world bring up regularly to frighten the West into believing that if they are not supported, then the Islamists will take over. The apparent ease with which the bogeyman "can hide itself, and can revive" is one such example. The government continues to assert that "*integrisme* has not died. Political Islam isn't dead, but once the [social] problems were resolved, people didn't need to follow what is irrational.'" Ben Ali will never in fact open up to the dialogue and pluralism that Jeribi claims already exists. If Ben Ali's raison d'être is to suppress the Islamist trend, and silence all opposition in the process, then it is clearly in his interest to ensure that elements of the trend remain present, or at least remain a threat. The organization has now been decimated in Tunisia, and yet the harassment of the family members of its 10,000 jailed adherents is ongoing. The only lawyer now prepared to defend the rights of the families of jailed Islamists is a communist, Radhia Nasraoui, who is herself subject to intense harassment and intimidation. With so many of them now in prison in Tunisia, the Islamists, whose political outlook was strongly condemned by the left during the 1980s, are increasingly viewed purely as one of many aspects of the country's dire human rights record. The weapons of repression available to the government have meanwhile enabled a well-protected army of "modernizers" like Jeribi and Benjaballah to securely occupy positions within the administration as part of the ongoing attempt to transform the reality of Tunisian life.

"Ignorance is the opposition. Cultural views are the opposition. It's a different culture that we are trying to introduce,"[8] said Soukaina Bouraoui, head of the Tunisian government agency responsible for promoting women's rights. "Perhaps between 40 and 70 percent of people have to change their mentality. It's necessary that peoples' own culture is changed. It's never been the case that the politics of the avant-garde have reflected the popular will. Change is always the work of a minority," she said. Political control intended to allow the pursuit of a cultural overhaul has plunged Tunisia into a maze of contradictions. Bouraoui says openly: "I don't know what is Arab in my identity, and how it is distinguished from the European identity." This kind of uncertainty has been the fuel for the Islamists' fire. The minority of which Bouraoui speaks is attracted by the European culture to which it has access and exposure. The majority, living in a country where the installation of a satellite dish is subject to strict government control, have had less such exposure and consequently look to the Arab root that is more familiar and accessible. "Ennahda gained influence because of the end of the [political] left," said Bouraoui, reasserting the purely political root of the movement, just as Ben Ali's approach has done for the past decade. So how is the question of identity mirrored by the political choices legally available to the population? "Everybody asks: What are we? And we reply: Arab, and Muslim. And 90 percent of Tunisians are happy in themselves. I don't think this question should be detached from the political and economic situation. Ninety-five percent of people are content with this government. Why? Because if the government gives them the minimum, most people are content with them."

Words, Actions, and the "Total Project"

The failure so far of most Islamist movements to secure political power has given secular regimes a breathing space in which to enact their own plans for reform. With the obvious exception of Tunisia, it is the force of the Islamists' message that has generally had the single strongest influence upon the incumbent, often formerly one-party regimes' strategies. The rise of the Islamists revealed characteristics of the Islamic world's population that had been denied expression during years of secular one-party politics. Since Ben Ali seized power in Tunisia in 1987, the number of mosques in the country has doubled, though they remain under state control. The reopening of Zaitouna University—while intended as a mark of Tunisia's modernization rather than a throwback to the Islamic past—had a symbolic importance in that it meant to incorporate that past into the superstructure of modernity. It would be convenient to be able to say that the secular regimes of the Islamic world had drawn upon the culture and religion of the past and attempted to use their resources to ease their countries into the "modern" age through a process of incorporation and acculturation. But this is not what has happened. The rift between the Islamists and the secularists is too wide for such a "liberal" process to have taken place. The incumbent regimes—in Tunisia, in Algeria, in Egypt, and elsewhere—have essentially used their resources to attempt to physically eradicate the Islamists as a first step toward clearing the ground in order to plant the seeds of a new system.

The central feature of the reformism that the secularist regimes have been forced or felt obliged to introduce since the early 1990s has been their refusal to clarify the specific elements of the political systems they ultimately intend to create. This contrasts sharply with the Islamists, whose agenda is at least superficially clear on issues of doctrine, though it remains highly ambiguous on the question of their commitment to democracy. The general refusal of secularist regimes to allow an evolution toward democracy, and their tendency to manicure a form of multiparty politics intended to exclude rather than include political trends that seek profound reform, has meant that the methods of the police state have remained central to their strategy. Multiparty politics exists in most of the countries in which Islamist movements have been active. But multiparty politics—a far cry from real democracy—has barely been allowed to nurture free speech, much less the translation of free speech into action.

On 22 November 1995 Rabeh Kebir, the leader of the exiled membership of the Algerian FIS, sent a letter to the newly elected Algerian president, Liamine Zeroual, acknowledging the latter's victory and seeking the reopening of dialogue intended to end the crisis wracking the country. Contacts between the FIS and the government had been curtailed in March 1994. These contacts, which had been conducted by Zeroual even before his elevation from defense minister to president on 30 January 1994, had collapsed under pressure for their curtailment from the *eradicateurs* within the regime, who had seized power in 1992. Most notable among those opposed to dialogue was General Mohammed Lamari, the army chief of staff, and Redha Malek, who was prime minister when Zeroual was first appointed head of state. Whereas Malek resigned on 11 April, when it became clear that Zeroual intended to boost attempts at reconciliation, Lamari was retained in his post and later became defense minister, a move viewed as an attempt by Zeroual to appease the hard-liners, whose presence within Algeria's security establishment forced him to walk a tightrope between the bitterly opposed sides.

Zeroual's task was complicated by the fact that not only were the hard-liners within the government opposed to dialogue but that the FIS itself set preconditions for talks that he could not meet. Meanwhile, the campaign of grotesque atrocities perpetrated by the Armed Islamic Group (GIA) against mostly civilian targets heightened the need to boost the morale of the military if the government were to enjoy any degree of support from a population it has failed to protect. In April, July, and August 1994 Abassi Madani, the jailed founder of the FIS, and his deputy, Ali Belhadj, between them sent four letters to Zeroual. They spelled out the conditions for their involvement in the process of finding a solution to the wave of violence into which the country had by then been plunged. On 13 September 1994 the two were transferred from prison and placed under house arrest, while three other detained FIS leaders were released altogether. Zeroual had meanwhile convened a "national dialogue" between the opposition parties and the government, and it was then that the FIS's demands tested the lengths to which the regime was really prepared, or able, to go in its apparent pursuit of reconciliation. Madani demanded that the FIS be allowed to reconstitute itself, that its leadership be reunited inside Algeria, that the declared state of emergency be lifted, that the trial of Islamists cease, and that the army return to the barracks. Zeroual rejected these demands. At the end of October the attempt at dialogue was abandoned, and Zeroual instead announced that the presidential election would be held by the end of 1995.

The following month the secular opposition parties, as well as Hamas and the FIS, met in Rome at a session intended as a broad attempt at national dialogue; it had become apparent that the government in Algiers was only prepared to hold such a meeting if it could control its composition, content, and outcome. Organized as an initiative of the Roman Catholic St. Egidio Community, a second meeting resulted in a declaration issued on 13 January 1995. The declaration demanded a return to constitutional rule, the legalization of the FIS, and the establishment of a broadly based national conference to oversee a short political transition that would culminate in elections. This "National Contract" was signed for the FIS by Anwar Haddam—the most hard-line FIS member outside the country—and Rabeh Kebir, and was a remarkable breakthrough. It did not insist that the FIS's previous electoral victories be respected but merely demanded a return to unrestricted multiparty politics. It also rejected the use of violence and unequivocally accepted democracy—both policies on which the FIS had been historically equivocal. The Zeroual government did not attend the meetings, and it did not sign the declaration. Consequently, the buildup to the 1995 presidential election was dominated by dramatic political polarization and intensifying violence. The government would not be "party" to agreements, as it attempted to project an image as "national savior" rather than partisan element; its very existence, reliant entirely upon military power, was built upon its need to control the entire spectrum of political life. To this end, the government embarked on a program of political innovation that rejected the calls for genuine pluralism made by the secular signatories to the National Contract. It also denied the FIS any access to whatever system might ultimately emerge out of the conflict that continued to rage in Algeria.

"I have never seen democracy provide a solution to a crisis. Never, in the modern era. The need is for a strong state. Then people will return to Algeria and the terrorism will stop." Such was the conclusion of a pro-Zeroual university lecturer, as we talked on the terraces of Algiers' main sports stadium while awaiting Zeroual's final address to his supporters a few days before the 16 November 1995 presidential election. Four days later Zeroual himself emerged from the modest villa in the center of Algiers that had served as his campaign headquarters to acknowledge his victory by deeming the election "a victory for democracy and the sovereignty of the country, against Algeria's enemies within and outside the country."

Then the FIS responded: "We think that this popularity you have gained could be a significant opportunity for both the authorities and the opposition to overcome the obstacles that have robbed the many attempts at national dialogue of their goal of securing a return to peace, liberties and national reconciliation." It was in these terms that Rabeh Kebir addressed Zeroual in his letter of 22 November 1995, acknowledging the election victory and the failure of the FIS's call for a boycott of the poll. But the government did not respond to the letter. Instead, for the next four months it watched the various Islamist groups turn on each other as they sought to reassess their respective positions following the election.

The government was also strengthened as the secular opposition parties, their election boycott having failed, were forced to modify their stance and distance themselves from the National Contract signed in Rome. On 6 April 1996, Zeroual reasserted his control over the political landscape by summoning representatives of eleven political parties and fifty veteran politicians to attend consultations that would lay the groundwork for parliamentary and municipal elections. The FIS was not invited.

"Democracy has limits. It cannot accept those who want to destroy it,"[9] Redha Malek, the virulently anti-Islamist former prime minister with close ties to the army, told me. "It's necessary to provide an alternative to those committing the violence. The notion of republicanism is more relevant now than ever, and it's necessary to ensure that it is an alternative and that those in favor of democracy can seize the advantage." The consultation was an attempt "to find the same sort of policy and government as in the past thirty years," one diplomat in Algiers said. This view was shared by supporters of at least one of the parties that had taken part in the election that had brought Zeroual to power; this party was thereby viewed by many as a willing accomplice in the government's strategy.

"These talks won't go far, because the government hasn't developed,"[10] said Mohammed Arezki Boumendil, spokesman for the Rally for Culture and Democracy (RCD) party, whose outspoken anti-Islamist leader, Said Sadi, had finished third in the 1995 presidential poll. Boumendil continued:

> Zeroual was elected to reconstruct the country. But in fact he is in the process of using the same old methods, taking into account the views of the old people who brought Algeria into the crisis. But he is in a position to invite who he wants to the consultations, and we have been invited, and we will probably go, because we know the terrorists well enough to know that there's no possibility of discussion with them and the state has a right to defend itself when it is threatened.

Zeroual's pursuit of his own agenda continued almost as if the throat cuttings, beheadings, bombings, and assassinations were not occurring. On 11 May 1996 he announced plans for constitutional change and elections, pursuant to the consultations held without the FIS during the previous month. The declaration, read by Zeroual to a gathering of those who had taken part in the consultations, acknowledged that the "current political system cannot satisfy the sensibilities and diversity which are manifest on the level of civil society. It has therefore become imperative, in order to meet the aspirations of the population, to cement the process of establishing a pluralist regime based on respect for public liberty."[11] More than a year later, on 5 June 1997, Zeroual honored his promise. By then the secular opposition had abandoned their hopes of forcing the government to engage in a dialogue that would create the conditions for a negotiated solution to the crisis. A parliamentary election was held, again excluding the FIS. The contest was waged among parties who had—even in the case of those who had signed the National Contract with the FIS in January 1995—all eventually come to accept that the division in Algeria right across the political spectrum was between those who believed in politics and those who didn't; between those extremists on all sides who long before had lost sight of what they were fighting for and those who had organized political parties whose very existence was anathema to those extremists. The political parties—the formerly ruling National

Liberation Front (FLN), the moderate Islamist Hamas party (renamed the Movement for a Peaceful Society or MSP), the vehemently anti-Zeroual Workers' Party—all participated in Algeria's second multiparty legislative election. And, just as had been the case with the presidential election two years earlier, accusations of ballot rigging erupted almost immediately after the polls opened. The regime, which saw Zeroual's four-month-old National Democratic Rally party sweep to victory with 40 percent of the vote, giving it 155 of the 380 seats in parliament, failed the democratic test on all counts. All the participating parties condemned the fraud, and within days the country suffered the most vicious upsurge of violence it had seen for many months.

Zeroual's only real achievement has been to transfer support from the FIS to the moderate Islamist parties—Hamas (now the MSP) and the even more moderate Nahda, which won 15 and 9 percent of the legislative vote respectively. His strategy has elevated the question of whether or not a change in the form of political representation is in itself adequate as a measure to resolve the crisis in Algeria. The voter turnout in 1997 was put officially at 65 percent, though this is widely disputed. Participation among the youngest of those eligible to vote was reckoned at less than 10 percent. The constituency of the armed militants remained disaffected. Zeroual had ultimately redrawn the political field, but not by using politics to allow the participation of all elements representing the reality of Algerian society. Instead, he had drawn upon the complicity of those politicians who had nowhere else to turn but to him, as a safeguard against the armed groups, who remain outside the political arena.

The same dispossession still prevails in Algeria that prevailed before the FIS rose to power and upon which it rose to power. There is diversity within the political "opposition," though opposition parties are unlikely to have an opportunity to influence the government to seek a solution to the appalling crisis facing the country. Politics is now part of the government's strategy. It is not intended to dilute the concentration of power, and in this sense Algeria has a multiparty political system without being democratic. More importantly, there are no signs that this partial opening of the political arena indicates any recognition of the social trends out of which the Islamist movement emerged. The current regime's ability to rig elections, maintain a state of emergency, control the media, and pay little more than lip service to genuine political pluralism is all-too reminiscent of the one-party system. The only difference is that the slightly enlarged political arena may mean that slightly fewer people feel alienated from the decision-making machinery. But as the political reforms are not intended to reach out to those conducting the armed campaigns, the impact of any new, democratic debate on the military conflict will undoubtedly be extremely limited, as the security forces that continue their campaign are answerable only to themselves and the president.

The improbability of a resolution to the crisis as a consequence of this partial reform of the political system was made evident five weeks after the election, when the government suddenly released the FIS leader, Abassi Madani, from prison. His release on 15 July 1997, five years into a twelve-year prison sentence, was part of a strategy of ongoing contacts between the government and the FIS, which had resulted in the FIS agreeing to a military truce in return for the release of its jailed leaders.[12] Within a few days of his release, Madani was again placed under house arrest after writing a letter to the secretary general of the United Nations offering his assistance in finding a solution to the crisis. The government's response was that he had overstepped the conditions agreed upon for his release and that the United Nations had no business involving itself in Algeria's internal affairs. It was clear that the solution sought by the government was not intended to open up Algerian society, but quite the opposite.

Despite the regime's treatment of Madani even after his release and the government's denial that it had made any deal with Madani on releasing him, the AIS—the armed wing of the FIS—announced a cease-fire beginning 1 October 1997 following a statement by its military leader, Madani Mezrag, that its militants should lay down their weapons "to foil the plans of those who are waiting for the opportunity to harm Algeria."[13] The harm erupted hours after the Muslim holy month of Ramadan began on 30 December. In the course of three weeks, more than 1,200 civilians were brutally murdered in attacks on villages in the north and northwest of the country, carried out by the GIA, not the FIS. The slaughter contributed to the hesitant expressions of concern that had been quietly uttered at the United Nations two months earlier. International silence on the crisis in Algeria stemmed both from preoccupation elsewhere and from the European tradition of leaving disputes in former colonies to the former colonial masters. The absence of a French initiative to find a solution prevented the idea of a foreign role from even arising, and concern over the death toll spanning five years barely warranted public expressions of concern. Algerian sensitivity to any French role had discouraged all efforts. France was condemned by Algeria for encouraging Italy to play a mediating role in October 1997, and the German government subsequently took the lead in raising the profile of the Algerian crisis.

After 30 December 1997, a combination of events triggered louder foreign calls for action. The strong pressure by FIS leaders abroad, as well as Abassi Madani's calls from within the country, gave meaning to the idea of negotiations by allowing the Islamist side to be clearly identified. The problem has remained that the FIS—and its armed wing, the AIS—is no longer the main perpetrator of the violence, most of it being carried out by the GIA, with whom no outside negotiators have made any meaningful contact. Also, beginning in October accusations that the Zeroual regime—or sections within it—had been responsible for allowing, encouraging, and even perpetrating some of the massacres of civilians radically altered the complexion of the conflict. A government overtly at war with its own already brutalized people threatened a much greater crisis than the conflict between the army and the Islamist factions.[14]

The GIA's Ramadan slaughter of January 1998 above all exposed a cynical indifference to civilian suffering on the part of the regime. On 22 January, Prime Minister Ahmed Ouyahia announced that 26,563 civilians and members of the security forces had been killed between 1992 and 1997, a figure that is less than half that of others based on media accounts from throughout the period, which put the total slaughter at around 66,000 dead, including Islamists excluded from the government's calculations.

The scale and manner of the January 1998 slaughter, which saw horrendous methods of killing and during which security forces apparently stood idly by, rarely managing to catch or kill the culprits, finally appeared to loosen the regime's grip on control of its own image abroad. The taboo—which French inaction had allowed—of appearing to meddle in Algeria's internal affairs was broken. Criticism of the regime's failure to protect civilians mounted. The outcome of the government's legislative program, which had begun with the 1995 presidential election and culminated in local council elections in October 1997, was that the crisis was raging even more ferociously than before. A mission sent by the European Union[15] met with government officials and in a later report demanded "greater transparency by the Algerian government, especially with regard to the situation in which terrorist groups continue to perpetrate cowardly and brutal attacks on innocent civilians."[16]

A Long, Slow Death

President Zeroual's failure to bring a solution to Algeria's crisis stems from a determination on the part of the country's *eradicateurs*, upon whom he must rely for his support within the security forces, not to encourage the moderation of the Islamist movements as a strategy aimed at eventually drawing them into the mainstream of Algerian society, but rather to destroy the Islamists by all means. A political "so-lution" is neither intended nor envisaged. The security forces' grotesque abuse of civilian vulnerability is intended to further dis-credit the Islamists and discourage any thought of dialogue with them. Even if some of the Islamist leaders are released and allowed to live freely, it is not intended that they should ever regain any of their lost influence. The weakness of this strategy stems from the fact that it groups all the Islamist organizations together—a strategy that many governments in the Arab world tend to follow for their own propa-ganda purposes even with full realization that there are significant dif-ferences between the organizations, particularly in Algeria, where the FIS and the GIA have fought each other.

Whatever the specifics, the common thread running through the policies of the secular regimes of the Islamic world is that they are un-likely to enter into meaningful public dialogue with Islamic political organizations. But although this is the basis of strategic relations be-tween secular and religious political trends, government policies have come to vary widely, as the diversity of the Islamist movements has inevitably emerged.

As befits the cradle of Islamic political and religious thought, Egypt has sought to incorporate certain elements of the Islamists' message into the mainstream while seeking to eradicate its military element and undermine its political element through restrictions and margin-alization. In the years immediately following his assumption of the presidency after the assassination of Anwar al-Sadat in 1981, President Hosni Mubarak permitted Islamic organizations easier access to the media and allowed the Muslim Brotherhood to play a political role, which enabled it to secure positions of leadership in the lawyers', doc-tors', engineers', and journalists' syndicates. Mubarak's policy was in-tended to incorporate the brotherhood's mainstream while isolating its radicals. But from early on this strategy caused great division within the government itself. Two schools of thought evolved, cen-tered around particular individuals. The Fouad Allam school, named after an army general of the Nasser period, viewed all Islamist groups as part of the same movement—ranging from the Muslim Brotherhood to the extremists—with the same aims and a strategy of providing each other with covert support. Opposed to this view was the Hassan Abu Pasha school, named after an interior minister of the early Mubarak presidency. Proponents of this school held that the Islamic groups should not be viewed as homogenous, that while some should be viewed as a threat to security others should be dealt with politi-cally, and that by co-opting the moderates into the mainstream the vi-olent groups could be marginalized.

The launch of violent attacks by the militant Islamic groups in Egypt since 1992 has brought the Fouad Allam school into the ascendancy. "I distinguish between the groups, but they have the same aim, which is to try and take power by force. Since 1928, when the Muslim Brotherhood was founded, their military wing has been trying to terrify society. They are following the same style [now],"[17] said Hassan al-Alfi, Egypt's former interior minister. He continued:

> We have so many terrorist organizations, under a variety of names. The difference lies in the financing and leadership. But they have the same aim. All of them are from the same organization: the Muslim Brotherhood. They are linked to all the terrorists who are linked to Islamic groups in other countries, and they are led from abroad by Mustapha Hamza and Osama Bin Laden. With Bin Laden, we know the way he moves. He is trying to unify all these groups to have one operation. They are all over the world.

Al-Alfi's view, which barely distinguishes between groups publicly committed to violence and those that have publicly rejected it, has been strongly criticized by both ardent secularists and moderate Islamists. Both believe that the government's refusal to seek political dialogue emanates from its growing weakness and its inability to meet the needs of the burgeoning population.

"Autocracy was achieved by welfare provision, but now the states can no longer sustain the populations that have been educated,"[18] says Saad Eddin Ibrahim, professor of sociology at the American University in Cairo. Ibrahim goes on:

> I have stopped trying to advise the president. You have to develop a strategy of isolating the militants by bringing in the moderate ones. We have been advising the president, but he thinks it's too intellectual. In the beginning he listened. But, like everybody who stays in power too long, he doesn't listen anymore. The government hasn't consolidated a consensus against the Islamic groups, and even though the Egyptian state has always managed to prevail, it's a question of the price that is paid.

Mubarak's attempts to incorporate elements of the Islamists' agenda into the political mainstream have meanwhile evolved in specific directions since 1992. Central to the strategy has been the identification of issues rather than political trends. The religious hierarchy has attempted to drive a wedge between the Islamist movement and the issues that define the religious credentials of Islam's practitioners. This strategy is consistent with the view that Islam is strictly a matter between the individual and God. However, this article of faith is of far less importance than the need to avoid the suggestion that the "institutionalization of Islamic revivalism"[19] marks a weakening of the government's independence from the Islamist movements. To this end, the institutions of Egypt's secular state have moved increasingly toward publicly upholding principles that draw their inspiration from the Koran, in a manner that the Islamists may view as a victory and the government may view as expedient.

Though many incidents preceded the emergence of this trend, the most dramatic example was the decision of a Cairo court in June 1995 to rule that a Cairo University teacher and distinguished writer on philosophy and Islam, Nasr Hamed Abu Zeid, should divorce his wife on the grounds that his academic writings had been construed as atheistic, that therefore he was an apostate, and that consequently he could not be married to another Muslim. The case had evolved over the course of two years, beginning when Abu Zeid filed and lost a lawsuit claiming his right to promotion to a professorship in the university's Faculty of Arts. Symbolic of the divisions within Egyptian society, two members of the appointments board had approved Abu Zeid's promotion. But the third had accused the professor of rejecting the fundamental tenets of Islam in some of his writings and had thus denied him promotion. The dispute gained momentum and finally Sunni Islam's highest authority, the then Grand Sheikh Gad Al-Haq Ali Gad Al-Haq of Al-Azhar, a government appointee, requested a report on Abu Zeid's writings. The report branded Abu Zeid an "infidel," and a group of Islamist lawyers then filed a lawsuit demanding that Abu Zeid be divorced from his wife. Although a high court at first rejected the lawyers' demand, the Cairo Appeals Court ordered the couple to separate. Abu Zeid and his wife have since fled the country.

The case raised the profile of one particular Islamist, Youssef al-Badri, who has since devoted all his time to bringing private prosecutions that have allowed the government to demonstrate the independence of the judiciary while also, in light of the judgments reached, been a sop to the Islamists. "Religion is an Egyptian invention. You cannot imagine any Egyptian man or woman without religion,"[20] said al-Badri, who masterminded the case against Abu Zeid. Central to his theory is that the Egyptian religious establishment, in the form of Al-Azhar, should take the lead in determining the policies of specific government ministries. It is this support for widening the power of the establishment, rather than overthrowing it in the manner endorsed by the militant groups, that has assured him of the ongoing if indirect support of the government. "I am trying to realize Islam through the courts. This is the advantage of Islam: Everyone is free to try and realize Islam in his own way. This is *ijtihad*." Despite his value as a "mainstream Islamist," al-Badri openly promotes the inclusion of the militant groups within the broad Islamist strategy and also criticizes the government that has allowed him to operate unhindered, claiming that it restricts freedom and "has moved miles away from Islam."

Debate within the Egyptian government on religious issues has on occasion reflected the divisions within society. While religious officials and the Ministry of Religious Affairs have been the guardians of conservative religious principles, other ministries have asserted altogether different lines of thought. Whereas the religious establishment condemned the cloning of human beings, the Ministry of Health argued that the issue was purely scientific. Even within the religious establishment, a welter of opposing views prevails. When the current Grand Sheikh of Al-Azhar, Mohammed Sayyed Tantawi, announced that he would donate his healthy organs for transplant on his death, other clerics condemned the practice. Tantawi also came to the assistance of another academic accused of apostasy, Hassan Hanafi, following the latter's condemnation by a group of academics at Al-Azhar University, the Al-Azhar Front of Scholars, of works it deemed "a destructive project against which the whole nation must mobilize." The government itself found its own authority undermined when Youssef al-Badri took the health minister to court and won a case reversing a government ban on female circumcision. Although the court's decision was made on the basis that the original ban had been issued by decree rather than enshrined in law, al-Badri claimed that the verdict was a clear victory for Islam, though the government continued to impose its ban in state hospitals.

Egypt, alone in the Middle East, has been able to draw upon a plurality of political, social, and cultural traditions that have enforced an undefinable but nevertheless functional cohabitation of contradictory forces. Civil society, of a kind Tunisia's secularists yearn for but are too anxious to unleash, has evolved for decades both in Cairo and elsewhere in Egypt. Pressure from opposing sides—the voices supporting Nasr Hamed Abu Zeid before he was forced to flee were as strong as those demanding his punishment for apostasy—has nurtured an environment of variety, intellectual dynamism, and public debate that is unique in the Islamic world.

What these pressures have not done is bring about a corresponding transformation of the political system. A state of emergency has been in effect—albeit halfheartedly in areas of the country unaffected by the Islamists' military campaign—since 1981. Egypt remains effectively a police state in which the multiparty system is feeble, the security apparatus is immune to public and international criticism, and the arrest and prosecution of alleged Islamist activists is conducted in an arbitrary and often brutal fashion. The government, meanwhile, remains intent upon bringing all the country's 55,000 mosques under state control—in terms of the appointment of imams—by 2002.

"The authoritarian state, the nihilistic opposition: the middle ground has been scorched in the two decades behind us. The ruler claiming everything, the oppositionist dispensing with all that has been built and secured by those who came before . . . Beyond economic repair (really a precondition of it), a modernist impulse will have to assert itself if rescue is to materialize,"[21] wrote the renowned Arab scholar Fouad Ajami in September 1997. The apparent failure of the state—in Egypt, as elsewhere in the Arab world—to replace failed nationalism with a new identity, coupled with the antagonism of the Islamists to all that the state represents, has trapped the protagonists within an ever-turning spiral. "Reform of the Arab political culture will begin when a system of limited authority encounters the oppositionist with limited, realizable goals—half-steps reform," Ajami writes, asserting that only in Egypt might such a process, stemming from the country's diverse political tradition, emerge to break "the vicious circle of total rule and nihilistic opposition."

The challenge facing the Egyptian government is to open the political playing field to all political players. It has not done so. In July and August 1997 alone, 353 alleged Islamists were tried by a military prosecutor, accused of involvement in violence and of belonging to banned organizations. These measures, as well as routine harassment and detention of the nonviolent Muslim Brotherhood, have offset whatever credibility the institutions of the state may have gained by, for example, passing court rulings that effectively bolster the Islamist cause. The benefits accrued directly to the government by such judgments are limited. Although the security measures—essentially confined to central and southern Egypt's rural areas, wherein the armed Islamist groups remain militarily active—are the result of government policy, the potential social and political benefits of this security are barely apparent to the mass of the population. The government simply appears incapable of solving its security problem. Meanwhile, it has also been unable to foster a "politics of restraint and pragmatism,"[22] which is the cornerstone of genuine pluralism. The government is in fact at odds with all the most salient trends in Egyptian society: the Islamists, with whom it cannot speak; the liberal intellectual elite, to whom it cannot justify its quasi-autocratic methods. It is a government without an identity, which has drawn upon its amorphous character to avoid definitively showing its hand. Its strategy is the major factor hindering political debate: "The government is itself enslaved. It is not free to act. Nor is it prepared to play the game from within the Islamic debate,"[23] says Mohamed Sid Ahmed. "The future is without hope, and it is being assumed that we're part of a new world order, when we're not. But if we are to get beyond this period it will be because of some sort of reform from within these Islamic groups."

"Unto You, Your Moral Law, and Unto Me, Mine"[24]

In 1992, as his country was plunging into conflict and as the opportunity for a peaceful solution was rapidly disappearing, the virulently anti-Islamist Algerian writer Rachid Mimouni began his last major work[25] with his own translation of the above line from the 109th sura of the Koran: "For you, your religion; for me, my religion."[26] It was a call for tolerance in a climate that had forced him into exile. Despite his own bias, Mimouni consequently concluded his work by writing:

> The Islamic tendency represents a quarter of national opinion [in Algeria]. It will last. The government and the democrats must take it into account. The dissolution of the FIS does not add up to a solution because such an administrative decision will not dissolve the electorate that supports the FIS. Even if the politics of repression is able to clear out the terrorist cells, it will not dismantle a movement born clandestinely, which can revert to clandestinity and can revive the organizational and propaganda methods that brought its initial success.[27]

Mimouni, who died in 1995 in exile in the Moroccan port city of Tangier, lived long enough to see the finest detail of his prophesy come true.

As is the predominant view among moderate Egyptian writers, Mimouni recognizes the need for accommodation, however strong his personal antipathy toward the Islamist trend might be. But most governments, who have watched Algeria explode and seen Tunisia remain peaceful since Ben Ali unequivocally crushed the Islamists, lack the mechanism for such an accommodation. "Sadat was . . . caught between two contradictory forces in Egypt: orthodox Muslims attacked him for reneging on Islamising legislation, and liberal Muslims for encouraging Islam. He tried to juggle his way out by offering contradictory concessions," writes Dilip Hiro.[28]

Governments—in Egypt as elsewhere—have now learned that they must avoid such contradictions. They have adopted the line that politics and religion should not be mixed. Such straight talking would be a comfort if it were not the case that religion in fact has much to say about politics and the running of the state. There is no escaping the strongly political elements of Islam. But the failure of the states of the Islamic world to open the political field and to allow experimentation is what has prevented a solution to the crises of varying intensity with which they are now faced. "The idea that 'Islam' as such provides an identity, explanation and moral code for all actions undertaken by Muslims is a clear simplification. . . . The set texts of Islam simply do not provide detail about how politics and social institutions should be organized,"[29] Fred Halliday argues. Why do millions of Muslims continue to subscribe to the various forms of Islamism which have emerged? The absence of alternatives must be regarded as a key reason. "In Algeria as in Egypt or elsewhere in the Arab Mediterranean, the Islamist currents . . . like the opposition forces, are the result of the incumbent regimes becoming worn out,"[30] writes François Burgat, asserting that the Islamists' appeal as the only credible alternative to the incumbent regimes stems from their ability to restore the links between dispossessed populations and a cultural-religious identity that has not been sullied by foreign—"modernizing" or "Westernizing"—influences.[31] Burgat indirectly criticizes the policy of the *eradicateurs,* whether in Algeria or elsewhere, as an unnecessarily brutal approach to a political challenge that could be met by a more sophisticated attack on the Islamists' own creed by opting to engage in a political debate rather than by treating the Islamists purely as an issue of security:

> The Islamist rhetoric contains an uncompromising ethnocentrism that strictly associates 're-islamization' with reactionism and regression, which is a major hindrance to the upgrading of the Muslim world, necessitating a dictatorial approach on the part of the "integristes." For this reason secular currents are not necessarily powerless in the face of the "integristes"; the "integristes" could see their ability to mobilize drying up, allowing secularists to take the initiative.[32]

The paucity of debate on fundamental issues, perhaps even the paucity of the fundamental issues themselves when they are subject to close scrutiny, has isolated the protagonists from each other and brought about the escalation of conflicts, which can only be resolved through dialogue. The absence of dialogue, except on the covert level intended to open or maintain channels of communication with the aim of deal making as the FIS and the Algerian government attempted in the latter half of 1997, encourages fundamentalism by limiting mutual understanding. The existence of common ground, even between the most ardent political adversaries, was demonstrated at the St. Egidio meetings held in Rome in 1994–1995 by the totality of the Algerian opposition. But the refusal of those in power to accept that their legitimacy was neither greater nor less than that of their opponents has deprived the nation of the dialogue which at that time could have begun to address the escalating crisis.

Elsewhere, the interests of Egypt, as perceived by the government, differ from the interests of Egyptians as perceived by the Islamists. Egypt's political direction has led to the state's primacy in the Middle East as a regional player that maintains a strong influence over the Palestinian leader, Yasser Arafat, but that also has diplomatic ties with Israel. Annually, Egypt receives $2.3 billion in financial assistance from the United States and considers itself a key U.S. ally in the region. But the tightrope the government walks is a fine one. Egyptian public opinion, across the social spectrum, is vehemently anti-Israeli. The close ties with the United States are a source of discomfort, due in part to the Israeli-U.S. network into which these ties draw Egypt. The country's regional, Arab identity appears to many to have been subsumed by global aspirations and the need for American financial aid.

Mohamed Sid Ahmed's view that Egypt, and perhaps the entire Arab world, has not become part of a "New World Order" stems from the prevailing opinion that although the states of the world are aligning and realigning, the populations beneath the ruling elites in developing countries remain as alienated from the political direction of their leadership as they have always been. The interplay between the West and the Islamic world, against the background of regional politics, prejudices, and interests, has driven the wedge even further between the rulers and the ruled. If Islamism has injected one vital element into politics, it is the phenomenon of mass mobilization, but mobilization rooted in cultural and religious values rather than in the globalism and homogeneity that are the essential characteristics of the post–Cold War global order. The closed political realm of autocratic politics in the Arab world has, not surprisingly, failed to turn the prospect of a "New World Order" into an appealing one for the underclass of that world. Owing to its role as the sole force able to mobilize public opinion in much of the Islamic world, the West generally responds to Islam—whether radical or moderate—as a threat to its interests, which are largely safeguarded by autocrats who have yet to prove their legitimacy among their own people.

It is in this climate that the politics of the Middle East, North Africa, and to some extent the broader Islamic world has evolved. Consequent to this internal political reality, popular Arab views of "globalism" have ultimately been at odds with the Western or Western-oriented proponents of this "big idea" for the future of the planet. Western policy in the Middle East is dominated by oil. But the political and military conflicts that have arisen *within* the region do not mirror this Western preoccupation. The wars of 1948, 1967, and 1973; the Lebanese civil war and the Israeli invasion of Lebanon; the Palestinian Intifada and the terrorist bombings in Israel, are all essentially local conflicts over territory and political power.

The initial motivation and consequent fallout of these conflicts have, inevitably, had an enormous impact upon the domestic politics of all the countries affected. The incumbent pro-Western regimes have had to balance these elements, drawing upon national "state" interests, domestic political concerns, and the practical questions of military power and security. The Islamists have meanwhile fully exploited this essentially political reality as a means of inculcating their movements with a practical sense of mission imbued with a religious gloss. Even within the upper hierarchy of the Egyptian religious establishment, the call for jihad to liberate Jerusalem from Israeli aggression has been publicly stated, despite being at odds with official government policy. The purpose of such calls is confusing. "The Arab political imagination will . . . have to steal away from Israel. That grand alibi for every failure under the sun has worn thin and ought to have lost what force it had in the time of the wars and of nationalism,"[33] writes Fouad Ajami. But this has not happened, and the issue of Israel remains explosive. But is this a consequence of Islamism, or something else? "The very concept of an 'Islamic threat' is itself a chimera, and to talk of some enduring, transhistorical conflict between the 'Islamic' and 'Western' worlds is nonsense. . . . In reality Islamic countries have pursued individual, nation-state interests, and as often as not fought each other,"[34] says Fred Halliday. He continues:

> In its political form, the Islamic movement is defined and determined by national states and rival political factions [rather than transnational forces]. This is so in the sense, first, that it remains the goal of these movements to capture state power and, second, that if and when they do so they use Islamic doctrine to bolster the interests of those states (Iran and Sudan are no exception). . . . There cannot be a great "Islamic challenge," not only because the Islamic states are, and will remain, much weaker than those of the West, but also because they do not represent a coherent, internationally constituted alliance.[35]

The widely demonstrated desire of Islamist movements to seize power within the context of the nation-state is a reasonable political ambition, but one that Western critics of Islamism rarely consider. Although the motivation behind the Islamist movements remains intellectually, practically, and politically set upon this goal, the view from the West is heavily influenced by its own sense of globalism, which seriously confuses Western interpretations of the true direction in which the Islamic world is moving. The *umma* is an important aspect of Islam, but the fact that efforts to revive it have failed is an issue that has been ignored by Western theorists. The entire history of twentieth-century Islam has been dominated by steps away from this "global" doctrine—ever since the failure of Sayyid Jamal al-Din al-Afghani to convince the leaders of the Ottoman empire to transpose their territories into a "community of Muslims."

The current view among Western conservatives who feel threatened by Islam and believe that it will at some point attempt to swamp "Western culture" emphasizes the conflicts that have taken place within and involving the Islamic world and explains these conflicts as resulting from the fact that those involved are Muslim. "Islam is a source of instability in the world because it lacks a dominant center. States aspiring to be leaders of Islam, such as Saudi Arabia, Iran, Pakistan, Turkey, and potentially Indonesia, compete for influence in the Muslim world; no one of them is in a strong position to mediate conflicts within Islam; and no one of them is able to act authoritatively on behalf of Islam in dealing with conflicts between Muslim and non-Muslim groups,"[36] Samuel Huntington concludes. His theory, based upon detailed statistical analysis of the number of wars in which Muslims have been involved, stumbles on two counts. First, it asserts the value of a definable "center" to a religion that clearly thrives on an enormous diversity and decentralization, which has allowed it to spread from North Africa to Southeast Asia, from central Africa to northern Europe and the United States. Second, and more important, Huntington identifies the conflicts in which Muslims have been involved as resulting from "Muslim conflict propensity."[37] Leaving aside the obvious slur against the perhaps 75 or 80 percent of Muslims who do not consider themselves Islamists, and the far greater proportion who, Islamist or not, have never engaged in violence and have no intention of doing so, his view takes no account of the historical roots of the conflicts that have involved Muslims and Muslim states. The failure of attempts to revive the *umma*, the emergence of a variety of Islamist movements as a response to a variety of colonial experiences, the revival of political Islam in response to failed experiments with nationalism and socialism, all emphasize the national rather than global characteristics of the Islamist movements.

The essential contradiction in Huntington's theory is that, although he argues that the "New World Order" will be characterized by cultural differences replacing ideological ones, he does not actually apply this argument to the Islamic world. He treats the Islamic world as if it were one single culture. But history has shown that there is no uniform "Islamic world." There are many countries that are Islamic, each with its own political, cultural, and historical identity. All of them have steered different paths, as his theory would show if he were to apply it on the micro level of states wherein Islam is the dominant religion. Instead, he applies his theory as if the Islamic world were one homogenous state, which it is clearly not. Although he is perhaps correct in asserting that the end of the Cold War has allowed cultural variety to emerge with greater flourish than has been the case for the past fifty years—not a very long time in world history—the real evolution of states and identities is taking place on a much more micro level than any part of his book suggests. The potential sources of conflict—Huntington's main preoccupation—are in fact far more localized.

Within the Islamic world this is particularly true, as secularist regimes "clash" with theocrats and modernizers vie with monarchists. But a civilizational conflict pitching Muslim against non-Muslim is not taking place. Nor will it, because the Islamic world is preoccupied with coming to terms with itself, its past, and on a secondary level its relations with the non-Islamic world. This is clear in the policies of governments toward the Islamists, as well as in their skewed relations with the West. This is nowhere more vividly illustrated than in the Islamized states of the Muslim world: Iran and, as the following chapter will show, Sudan.

7

The Book and the Gun

Sudan

PLUMES OF SMOKE FROM BURNING INCENSE curled into the hazy blue-gray afternoon sky, as the magnificent red blaze of the sun cast the shadows of the singers and dancers onto the harsh rock and sand of the graveyard. Dry, gnarled young trees stood motionless in front of the conical dome of the saint's *qubba*, or tomb. Roughly hewn, white-painted stones marked the hundreds of graves that were scattered across the plain surrounding the saint's tomb. Lines of men, bare-headed, dressed in fine white cotton *jelabias*, filed between the graves toward the incense burner. The raging sun burned the land and the men shielded their eyes as they gathered in an ever-growing circle on the plain, leaving an open space in their center. The slow setting of the sun dictated the timing of the ritual, which slowly gathered pace on the edge of the Sudanese city of Omdurman, one of the three cities (together with Khartoum and North Khartoum) that, divided by the confluence of the Blue and White Niles, form the Sudanese capital. The rivers, the desert, and the ritual mark the confluence of cultures and religious practices by which Sudan has evolved, through dramatic phases of history, through invasions, and through ideologies, which have both enriched and devastated the country's land and people. Sudan is a crossroads of civilizations, where a rich cultural heritage has imposed a great weight upon the course of change, new ideas being forced to coexist with what has been inherited from the past, the political elite being drawn from a religious-political ruling class with an enduring attachment to power.

On Friday afternoons, after the scorching midday sun has passed overhead, Sufi adherents raise green and red and black flags on tall canes as they gather on the plain on the edge of Omdurman, to venerate their saints and remember the dead buried in the graves scattered as far as the eye can see. The mystics of the Islamic religion, gathering in circles on the open plain, watching the sun as it dictates to them the time for starting their ritual as well as the time it will reach its end, brandish a tradition that more than any other confronts the Islamist modernists, revivalists, and militants. As the sun begins to slip over the horizon, the gathering of men begins to sway, arms linked, to the sound of drums beaten furiously by bony hands. The devotees, two, three, or four hundred of them, sway in a great wave, slowly circulate en masse around and around the space in their center, and begin to chant in a loud, deep, uniform voice, as the drummers' pace grows faster until their hands can barely be seen as they beat the taut animal skins. The waves of movement become greater, the men stride in unison, their arms tightly linked; they step into the circular space and then back out, and as they move their voices rise and fall, louder and softer. From among them an ancient, gray-bearded man steps into the circle swinging a copper burner billowing smoke from glowing incense. Dressed in the green and red colors of the sect, he slowly circulates close to the crowd, dousing the gathering in the sharp odor of sandalwood, his cracked and lined face emerging from within the billowing smoke. The devotees' chanting grows louder, and into the center of the circle step men in the same colors—the "whirling dervishes."[1] Slowly they begin to spin on their feet, twisting on the sand and rock, turning faster and faster until the sand and dust rise into the haze of the incense, as they spin and spin and spin, the drummers beating out a hypnotic rhythm while the chanting devotees encircle the gathering, doused in a haze of sand and dust and smoke.

Devotion, the veneration of religious mystics, and a belief in supernatural powers have distinguished the Sufi orders from the dawn of Islam in the seventh century. Islam reached Sudan in the late tenth century, when a representative of the Fatimid dynasty, which had conquered Egypt in 969, visited the Nubian king at his court in Dongola and sought his conversion to Islam. The attempt failed, but a small Muslim presence was established, which influenced the area's religious direction over the centuries that followed. The Sufi orders became a more firmly established part of Sudan's religious identity during the period of the Muslim Funj sultanate (1504–1821) with its capital at Sennar. Islam flourished and established strong direct roots with the Hejaz, the western part of the Arabian peninsula where the two holy cities of Mecca and Medina are located. Religious figures moved directly from the Hejaz to Sudan, where their influence and personal esteem evolved into veneration and the establishment of Sufi orders devoted to the celebration of their acts and teachings.[2] J. Spencer Trimingham writes:

They initiated their followers into the Sufi path they themselves followed; but since Sufism at this time was at a very low ebb, for mysticism in Islam is not only its highest but also its most degraded form, it was materialized in the form of the cult of mysterious powers, now Islamized in the form of *baraka* (supernatural powers), therefore personal allegiance and abject reverence for the shaikh was the thing that mattered. . . . During their life they enjoyed royal favor and the adoration of the people; and after their death they became intercessors with God and their tombs places of pilgrimage.[3]

The *Sufi tariqas*, the groups of adherents who over time evolved into orders under the guidance of a sheikh, formed a thriving religious environment in Sudan. Scholars traveled throughout the area, and their influence led to the creation of numerous *tariqas*, which exerted influence in all areas of life. "Initiation was purely an act of blind submission to the shaikh. The great aim was to increase the power of the orders by augmenting their numbers and centralizing the organization."[4]

Politics abruptly intruded into the life of the religious orders after the invasion of Sudan in 1820 by the Ottoman viceroy, or khedive, installed in Egypt. These forces used their military power and an array of European adventurers and mercenaries to further their territorial conquest as far south as the border with present-day Uganda by 1870. The religious orders in Sudan were legally recognized by the Ottoman rulers, and the sheikhs became a conduit through which the new rulers exercised much of their authority. Three notable Sufi orders—the Majdhubiyya; the Idrisiyya; and the Mirghaniyya, or Khatmiyya—became key allies of the Ottoman rulers in Cairo. Administrative authority within the Ottoman possessions in Sudan was exerted through governors, employed as the private employees of the khedive in Cairo. The governors' sole necessary qualification was proof of an ability to impose a degree of order on areas of the country that had traditionally had little if any contact with areas beyond their own tribal territory. A key player in extending Ottoman influence was an English soldier, George Gordon, who was appointed governor general of the Sudan by the khedive in 1877. Gordon's power was dependent on that of the Ottoman empire, which was itself in decline when he was appointed. The collapse of Ottoman power in Sudan was marked by the eruption of a revolt in 1881, led by Muhammad Ahmad ibn 'Abdallah, who in June that year dispatched a series of letters to the rulers and administrators of Sudan declaring that he was the Mahdi.

The tradition of Mahdism is rooted both in orthodox doctrine and social movements throughout Islamic Africa and elsewhere. The Koran foresees the arrival of a restorer of faith just before the Day of Judgment:

And, behold, this [divine writ]
is indeed a means to know
[that] the Last Hour [is bound to come];
hence, have no doubt whatever about it, but follow
    Me:
this [alone] is a straight way. And let not Satan bar
    you [from it]—
for, verily, he is your open foe.[5]

The Koranic reference to a second coming also led to the adoption of beliefs in the conditions—largely social and political—that would prevail before the second coming. Muhammad Ahmad "was the 'leader,' thrown up by the times, of a peculiar type of Sudanese nationalism. Behind all was his very real and unwavering belief in his divine call—a belief which exercised a compelling influence on others."[6] Mahdism catapulted the power of Sufi mysticism and veneration, into which Muhammad Ahmad had been inducted from an early age, directly into the Sudanese political arena, although Mahdism itself—because of its historic import—was not a Sufi movement. The declining power of the Ottomans and the irascibility of Gordon combined to bring a crisis of leadership, which Muhammad Ahmad seized upon. He was able to focus the anti-imperialist aspirations of the Sudanese people onto his role as the religio-political redeemer promised in the Koran. He gathered followers, called the *ansar* after the "helpers" of the Prophet Mohammed but who in Sudan were farmers and cultivators, and divided them into sections united under red, black, or green flags. He rebutted accusations that he was mad and stressed that his divine role was inspired by a direct call from God: "The Prophet told me that I am the awaited Mahdi and appointed me to succeed him by repeatedly making me sit in his chair. . . . The Prophet said to me, 'God has made for you a sign of Mahdiship,' and it is the mole on my right cheek,"[7] he told his followers as he garnered support for the military revolt that swept through much of the Ottoman territory between 1881 and 1885, when Khartoum fell to the Mahdist forces and Gordon was killed, his severed head raised on a tree stump.

The Land of the Mahdi

The Mahdist revolution was a remarkable attempt to create an Islamic state. Certain Mahdist characteristics drew on Sufism, such as the exultation of the role of the leader. But the revolution also sought to diminish social divisions by undermining tribalism and pursuing the creation of a definable "state" led by the Mahdi; it set about banning traditional rites that had tribal origins. The Sufi "dervish" religious orders, so called because they grouped the poor—*darwish* or "dervish" in Arabic—into orders committed to the devotion of saints, were abolished because their identity corresponded with that of the tribes.[8] Muhammad Ahmad superseded Sufism and modified the pillars of the faith to place himself within the hierarchy of devotion, by proclaiming himself the "Mahdi of Allah and the representative of His Prophet." Such claims were in direct opposition to the ulama, the orthodox religious hierarchy, which stressed the direct relationship between God and the individual Muslim, with no intermediaries. On the basis of his divine purpose as the guide to be followed as the Day of Judgment approached, Muhammad Ahmad instituted reforms that diverted his followers from the religious path that had been followed since the time of the Prophet. Because he was the Mahdi, devotion to him meant that the haj, the pilgrimage to Mecca, was no longer necessary and was therefore prohibited. After his death in 1885, the haj was replaced by visits to his tomb in Omdurman. The devotional purpose of the haj was replaced by jihad, the holy war in defense of Islam, on the back of whose success the Mahdist state had been established. Other innovations included the banning of many traditional rituals that had been subsumed by or had themselves subsumed Sufi practices that had evolved over the previous 350 years; the use of tobacco, the practice of magic, processions, marriage and circumcision feasts, and mourning and visits to saints' tombs were all banned despite their strong popularity among the population, which ensured their clandestine practice during the *Mahdiyya*[9] and under the rule of Muhammad Ahmad's nominated successor, Khalifa 'Abdallahi.

Famine, war, and pestilence dominated 'Abdallahi's caliphate. Conflict in the western region of Darfur, a long-running dispute with the neighboring kingdom of Ethiopia, and the imperialist ambitions of the Anglo-Egyptian administration in Cairo, which had come to assert great influence over the Ottoman rulers, all undermined 'Abdallahi politically. "Far from destroying the [British] government, the fall [in 1885] of Khartoum gave it a new appetite for power."[10] In 1898, the British took revenge for the death of General Gordon. But their strategy and colonial policy had little or nothing to do with the ambition of jihad that united the Mahdists.

On 8 April 1898, Major General Horatio Herbert Kitchener, the commander of a combined army of British, Egyptian, and Sudanese troops, attacked the Mahdist army outside Omdurman and annihilated it in fifteen minutes, using modern weapons against spears and clubs. Kitchener halted, and the remaining Mahdist forces retreated.

The two sides dug in, and the British were sent 25,000 men and sup-plies as reinforcements. On 1 September, Kitchener began bombarding Omdurman, destroying Muhammad Ahmad's tomb. The following day the two armies engaged for two hours, after which the Mahdists retreated, leaving 2,000 of their comrades dead or dying on the battle-field, as Kitchener yelled: "Cease fire! Cease fire. What a dreadful waste of ammunition!"[11] That night Kitchener was firmly ensconced in Omdurman. Four days later he razed the Mahdi's tomb, scattered his bones in the Nile River, and began the campaign to bring the entire former territory of the deposed Ottoman khedive, seized by the Mahdists in 1881–1885, under Anglo-Egyptian rule.

The purpose of this exercise was to ensure that France, Great Britain's primary colonial rival in Africa, did not succeed in claiming this same territory. On 17 September 1898, this rivalry erupted at the Nile village of Fashoda, where French troops laid claim to "parts of the upper Nile abandoned by Egypt and therefore without a legal owner." Over whisky and soda aboard a gunboat, Kitchener warned his French rival, Captain Jean-Baptiste Marchand, that a refusal to depart could lead to war. Eventually the French backed down, and from that time until full independence in 1955 Sudan remained under Anglo-Egyptian rule, with authority wielded by a British governor general in Khar-toum.

As before, religion has forged the course of Sudanese politics, di-rectly or indirectly, since independence. In 1938 the Sudanese clamor for a voice in discussions over future independence resulted in the for-mation of the Graduates' General Congress (GGC), whose first general secretary, Isma'il al-Azhari, formed the Ashigga party,[12] which favored a postindependence Sudanese union with Egypt. In 1943, the Ashigga won the support of the head of the Khatmiyya Sufi religious order, Sayyid 'Ali al-Mirghani, whose ancestors' close ties with Egypt had played a key role during the Ottoman period before the Mahdist re-volt. The Ashigga-Khatmiyya alliance, which fought and won an elec-tion for a constituent assembly in 1953 under the banner of the Na-tional Unionist Party, was a direct assault on the growing influence of Sayyid 'Abd al-Rahman al-Mahdi, the son of the Mahdi, Muhammad Ahmad; the former had inherited the position of leader of the Ansar religious order and had played a key role in negotiating the end of An-glo-Egyptian rule. In 1940 the Ansar won control of the GGC but later lost control to the Ashigga. By the time of independence, on 1 January 1956, Sudan's political environment was dominated by Sayyid 'Abd al-Rahman al-Mahdi's political ambitions, which after 1945 he had chan-neled by patronage into his newly established Umma Party, led by his son Sayyid Siddiq al-Mahdi; the Ashigga-Khatmiyya leadership feared that the Umma would attempt to establish a new Mahdist state. "The events surrounding the factionalization of the [GGC], which had shown promise as a secular body, illustrated the fundamental if much-deprecated fact that the sectarian leaders retained the keys to political strength."[13]

Civilian rule under the prime ministership of al-Azhari lasted until 17 November 1958, when Major General Ibrahim Abboud led an army coup, largely in response to the chaotic and unworkable civilian coalition government, which al-Azhari had failed to strengthen or steer toward addressing Sudan's severe economic and social problems. Countercoups within the army followed but were suppressed by Abboud, whose consolidation of power witnessed the emergence of the political forces that have dominated the country's direction ever since.

Sayyid Siddiq al-Mahdi died in 1961, and his religious-political role was assumed by both his brother, Sayyid al-Hadi, who became the leader of the Ansar, and his son, Sayyid Sadiq al-Mahdi, who became leader of the Umma Party. Also emerging as political forces during this period were the Communist Party, and the Muslim Brotherhood, led by a law lecturer at Khartoum University, Dr. Hassan al-Tourabi.

As potent as the machinations of the northern Sudanese political parties centered in Khartoum, however, was the growing mobilization of the southern Sudanese. After 1922, the British had effectively barred northern and southern Sudanese—Arab and sub-Saharan African populations, respectively—from each other's essentially tribal areas, deeming the south an officially "closed area." The British aimed to incorporate southern Sudanese affairs into its East Africa and central Africa policy. At all costs, they did not want to see the emergence of a homogenous Sudanese identity that could give rise to aspirations for independence. A separate educational system, run by Christian missionary societies, took root in the south, and the English language was widely taught and its use encouraged, unlike Arabic, which did not even appear on school curricula.

Even before independence, a southern Sudanese consciousness, particularly heightened by the south's almost routine exclusion from the negotiations that led to the final settlement of the terms of independence, was emerging. In 1955 a battalion of southern troops refused to open fire on striking southern workers; following their mutiny these troops went underground and formed the nucleus of what became known as the Anya Nya movement, named after a poisonous plant that grew in Kordofan province. In 1964 this group reemerged as a focus of southern opposition, attacking the southern town of Wau and taking the Abboud government by such surprise that it eventually fell from power. For the following five years, the Khartoum government fell into the hands of a succession of coalitions, led from July 1966 to May 1967 by Sadiq al-Mahdi as prime minister.

The Umma Party's main rival, the Khatmiyya-led Democratic Unionist Party (DUP),[14] won parliamentary seats but failed to create a coalition capable of running the country. In May 1969 civilian rule was once again sidelined when Colonel Gaafar Nimeiri seized power in a bloodless coup. But Nimeiri's pursuit of large-scale development programs, as well as his introduction of Islamic-oriented policies in the justice system, failed to alleviate the country's widespread poverty or to appease the civilian political establishment. Despite the Muslim Brotherhood's nominal support for the Nimeiri regime and Nimeiri's appointment of its leader, Hassan al-Tourabi, as attorney general, none of the recognized Islamic parties were consulted on the Islamization program, a program that Sadiq al-Mahdi meanwhile strongly condemned. The effect of the worsening political and military crisis in the south with the 1981 launching of a full secessionist war by the Sudan Peoples' Liberation Movement (SPLM), coupled with unceasing economic hardship in the north, combined to bring down Nimeiri in a 1985 military coup. Civilian rule was restored in 1986, with Sadiq al-Mahdi installed as prime minister, but subsequent elections produced a hung parliament that was unable to produce a stable government. The Umma Party, the DUP, and al-Tourabi's National Islamic Front (NIF)—the party he had formed from the less conservative elements of the Muslim Brotherhood—vied for cabinet posts. Still, the war in the south remained the key factor in ensuring the continued instability of the Khartoum government, regardless of who was in charge. In 1989, al-Tourabi was appointed al-Mahdi's deputy prime minister, an appointment that, given the NIF's strong support for the institution of Islamic *sharia* law throughout a unified Sudan, was unlikely to please the SPLM. War raged in the south, and al-Mahdi was overthrown in yet another bloodless coup on 30 June 1989, this time by army officers led by Brigadier Omar Hassan al-Bashir, who announced that his primary objective was to bring an end to the southern conflict.

The Corridors of Power

"I do believe there's a revival in all the Islamic world. There's a renaissance of Islam. But we don't meddle in the internal affairs of other Muslim countries, because we don't want others meddling in our affairs. There is a renaissance of Islam, and these countries are retarding this. But we believe eventually that our view will be triumphant."[15] President al-Bashir sat serenely in a grand armchair in a large office on the upper floor of a nondescript concrete government building off a tree-lined street on the edge of Khartoum. "In Sudan there is a freedom of creativity, and everything is open to debate." The brigadier, who became a general when he seized power, was dressed in a gray double-breasted suit rather than the military uniform in which he was portrayed in his official photograph.

Al-Bashir had forged an alliance with al-Tourabi's National Islamic Front soon after seizing power. In 1991 the military government began introducing elements of Islamic *sharia* law into policy. "Our guiding principles are constant and have nothing to do with the conflict in southern Sudan or the economic situation," al-Bashir told me. "On the contrary, we know that these guiding principles address many of the grievances that have led to the conflict. When you try applying Islamic ideas, it could be that there are points of convergence between Islamic thinkers, and differences as well. You find different points of view, to the extreme right and the extreme left. Our way is mediation."

"Mediation" in Sudan since the 1989 coup, and more specifically since the launch of the Islamization program in 1991, has been dominated by the lessons gleaned from the political failures of the country's postindependence history. It has also been heavily influenced by the weakness of a political system dominated by the religious-political elite, which drew its power from the religious orders established during precolonial times. "Our most serious problem in Sudan since independence has been the search for stable government. We have had a formal democracy ruled by tribal families. Then a military dictator [Nimeiri]. Because there's now a religious spirit, the military can't rule the government,"[16] Hassan al-Tourabi explained when we first met in 1993. He went on:

> You can't have democracy without basing it on the spirit of the people. Throughout Africa there are parties, but they are tribal actually. And Islam is based on democracy. In the new Sudan there is no following of the [religious] sects and their relevant political parties. Revolutions run against the old order, and people don't join those sects anymore. People worked for them for the hereafter. But now people know that in the hereafter they don't get anything for working for these people.

Al-Tourabi's rejection of the old order, his alliance with a section of the army in which political Islam has strong roots, and his readiness to confront and reject a religious and cultural heritage while paying little heed to its residual importance for the Sudanese set him on an extremely isolated path. The Muslim Brotherhood, from which he extricated himself, as well as the religious conservatives of the Ansar and Khatmiyya sects, view him suspiciously. "All this government has to claim that it is Muslim, is that it prays," one conservative religious leader told me in 1993, when we met after I took a circuitous drive to his modest house in North Khartoum in order to avoid detection by whichever branch of the security forces my accomplice expected was trailing us. Other religious critics of the government during its first years in power found its religious credentials overshadowed by the personality of al-Tourabi, whom they saw as casting a pall over whatever claims the regime had to be pursuing an Islamist path.

"I haven't been deceived by anybody throughout my life, with the exception of Hassan al-Tourabi,"[17] said Hibir Yussuf al-Dayim, who succeeded to the leadership of the Muslim Brotherhood in Sudan after al-Tourabi's departure. He recounted an incident in which al-Tourabi had told him that the only way to instill Islamic fervor into army officers was to give the impression that you were a sheikh, a religious leader, who could tell the future. "I told him that I couldn't do that—because I was not a sheikh. I think he is a pretender," said al-Dayim. "But if he has an idea he will try and pursue it to the end of his ability. And he is patient enough to do it little by little. But I think he is very weak [to resist] in the face of power."

Asked bluntly whether the Islamic state exists, Abel Aziz Shiddo sucked on his pipe and replied: "No." The justice minister of Sudan's Islamist government sat in the near-frozen environment of his ultra–air conditioned office. High up on the walls were black-and-white portrait photographs of his respectable-looking predecessors staring down at the new incumbent. "We are a people looking for an identity, and I believe religious values are a way of looking for that identity," he said.

Candor flickered in those first years of the regime. I never saw Mr. Shiddo again, though he remained in his post until his appointment as deputy speaker of the National Assembly in 1996. But the question of a search for identity was not one that came up frequently in the conversations I had with other leading members of the regime. The identity was Islamic. The search was not a pursuit of faith, and it was not a pursuit of personal identity. The quest was to create an Islamic identity for the apparatus of the state. Having rejected the models of the past—in particular the Mahdist state, whose descendants had reemerged during the democratic period but failed to rule the country with any success—the regime could only look to the future. Sudan's political heritage was rejected as a failure. The western democratic models that had influenced Sudan between 1956 and 1989 had collapsed. The traditional ruling elite had failed to lead. The previous military interventions had not brought stability. What was left?

"Democracy is a relativism. We believe in absolutism in some areas, because we are religious people. Sudan is not exactly paradise, but it's getting better,"[18] Baha al-Din Hanafi, the director of President al-Bashir's political department, told me. "I think Sudan is an Islamic model. The West will never find a better Islamic model with which to conduct a dialogue. We don't believe in violence and terrorism, and the West will never find a more rational political Islam than in Sudan," he said. The Sudanese government's obsession with what the West thinks of it has strongly influenced the manner in which it has responded to Western criticism. Politically, Sudan is irrelevant to the non-Islamic world. Since 1989 it has had little strategic significance. The country's *potential* as a market for Western goods is perhaps great, but is currently negligible. Its oil reserves are substantial but have yet to come on-stream. Sudan's influence in U.S. Middle East and Persian Gulf policy is nonexistent, as Khartoum has little positive impact upon the views of other Arab states. And the West does not really seek a dialogue with Sudan on issues of religion. The government's pursuit of such a dialogue is raised as an issue because it is absent. The West is portrayed as closing the door on Sudan because of its religious path. In fact the West, particularly Britain, has largely closed both eyes and ears to Sudan's Islamization and the conduct of the regime, due to its strategic irrelevance, poverty, weakness, and internal conflict. As I shall discuss later in this chapter, it is Sudan's foreign policy that has raised the country's profile. But as an "Islamic model" in search of a leading role in dialogue with the non-Islamic world, Sudan has had few of its offers taken up.

Establishing the identity of who really runs Sudan is a major undertaking, and the closed government has intensified outside suspicions of both its practice and aims. In 1993 five members of the fourteen-member ruling cabinet were members of al-Tourabi's National Islamic Front, though Baha al-Din Hanafi insisted, confusingly: "There's no official presence or influence of the NIF. Tourabi has nothing to do officially with the government. He has his PAIC,[19] in which he tries, like everybody else, to influence the government and society. He has no official role. Most people look to him as a bigger thing than even the government."

In a 1985 general election the NIF had won fifty-one parliamentary seats, compared with ninety-nine for Sadiq al-Mahdi's Umma Party and sixty-three for Osman al-Mirghani's DUP. Al-Tourabi did represent a break with the past practice of concentrating political power in the hands of the two traditional religious-political movements. He also defended his behind-the-scenes role: "I'm not interested in political office for myself," he told me. "Sudan has lost most of its intellectual leadership, who have gone abroad. People don't have to join the government to play a role." But three years later he was elected to the National Assembly and appointed speaker. His influence had radically shifted by 1997, but in the early years of the al-Bashir regime the fundamental question was whether it had been the political nature of the traditional movements that had led to their failure to govern the country effectively, or whether it had been the religious position their leaders—or their leaders' forefathers—had occupied. Was religion a dead weight on the practice of politics, which had denied the chance of leadership to those seeking alternatives? The fact that al-Tourabi is married to Sadiq al-Mahdi's sister Wisal and is very much a part of the social establishment—which in Khartoum is determined by whether one is routinely invited to establishment weddings, which al-Tourabi is—has prevented the total demarcation of the old and the new. What has changed is the NIF's use of political weapons to monopolize religious issues, avoidance of which had since independence provided some common ground among the religious-political parties.

"The main political parties were committed to Islamization, but the Islamic program had to be nonpartisan. Before it was implemented there had to be a bill of rights clearly defining the rights of non-Muslims,"[20] said Sadiq al-Mahdi. The military guard, which had been posted in a green tent and armed with a heavy-caliber machine gun mounted on an armored personnel carrier at the end of his street in Omdurman, had been dozing as we drove quietly past on the sand road that stretches along the length of the grounds surrounding the house of the great-grandson of the Mahdi, who had fought the British and whose Ansar followers had decapitated the defeated General Gordon in 1885. A long, neat lawn spread out from beyond the terrace of the large house. A gravel path encircled the lawn, which was wilting in the soaring heat, leading to a summer house draped in the fantastic blossoms of bougainvillea. It was cool inside, with the scent of the blossom, the hum of bumblebees, and the occasional whiff of sand dust turned up by a rare breeze dousing the place with the timeless air of the desert. Sadiq al-Mahdi strode into the shade, his big frame clothed in a fine white *jelabia*, a round skullcap perched on the crown of his large head. He tucked a leg beneath him where he sat and talked animatedly, a living symbol of a vast country's mysterious, dramatic, awesome history.

"The NIF, with its military allies, has really put aside all those principles," he went on. "According to the Koran, there's no way of establishing Islamic authority by a coup d'état, because anything that is based on compulsion is null and void."[21] Since the 1989 coup, Sadiq al-Mahdi had been under house arrest in his compound, allowed out only on rare visits to see members of the government, his sister—at the house of his tormentor and brother-in-law, Hassan al-Tourabi—or to see the other of his two wives, who lived nearby in Omdurman.

Many of the statements made by the government in the days before I first met Sadiq al-Mahdi seemed to be undermined by the fact of his house arrest. But his arrest was only the most visible sign of the government's general attitude toward detractors, critics, and political opponents. The explicit Koranic rejection of compulsion, expressed in the 109th sura,[22] appeared to have been overridden by the interests of political control. Even so, confusion lay at the heart of the official government line with regard to how the "freedom of creativity" that President al-Bashir had proclaimed tallied with the admission made to me by his political director, Baha al-Din Hanafi, that "there have never been more than 150–200 political prisoners." Hanafi's statement itself contradicted not only the president but also Mohammed al-Amin Khalifa, then the speaker of the transitional National Assembly, who had told me: "Anybody is free to give us his ideas," but then had qualified his claim by adding: "If they are wrong we will reject them."[23]

The fine line the government had trodden since the army-NIF alliance had been established in 1991 led to the creation of parallel organizations not only within the military forces but in all areas of the power structure. The early 1990s witnessed the eclipse of President al-Bashir as a real decisionmaker and his transformation into a front behind which lay the internal power structure of the NIF. His role was merely to sign decrees, on occasion after events—such as the execution of army officers allegedly involved in a 1992 coup attempt—had already taken place. Al-Tourabi dominated the daily decisionmaking process, in coordination with the foreign minister, Ali Osman Taha; the minister of state for foreign affairs, Ghazi Salah Eddin Atabani; and other key National Islamic Front figures. The NIF had itself been officially disbanded and renamed the Islamic Movement, though its key personnel remained the same. The inner circle of decisionmakers—the Higher Committee—was chaired by al-Tourabi. Its decisions affected all areas of government, and it planned all future policies. The committee's long-term strategy was to install NIF supporters in all areas of government and in the armed forces. By 1995, up to a thousand senior non-NIF army officers had been dismissed from the army[24] as part of the government's attempt to shape its political identity. Ultimately, the intention was to replace the army with a popular defense force loyal to the NIF. In the police force, an estimated five hundred officers had been dismissed by 1995, with the same aim in mind, the intention being to replace the state police with the "Popular Police" by 1999. In the civil service the aim was the same—to install a service totally loyal to the NIF by 2000.

To protect its transition toward totalitarianism, the government had by 1993 created a security service tasked with destroying the power of the political opposition. Naf'i Ali Naf'i headed an NIF-run department within the security apparatus—the Security Group—which effectively controlled all state security departments. The same group controlled a series of "ghost houses" in Khartoum, residential villas in which opponents of the regime were held incommunicado for long periods of time without the government being required to announce that an arrest had even been made.

"Where society can manage, government has no business interfering. . . . Where society on its own manages to realize social justice, for example, then the government does not need to interfere," Hassan al-Tourabi wrote in 1983.[25] The role of government in the creation of the Islamic state—as opposed to the maintenance of that state once it has been established—varies, al-Tourabi argues, according to historical circumstances and the ability of the government to physically communicate with all those living within its domain. It has at its heart the assumption that:

> the freedom of the individual ultimately emanates from the doctrine of *tawhid*[26] which requires a self-liberation of man from any worldly authority in order to serve God exclusively. Society, and particularly those in power, is inspired by the same principle and the collective endeavor is not one of hampering the liberty of an individual but of cooperation toward the maximum achievement of this ideal. To promote this cooperation, the freedom of one individual is related to that of the general group. The ultimate common aim of religious life unites the private and public spheres; the *sharia* provides an arbiter between social order and individual freedom.[27]

Political power lies at the heart of al-Tourabi's program. Despite having, until his election to the National Assembly in 1996, no official government post, his intention was to apply his understanding of the Islamic *sharia* in a way that suited the needs of the government over which his ideological influence has reigned supreme: "Any form or procedures for the organization of public life that can be ultimately related to God and put to his service in furtherance of the aims of Islamic government can be adopted unless expressly excluded by the *sharia*. Once so received, it is an integral part of Islam whatever its source may be,"[28] he wrote. Al-Tourabi has subsequently practiced what he preached. His philosophy effectively advocates unrestricted religious and therefore political power for those pursuing the creation of an Islamic state. The assumption is that compulsion is unnecessary where the exercise of that power reflects the popular will. Today in Sudan the government looks to the future, whereas the population assesses its next move by drawing upon the lessons of past failure. The two are looking in different directions. Meanwhile, the war that has brought more than one Khartoum government to its knees is edging closer to the seat of power.

"They Have Learnt Silence and Patience from the River and from the Trees"[29]

Twisted trees rising in a thick, dark forest were the pillars. Lines of earth piled in long, neat mounds were the pews. A roof soaring high above the ground was woven from dry grass. The forest of pillars inside disappeared into the gloom that rose where the light from the two-foot-high entrance failed to reach. The Presbyterian church at Ayod had the grandeur of a cathedral: The trees, two or three hundred saplings arranged in lines and driven into the ground, held up the roof of grass. A low wall of mud rose out of the earth, while the grass roof swept almost down to the ground.

In the wilderness of southern Sudan, the church rose almost as high as the grand trees that, alone in the dry miles of desolation, burst onto the horizon. Southern Sudan, the forgotten battlefield of a forgotten war, is a dead land during the dry months. The war comes and goes; at least a million people have died from starvation, disease, and fighting since 1981, when the Sudan Peoples' Liberation Movement went to war with Khartoum, demanding that the rights of the southerners, the Christians, the animists, the Africans, the non-Arabs, the non-Muslims, the English-speakers and Dinka-speakers and Nuer-speakers and all the other identities, be recognized and respected. Sadiq al-Mahdi, during his brief premiership in 1966–1967, had attempted such reconciliation, but he had fallen from power before anything could be done. By 1981, the desperation of southerners and the weakness of northerners had entrapped the country.

"Somebody who believes in politics is believing in politics. Somebody who is a believer believes in religion."[30] Pastor Peter Rit Machar stood on the threshold of the magnificent church looking out over the desolation of Ayod, at a child crawling naked across the harsh earth, slowly crawling, watched by a flock of vultures pecking at the waters of a stagnant pool. "But Christianity is also politics. Just like Islam. So, the solution: We don't know. We don't know. But we Sudanese cannot solve our problem for ourselves. Because of these two religions we cannot solve our problems for ourselves."

War has devastated southern Sudan. The people who have not fled as refugees, either to the north of the country or to Kenya and Uganda, survive on sporadic supplies of foreign food aid. They live beneath the great trees, in the crumbling ruins of villages destroyed at first during fighting between the SPLM and the Khartoum government, but later in fighting between factions of the southern movement, which turned on each other in 1991.

"We have no friends. We are unable to mobilize others to support our cause. We are, by force of history, jammed into the present situation. The question is: how do we extract ourselves? The minimum is the separation of the two states."[31] John Garang, the leader of the SPLM, talks as much with his tiny, sparkling eyes as he does with his clear voice as he outlines the options for the wilderness over which his army has tried to rule. He is a realist, knowing that he cannot win the war on his own, knowing also that the Khartoum government would only accept a compromise if it were forced to in the interests of its own political survival. By 1993 he had reached the conclusion that the northern Muslim population was split and that a new southern strategy could incorporate this growing antigovernment tide among northern Muslims. "The NIF regime is the climax of all the policies of the Islamists. It is the highest stage of these parties, since 1956," said Garang. "It's a blessing in disguise that the NIF took over, because it is exhausting all the political resources of the extremists. The NIF has used the last card to suppress us: jihad."

Is there a jihad in the south? I asked Hassan al-Tourabi in Khartoum a month later. He replied:

Oh yes. But jihad doesn't mean Muslim and non-Muslim. You don't use the word only to energize sentiment. You use it to control the army. Here jihad is a strict word: using force to stop force. But [there is jihad] in the south, because this is a nation. That's why it's used. Many people think the south is non-Islamic. In fact there are many Muslims in the south. And the jihad spirit is deep within the Mujahideen fighting in the south. If somebody uses force against you, you use the same force.[32]

At a crossroads close to the government's foreign relations office in Khartoum, a small brass band had struck up a stirring tune. A group of men, some old and gray, the rest in their late teens, were marching on the spot. A group of women watched them as they paraded proudly, their backs straight, their arms swinging. I was told that they were going to the battlefront, the latest troops of the Popular Defense Force, the PDF, being sent to fight the SPLM.

"There's no formal relationship between the army and the Popular Defense Force. The army does the fighting. In the PDF, we are trying to prepare the people in case they come under attack," Baha al-Din Hanafi, President al-Bashir's political adviser, had told me in 1993. But the PDF, the foot soldiers of the government's ideology of jihad, were in fact being dispatched to the front not as a defensive measure but as frontline troops. It was this military strategy, which gave the government's most loyal supporters the opportunity to demonstrate their faith, with even junior government ministers going to fight and often being killed, that had provoked the groundswell of opposition to the government among the northern population of which John Garang had been speaking.

"Public opinion in the north is agreed—the war must stop by all means, and if it takes [southern] self-determination, then so-be it,"[33] said Sadiq al-Mahdi when we met again in 1995. His views had changed since our previous meeting, as it had become clear that the only way to confront the NIF government in the north was to harness the impact of the war in the south to the internal politics of the north religiously, socially, and politically. The government had to be shown to have failed on all counts. "The Islamic program has lost any credibility among the majority of Muslims, and is no more than the partisan program of the NIF, supported by force. There's a clear cleavage between the northerner whose identity is Islamic and the southerner whose identity is African, and this was accentuated by British rule. But never before has there been a call for jihad."

The military campaign in the south, which in 1993 was costing the government $1 million a day[34] and which had caused most of Sudan's postindependence governments to weaken and collapse, was intended to mobilize the army and to instill army discipline, according to Hassan al-Tourabi. There is no certainty that the north even needed a unifying call of jihad to unite the population behind the government. It was notable that al-Tourabi had referred to the southern campaign as a jihad "because this is a nation"; jihad in the interests of the nation—not of the *umma*—was the kind of innovation that al-Tourabi's critics among the religious establishment found intolerable, because these innovations had no Koranic basis and appeared to be purely opportunistic. The creation of the PDFs, and their existence parallel to the regular army, created two systems of control whose coordination was dependent upon the maintenance of the NIF-army alliance. But the durability of the alliance, whose government was the first in Africa to have created an Islamic state since the Mahdist revolt 100 years earlier, was coming under increasing pressure.

Two events have shaken it. In November 1996 Sadiq al-Mahdi escaped. His son organized his departure. During hunting trips to eastern Sudan with his cousin, the son of Hassan al-Tourabi, al-Mahdi's son had secretly mapped out a route to neighboring Eritrea. Late one evening, the day before the wedding of a family member—when al-Mahdi would be least expected to flee—the Umma Party leader arrived back home from a visit to his second wife. The soldiers at the end of the street, as had been their habit, left their post on seeing him arrive home. Less than an hour later, al-Mahdi slipped out the gate and began the long drive east, first by road then across the desert, until he reached the Eritrean border and made his way to Asmara, then on to Cairo.

His escape was followed by a second event, which exposed the government's vulnerability to the ongoing war in the south. On 21 April 1997, the government signed a peace accord in Khartoum with five southern factions. Central to the accord was the government's agreement to the holding of a referendum on southern self-determination. John Garang was not party to the accord, which grouped factions whose military ability had diminished over the years but who still had a presence in the south. For the government, the accord marked an end of the jihad and a recognition that it could no longer justify sending the ill-trained martyrs of the PDF, or the regular army for that matter, to fight a war that had become unwinnable and unpopular. For some northerners the accord marked a capitulation to the demands of southerners, and it consequently weakened the government's reputation considerably among its natural constituency: the northern Muslims.

The accord, which had been in the cards for more than a year, united the government militarily with the weakest of the southern factions, with which it agreed to hold joint military maneuvers against the SPLM. The accord marked the opening of a new phase in the administration of the Islamic government. Al-Mahdi fled in order to lead the political arm of a united opposition movement operating from exile in Eritrea. The National Democratic Alliance (NDA), as it was named, was the result of three years of negotiations by John Garang's SPLM with disaffected northern Muslims who had fled the regime—many of them from the senior ranks of the Sudanese army. Just as the successive governments in Khartoum had never before used the jihad as the rallying call for the southern war, so the northern Muslims had never before united with the southerners in a common front against Khartoum. The traditional support the SPLM had received from Uganda was, from late 1996, supplemented by the support of the NDA from Eritrea and Ethiopia. In 1995 the United States had provided Uganda and Eritrea with $20 million in assistance aimed at improving their security in areas vulnerable to attack from outside. Effectively this meant attacks by groups known to be operating from Sudan, drawing the United States into a proxy conflict with the Khartoum government.

"The government is now weakening the position of the entire north, because they have given in to the people in the south. They are taking the north for granted, without coming to terms with Sadiq and

[DUP leader Osman al-]Mirghani. The solution is to strengthen the north by reconciliation within the north. Then the southerners would be more realistic. Garang would not then aspire to rule the entire country, because he wouldn't have the alliance with Sadiq."[35] Al-Tayib Zain Al-Abdin sipped a glass of fruit juice at his house near Khartoum's airport as he articulated the crisis facing the northern Muslims: "The war in the south has continued for longer than anybody imagined. The army has failed to defend itself. So now the page has turned. It's become a story of failure rather than success, which is why the government has made this agreement," he said, referring to the 21 April 1997 accord. "The government has been pushed to this agreement by the circumstances. They don't have much room. When it comes to politics, the survival of the government is their number one goal. It is prepared to accept anybody who is prepared to join it, but not anybody who is going to compete with it in the north—who poses a threat to the survival of the government. It is not going to compromise power for the sake of principles."

Al-Abdin, a professor of political science at Khartoum University, had been a long-time associate of al-Tourabi and a member of the NIF. He, like many others, had drifted away after 1989 when the reality of what it meant to be allied with the army became clear. But within less than a decade, the alliance between the NIF and the army had begun to falter. Whereas in 1993 al-Tourabi had been formulating and executing policy, in 1997 he was an isolated figure. Al-Bashir, previously a rubber-stamp president, became an elected head of state in the same 1996 election that brought al-Tourabi into power as an elected member of the National Assembly, and he began to assert himself. Decisionmaking had shifted from al-Tourabi's grasp to the presidency, where Zubeir Mohamed Salah, the vice president; Magzoub al-Khalifa, the governor of Khartoum; Ali Osman Taha, the foreign minister; and al-Bashir himself formed the primary policymaking body, within which Ghazi Salah Eddin Atabani and al-Tourabi himself were involved but less influential. Al-Abdin said:

> Now, all the senior officers are in Bashir's camp. None of them are siding with Tourabi. He is associated with many of the policies which went wrong. He is a visionary, and he does represent a more forward-looking Islam. The people that criticize him are far more conservative than him on the issues of women, and on the rights of non-Muslims. But he has miscalculated the moves the government has taken, and the military people are now more in charge than they used to be.

In an enormous office down a dingy corridor in the mazelike, Chinese-built national assembly building on the banks of the river where it flows past Omdurman, I saw Hassan al-Tourabi again. Still smiling, his slightly protruding front teeth were bared in the grin of his neatly clipped beard. Sentences darted out from a face alternating between expressions of serious concern, appeasement, conciliation, and defiance. He judges first whether his discussant really knows anything of the subjects under discussion. Then, like the teacher he once was, he takes them through their paces. For a man about whom never a good word has really been spoken in the West, al-Tourabi remains remarkably open to the Westerners who arrive on his doorstep. A distinguished member of society, he is courteous and often disarming in the manner in which he delivers his lines. Only afterward, when one is back out in the sun, do the implications of his words begin to dawn.

"As you successfully realize your goals, things change, of course. There's more consideration to reality. Religion is not abstract. There's not a new generation coming up which is more secular. I'm not an abstract scholar, and I don't want to be a religious person in isolation in a monastery. I don't want to grow into a pope or an imam,"[36] he told me as we ended our conversation, his mind clearly on the future, the problems of the present obviously mounting in a way that had already diminished the government's power to control them.

The Dangerous Game

Rusted metal sheets welded into a five-foot-tall sculpture of an iron fist stood red-hot as the heat rose to 104 degrees in the garden of the Hamas militia office, hidden in a maze of sandy streets on the edge of Khartoum. Neat coils of barbed wire topped an iron fence surrounding the Palestinian group's two-story building, where the children of the Palestinian diaspora played beneath giant-sized currency notes of their nonexistent state, encased in plastic on the wall as the backing for clocks whose three hands ticked in the red, green, and black of the Palestinian flag. Security was tight, the soft drinks were warm, and Mounir Said, the representative of the Palestinian Hamas Islamic Resistance Movement, brushed away the flies that droned incessantly in the hot building.

We talked about Sudan and its role as a haven for organizations like Hamas, whose rejection of the Oslo peace accord with Israel[37] was bringing it into direct conflict with the Palestinian Liberation Organization, which for its part was seeking to patch up a deal on the future of Palestine before the chance was lost. "We have an Islamic project. Sudan has the same project, and we are going to carry out this project in all Islamic countries,"[38] said Said. "We feel about Sudan the same

that they feel about us. We respect one another. Arabic countries are
going through a difficult time now, and the rulers of the Arabic countries are not in touch with their people. In Khartoum we lecture in the
schools and universities, and mount exhibitions to show what Hamas
is doing, to make people know that we are still struggling against the
occupation of Palestine by the Israelis."

Part of the unspoken terms to which Hamas agreed before it established itself in Khartoum was that it would not carry out its operations outside Palestine. The same has generally been the case with
other organizations that have a presence in Khartoum. The Lebanese
Hezbollah, the Abu Nidal Group, the Popular Front for the Liberation
of Palestine, the Algerian Islamic Salvation Front, and others have visited Sudan, usually for conferences of al-Tourabi's PAIC. But the Khartoum government has discouraged activities by these groups—against
foreign embassies in the city, for example—that would jeopardize its
own relations with the countries involved. Said continued:

> We are a wise movement. We know that Israel is a very strong power, and
> that we Islamic people are not in a strong position. So we are creating
> good relations with all Arabic countries, by carrying out our operations
> only in Palestine. We never do anything outside Palestine. We don't have
> many important targets outside Palestine. The Israelis have many impor-
> tant things outside Palestine. We have been talking about not taking the
> war outside Palestine. But if they want us to take it outside Palestine,
> then we will. We have told the Israelis this. Also, there's no need for
> those of us in Sudan or Iran to be fighters. So there's no problem for us to
> live above ground rather than underground. But we will take the war out-
> side Palestine if they want us to.

Sudan, unlike Egypt, Jordan, Syria, and Lebanon, allows Palestinians
to travel unhindered to the country. The neighbors of the Palestinian
territories, in particular Egypt, make such movement extremely difficult. Meanwhile, scores of Palestinian students are now studying at
Khartoum University. Perhaps easing the Sudanese government's position has been its not altogether negative attitude toward Israel. Khartoum's Islamic agenda has not prevented it from allowing Sudanese
businesses to establish economic ties with Israeli companies, though
it has no official diplomatic ties with the country. Sudan's geographical distance from the heart of the Middle East has confined it to the
periphery of Middle Eastern affairs. Its historical identity in the eyes
of many Arabs is as an appendage of Egypt rather than as a distinct
state. Arab states have generally followed the influential Egyptian line
on Sudanese affairs, the twenty-two-member Arab League—to which
Sudan belongs—supporting Egyptian objections to even considering

the division of Sudan, even if this were to bring an end to the southern war.

"The challenge now is the neighborhood. To the east, the south and to the north. It's obvious that some international forces are seeking to undermine the Sudan,"[39] Hassan al-Tourabi told me. Sudan's problems were its immediate neighbors rather than conflicts further afield in the complex theater of the Middle East. In 1995 he had told me that he was able to "talk with" the Islamic Liberation Front (FIS) and the more radical Armed Islamic Group (GIA) in Algeria, and that he had some influence with the PLO; he said that "if there was more freedom [in Egypt], Islam would express itself more in public life. Instead, people are jailed, and the world doesn't seem to care."[40] But two years later, his role had diminished as the government focused its attention on its own foreign-backed dissidents, who had secured the support of countries now intent upon overthrowing the regime in Khartoum in revenge for its support of their own opponents.

"I saw the Eritrean opposition in Khartoum. They held security meetings with the NIF, which has given them financial support, vehicles, and weapons,"[41] said Mohamed Ahamed Abdelgadir al-Arabab, a former Sudanese state minister who fled the country in 1995, having been directly involved in the establishment of Sudanese military training camps for foreign groups before he fled. He elaborated:

> They established training camps for the Eritreans at Kassala and Gedaref, and in the Markheatt mountains near Omdurman, where there was a terrorist military training camp for several nationalities, and another at Jebel Awliyaa in the south of Khartoum. Other camps were at al-Gash river in Darfur, the eastern mountains of southern Kordofan, in Sennar state, the Mazmun mountains, the Kardus forest, and in the far north. All of these areas have military training camps for foreign extremists, as well as housing the Sudanese PDFs. At Hajyosif there's a camp for a regiment which has been specifically trained for the assassination of politicians. There are also four hundred teenagers there, who have been trained for the killing of domestic opposition leaders and non-NIF people. By 2002 they will have executed their entire plan, the secret plan of the NIF, and the PAIC will become the leader of world Islam. The PAIC will support the extremists throughout the world, to allow them to seize power in their own countries, to change governments and replace them with Islamic groups. They are planning to do this in Eritrea, Somalia, Ethiopia, Chad and Niger, and elsewhere. There are ten countries in all.

Al-Arabab had been the head of the Sennar state security council, and in this role he had been instrumental in preparing the military camps for training. He had been under pressure to join the NIF, but resisted. Meanwhile, the government had found willing recruits in the border areas to the east, particularly among the Eritrean refugees who had been living in Sudan for up to thirty years. Among the movements to which Sudan had provided weapons was al-Jihad al-Islamiyya, the Islamic Jihad.

"Our al-Jihad al-Islamiyya movement was founded in 1990, and it's very powerful inside Eritrea. The aim is the liberation of Eritrea, and the domination of Islamic morals. Now, we have fighters inside Eritrea, and after victory they will establish the Islamic government."[42] Idriss Mohamed Idriss was excited as he spoke inside a large, grass-walled and grass-roofed hut, whose walls were hung with colored cloth, at the Kashm al-Girba refugee camp in a desert landscape scattered with large boulders, somewhere among which lies Sudan's border with Eritrea. The Eritrean government had demanded that Sudan prevent Eritrean dissidents from using the camps as a base for their activities. But the calls were ignored throughout 1995 and well into 1996. Four Eritrean organizations—not all of them Islamist—were said by the refugees at Kashm al-Girba to be operating inside Eritrea. "The Eritrean Muslims have been strongly influenced by the way in which Sudanese Islam has been practiced since 1989,"[43] said Sheikh Mohamed Ismael Ali. "Because Sudan is ruled by an Islamic government, we feel secure, and that Islam has a new life here. That's how we have been influenced by the government in Sudan. That's why there will be Islamic rule in Eritrea. When people go back from the camps in Sudan, they will want there to be Islamic rule in Eritrea," he told me.

Sudan's policy was not something its architects felt the need to conceal, despite the consequences for their relations with countries that had fallen under Khartoum's spotlight. "Some countries are more wary of us than others,"[44] said Ghazi Salah Eddin Atabani, Sudan's minister of state for foreign affairs until 1996. He continued:

> For example, Saudi Arabia is a corrupt system which corrupts Islam. It's decadent. It represses women, and can't accept these changing, modernist ideas. At the same time, they are not providing an Islamic government. The problem for the royal family there now is their relevance. They don't have the right mindset, nor will they accept new ideas because they are so corrupt. . . . The role we are playing is one relating to the revivalist model, which is what makes Sudan central to the revivalist model. The Islamic model is considered incomplete until its political component is implemented. So, it's the first time that a revivalist movement has been both fundamentalist in the way it perceives things and views life, while at the same time being a modernist movement.

The determination to strengthen the policy and its effectiveness within Sudan, as well as bolster its influence outside the country, had, by 1995, inspired a rare degree of coordination among the often fractious countries of the region within which Sudan's influence was being felt. The United States had become determined, since including Sudan in 1992 on its list of states that allegedly sponsored terrorism, to enhance the effectiveness of the opposition to Khartoum. But as one U.S. regional strategist said of assistance to Sudan's neighbors: "You do what you need to do, and we will help them. But it's a very dangerous game. Something has to be done to change the course of Sudan's policies. If they don't change their internal policies, their human rights policies, then they're digging their own grave. This is just one step short of saying that we will provide the bullet."[45]

Within a year of my discussions about the future of Eritrea with the Islamists in the Kashm al-Girba camp, the border area around the camp had become a war zone. The NDA, the Eritrea-based Sudanese opposition force that Sadiq al-Mahdi joined in November 1996, began attacks in the border area in early 1997. These attacks were coordinated with a renewed campaign in the south led by the SPLM. Khartoum was being squeezed. The training camps in the east had been closed, and the government took steps to try and appease its critics. In 1996, the Saudi Arabians used their influence with the United States to demand and achieve the expulsion of Osama Bin Laden—their most outspoken critic—who had been living in and operating from Khartoum since 1993. The Sudanese government then sought to repair its relations with foreign donors by agreeing to a series of measures that would prevent an increase in the repayment of arrears of its debt to the International Monetary Fund. It then began sending out feelers to Egypt in an effort to repair the damage done by accusations that Khartoum had harbored the assassins involved in an attempt to kill President Hosni Mubarak in Addis Ababa in 1995.

Suspicion of the Khartoum government had become too deep for these measures to have any rapid impact. "Sudan is a gathering place for all the world's terrorists, and they are going to destabilize us with any means. They have intentions for the whole region,"[46] Saleh Kekia, Eritrea's foreign minister, told me in Asmara. His view was echoed along the length of the Nile valley: In Kampala, the Ugandan minister of state for security, Colonel Kahinda Otafi'ire, told me the same thing, claiming that Ugandan groups—Islamic and non-Islamic alike—had received facilities and supplies from Sudan. Asked if this were true, Ghazi Salah Eddin Atabani said: "We have never had the chance." Asked if Sudan would provide that assistance if it could, he replied: "Yes. Sure."

The Sudanese government has attempted to create an Islamic state in which policy is inextricably linked to the mechanism of government. This is illustrated in the practical application of its military-Islamist alliance, the personalities of the key decisionmakers, the image of Sudan within the Islamic and Arab worlds, and the country's ambiguous relationship with sub-Saharan Africa. The Islamic *sharia,* a judicial system that theoretically can only be introduced once the government of a given Islamic state has all but perfected the provision of social and economic needs to the general population, has had a partial impact in Sudan. The poverty of the country means that the required level of prosperity, beyond which crimes of theft can legally be punished by amputation, has not yet been reached. Consequently, the courts have only ordered four amputations since the introduction of the Islamic program. Women have played a more active political role in Sudan since 1989 than previously, though within the context of the system and rarely as voices allowed to proffer alternatives. The Family Law, introduced in 1992, allowed women greater influence in the upbringing of children and provided more straightforward credits to women wanting to launch small businesses. But these issues are likely to go down in Sudanese history as the few specific benefits accrued during a period in which Sudan became an international pariah rather than a model for other developing countries with Muslim populations.

"In Sudan the regime will fall, because it has lost its friends among the Islamic movements,"[47] Karim Omar, the former Afghan Mujahideen, told me in London. "When the U.S. forced Sudan to expel Bin Laden, it did so. It was also forced to close many of its Islamic training camps, and it forced young militants to leave. This means it hasn't the courage to see its Islamic program through. So, it's weak, and taking these measures hasn't in the meantime led to it strengthening its ties with other countries."

In fact, the Sudanese government's apparent reassessment of its aims has brought about some easing of the foreign pressure pitched against it. Unsurprisingly, given the inextricable bonds of history and common experience, the first country to seek a rapprochement has been Egypt. Despite the accusation that Khartoum had harbored at least one of the attackers held responsible for the attempted assassination of President Mubarak in 1995, Egypt regards Sudan as too valuable a neighbor to lose. Central to Egypt's policy with regard to the entire region of northeast Africa is the question of the division and management of the Nile River waters. By a 1959 agreement, Egypt is allotted 55.5 billion cubic meters of Nile irrigation water annually, while Sudan is allowed 18.5 billion cubic meters. Both countries draw most of their water from Ethiopia, the source of the Blue Nile. Ethiopia has become increasingly angered by its own exclusion from any water-sharing agreement. Pressure for a renegotiation of the water agreement has mounted. The discussions will become a major issue: of security, of regional politics, and of development. Egypt will need the support of Sudan in these discussions, and it is due to this that Egypt has become increasingly keen to restore ties with its neighbor.

Perhaps, for Sudan, the apparent curtailment of its efforts to diffuse its message across its borders and beyond will last a bit longer. Much will depend upon the alliance in power, as the decisionmakers drift away from Hassan al-Tourabi and gather more frequently in President al-Bashir's office. For al-Tourabi, a wide gulf remains between reality and his articulations, which take whatever form he prefers that reality to mean. Smiling as we ended our last meeting in 1997, he said: "If most of society becomes like me, that will be my success."

8

From Dual Containment to Double Standards

The United States, Islam, and the Middle East

For more than seven years the United States has occupied the land of Islam in the holiest of its territories—Arabia—plundering its riches, overwhelming its rulers, humiliating its people, threatening its neighbors, and using its bases in the peninsula as a spearhead to fight against the neighboring Arab peoples. Though some in the past have disputed the true nature of this occupation, the people of Arabia in their entirety have now recognized it. There is no better proof of this than the continuing American aggression against the Iraqi people, launched from Arabia despite its rulers, who all oppose the use of their territories for this purpose, but are subjugated.[1]

Thus began the declaration of war against the United States issued by the exiled Saudi Arabian Islamist leader, Osama Bin Laden, from his base in southeast Afghanistan and published in the London-based Arabic daily newspaper *Al-Quds Al-Arabi* on 23 February 1998. The declaration threw back into the face of Western policy makers the already flawed and unconvincing logic of U.S. involvement in the region. It turned on its head the very idea—first expressed through the launch of Operation Desert Shield, which was aimed at deterring an Iraqi invasion of Saudi Arabia following its invasion of Kuwait in August 1990, and then by the war that followed—that the United States was acting on behalf of the regional states it portrayed as its allies.

Apparently Bin Laden's message was even sympathetic to the Saudi Arabian leadership, the royal house of Saud, whose decadence he and his associates had heretofore condemned. Now, these same rulers were the hapless victims of U.S. imperialism. Bin Laden's historical emphasis shifted the parameters from the political to the religious. Whereas Arabia had been the cradle of Islam in the seventh century, Iraq had subsequently been its political heartland for more than 500 years. The onslaught against Iraq was an onslaught against Islam's historical and spiritual heritage, as if it were an attack on the holy city of Mecca. "For Muslims, no piece of land once added to the realm of Islam can ever be finally renounced, but none compares in significance with Arabia and Iraq,"[2] wrote Bernard Lewis, following the declaration of Jihad, in an attempt both to elucidate Bin Laden's perspective on the political import of U.S. policy in the Middle East, and to contextualize that perspective against the background of political Islam.

To what end does the United States have a policy in the Middle East? Is this policy consistent with the political and religious aspirations of the people of the Middle East? In short, how do U.S. interests coincide with, complement, and correspond with the direction sought by the countries of the Middle East with whom it is involved? These issues have become increasingly important as radical change takes place in the major countries of the region whose political agendas or Islamic identity have clashed most dramatically with the West. Iraq, Iran, and, to a lesser extent, Sudan—the "rogue states," as they along with Libya are sometimes called—present the most significant challenges to U.S. policy makers in the Middle East. The policy of the "dual containment" of Iraq and Iran has been confronted by the double standard implicit in that policy. Although Israel's religious fundamentalism, its possession of a nuclear weapons capability, and its ongoing extra-territorial military occupation are tolerated by the United States, the same is not true when Arabs and Muslims aspire to similar goals. Such Muslim countries become rogue states, confrontation with which in the past twenty years has been both cause and consequence of the U.S. role as the apologist for Israel's policy towards its Arab neighbors.

Now, as the Islamic states of Iran and Sudan undergo radical shifts of policy, how will U.S. policy adapt to the new reality, which has determined that, at least in the case of Iran, a "dialogue of civilizations" must now take place with the West, creating new potential for normal ties?[3] The bearing this new reality will have on U.S. policy will be significant. The religious issues affecting the region—in particular the Israeli occupation of East Jerusalem, wherein lies the al-Aqsa mosque, the third holiest site in Islam—cannot but have a strong part to play in this civilizational dialogue. But when the discussion comes to rest on the level of practicalities, will the United States continue to accept that the absence of normal ties with the Islamic world is a price worth paying for its continued support for Israel?

Any analysis of U.S. policy in the region must start with an understanding of how the United States relates to the countries with whom it has sought to work closely in order to pursue its regional policy. The roots of this policy, and its impact upon political Islam, were firmly planted in the 1960s, by consecutive U.S. presidents, from Eisenhower to Nixon:

> From the start, Nixon and Kissinger viewed the Jordan crisis of 1970 through the narrow binoculars of the East–West conflict and gave little thought to the stresses and strains in the Arab camp in the wake of Israel's 1967 victory or to the problems posed for Arab regimes by Palestinian impatience. America's worldwide ambition to keep on top of the Russians was confused with Israel's regional ambition to keep on top of the Arabs. Israel was promoted to a privileged place on the U.S. side of the superpower struggle for having, in Washington's perception, faced down not just the Syrians but the Russians as well. . . . Not only was Israel thereafter entrusted with keeping the peace in the Middle East on America's behalf, but the crisis served to launch the "strategic relationship" between the two countries which was to have consequences extending far beyond the Middle East.[4]

U.S. policy in the region is that of a feigned equanimity, which oozes from the public statements of U.S. foreign policy makers in regard to the Middle East: "[We] must fortify the international system by helping transitional or otherwise troubled states become full participants. This is essential to maintain the momentum of democracy's recent advances and create more anchors for regional stability and growth. To this end, we are encouraging rivals in areas such as the Middle East and South Asia to settle their differences peacefully," wrote Madeleine Albright in 1998.[5] At heart, this encouragement demands that the Palestinians end their use of violence as a strategy for insisting that Israel abide by UN resolution 242, whereas Israel is allowed all means at its disposal—military, logistical, bureaucratic, financial, and even the threatened use of its nuclear weapons capability—to impose its will in the occupied land.[6] In this way, Israel ensures that the final outcome of such a "peace process" works entirely in its favor, and in doing so safeguards U.S. interests in a manner that truly independent Arab states are unlikely to do, particularly once their need for U.S. ties in pushing the peace process forward has diminished. In practice there is no equanimity, and both the Arab states and Israel know this.

With regard to Palestinian–Israeli issues, U.S. policy, like Israeli policy towards the Palestinians since the signing in Oslo of the Declara-

tion of Principles in 1993, has been dominated by the imbalance in favor of Israel.[7] This policy has not been offset by the U.S. need for Arab
support for the peace process as a whole. Although the peace process is
a strategic necessity for the United States, its real, long-term success
from the U.S. perspective will be determined only by the extent to
which Israel both emerges as the dominant economy in the Middle
East and uses this economic power to assert a dominant political role
that can forever divide Arab opinion. The historic circumstances are
well understood by Israeli policy makers. Israel embarked on the peace
process in the knowledge that "[the] United States was being courted
by almost every country in the area. . . . Many Arabs had begun to
view Israel as a potential partner in their endeavours."[8] Whether Arab
states regarded Israel as a back door to improving ties with the United
States is debatable. But it has rarely been lost on Arab states that their
political relations with the United States are defined almost entirely
by their position in regard to the peace process and, therefore, in regard to Israel itself, whereas strategic relations are defined by the U.S.
need for Arab oil.

> Until the need for oil, the Cold War, and the desire to manipulate the out-
> come of the Arab–Israeli conflict forced it into the open as the dominant
> power in the Middle East, republican non-colonial America was accept-
> able to the Arabs. Even in the late 1930s the Arabs believed in America's
> neutrality on the problem of Palestine. . . . But America discarded its ide-
> ology, followed oil interests, turned a blind commitment to anti-commu-
> nism into a wish to involve all people in this issue and manifested a de-
> sire to please Zionism and win elections at home at the expense of the
> Arabs. America has, during the past four decades, followed its replace-
> ment of the old, tired colonial powers by adopting policies similar to
> theirs. In the process America became colonialist and made the Middle
> East unsafe for democracy.[9]

Democracy, meanwhile, is barely on the agenda in the Middle East.
The pursuit of such an ideal, and the references made to it by
Madeleine Albright, amount merely to being one more stick with
which to beat the Arab states. The ongoing, opportunistic dialogue the
United States enjoys with its closest Arab interlocutors is entirely reliant upon the total absence of democracy within those states. Public
opinion in Egypt, in particular, remains rigidly anti-Israel and immensely skeptical about the peace process; if there were to be a democratic election, Egypt as a whole would not deliver the support that its
most recent presidents—Anwar al-Sadat and Hosni Mubarak—have
given to the process. Equally, the emergence of democracy in the Arab
states would force Israel to treat Arab governments with a greater de-

gree of seriousness, something successive Israeli governments have refused to do on the basis of their own perceived superiority. Israel's
"democracy" looks down upon the variety of despotic regimes by
which Israel is surrounded but with which it must engage.

"To protect our interests, we must take actions, forge agreements,
create institutions, and provide an example that will help bring the
world closer together around basic principles of democracy, open mar-
kets, law, and a commitment to peace," writes Madeleine Albright.[10]
But the ideals set forth by U.S. policy makers increasingly seem to reflect an uncertainty about how to evolve appropriate responses to the
way the world is actually going. Referring to U.S. strategy at its most
combative, Samuel Huntington writes: "In the unipolar moment at
the end of the Cold War and the collapse of the Soviet Union, the
United States was often able to impose its will on the other countries.
That moment has passed. The two principal tools of coercion that the
United States now attempts to use are economic sanctions and military intervention."[11] Huntington advocates a policing role for the leading states of each region, "while American intervention could then be
restricted to those situations of potential violence, such as the Middle
East and South Asia, involving major states of different civilizations."[12] What Huntington does not say, though it is consistent with
his thesis of looming "civilizational wars," is that his proposal implies
that the United States should rush to the defense of Israel—as it confronts its Muslim, Arab foes—on the basis of a civilizational link that
supersedes the preoccupation with oil (which Said Aburish identifies
as having captured the center of U.S. policymaking).[13] Now, the imperative is to thwart the foes without alienating the allies. In so doing,
U.S. policy has become an opportunistic juggling act, failing to incorporate the interests of supposed Arab allies, isolating both the United
States and allied Arab leaders from the population of the Arab world
across all classes, and entirely dependent upon hi-tech bullying.

Baghdad's Last Smile

As he died slowly on a soiled hospital bed, Latif Abdelsettar's eyes
spoke silently of the victim that he was. One of the twelve new cases
of child leukemia arriving each week at the Saddam Hospital in central Baghdad, the five-year-old boy was presumed unlikely to survive
the sanctions that denied him adequate medication. The emergency
unit of Saddam Hospital possessed four syringes. Each was used up to
fifty times per day, according to Dr. Kasim al-Taie, the hospital's chief
resident doctor. The one incubator in the pediatric wing broke down

at least twice a day, and the one electrocardiograph had been confined to the corner of a ward, having stopped working in 1996. "We ration the main medicines. If we ration things then the monthly supply can last for one week, but if we hand things out liberally, they would last two days. Even so, there is a gap of three days every week when we have no antibiotics," said Dr. al-Taie.[14] The boy's parents had spent 95,000 Iraqi dinars on his medication.[15] Their joint monthly salaries were 9,500 dinars. They had sold all their furniture and borrowed money from relatives to pay for the treatment. The medicine they bought was smuggled from Jordan by a taxi driver. Each batch took a week to arrive, one of thousands of examples of how sanctions were broken to ensure the survival of at least some of the population.

"I reckon 50 percent of the medicine we use is smuggled in from Jordan,"[16] said Hussein Fadelrahim of Baghdad's Central Hospital for Children. He was overseeing the funerals of thirty-six children whose average age was six months and who had died from a variety of preventable diseases. Beneath the driving rain, a convoy of small taxis had parked on a street lined on one side with trees and on the other by a series of buildings, one of which was a United Nations office, outside of which a noisy protest had been staged. Women dressed in black bore photographs of the dead. The children were being given a last taste of dignity before being consigned to the oblivion of international strategic calculations. Each taxi bore a rough, wooden coffin just large enough to hold a small child. Photographs attached to the coffins showed young children, babies, the dead victims of a brutal war of nerves.

"It would be a mistake, I think, to reduce what is happening between Iraq and the United States simply to an assertion of Arab will and sovereignty versus American imperialism, which undoubtedly plays a central role in all this. However misguided, Saddam Hussein's cleverness is not that he is splitting America from its allies (which he has not really succeeded in doing for any practical purpose), but that he is exploiting the astonishing clumsiness and failures of U.S. foreign policy," wrote Edward Said of the crisis in February–March 1998, while the babies of Baghdad were being buried.[17] Said asserted that by that point in the war of attrition against Iraq, which had been ongoing since the end of the Gulf War in 1991, 567,000 Iraqi civilians had died "mostly as a result of disease, malnutrition, and deplorably poor medical care."[18] An article in *Foreign Affairs* in May/June 1999 stated: "By 1998 Iraqi infant mortality had reportedly risen from the pre-Gulf War rate of 3.7 per cent to 12 per cent. Inadequate food and medical supplies, as well as breakdowns in sewage and sanitation systems and in the electrical power systems needed to run them, reportedly cause an increase of 40,000 deaths annually of children under the age of 5 and of 50,000 deaths annually of older Iraqis."[19]

In a devastating critique of the U.S. policy that has led to the plight of the Iraqi population, Said explains that the readiness of the United States to induce such suffering is reflective of the U.S. disdain toward Arabs and the Arab world. Said argues that the refusal of U.S. policy makers to pursue any kind of balance in their Middle East policy has fed the fire of a more general potential "Arab/U.S. crisis," the conditions for which are exacerbated by the fact that "the notion of an Arab people with traditions, cultures, and identities of their own is simply inadmissible in the United States."[20] Said's view that "clumsiness and failures" are intrinsic to U.S. policy verges on the charitable. In fact, U.S. policy is direct and successful; at its heart lies the ongoing need to ensure the oil supply. Implementing this policy is relatively straightforward, because the Arab states need the U.S. market as much as the U.S. needs the oil.

More complex is the U.S. need to strengthen Israel. In the wake of the Oslo accords, the Palestinian Liberation Organization was no longer available as a bogeyman, as it had come on board as a partner in the U.S. strategic vision for the region. Yasser Arafat, the terrorist, became President Arafat, the peacemaker. Meanwhile, Saddam Hussein was transformed from the pro-Western bulwark against Iranian interests to the villain, at least in Western eyes. The failure of Oslo to bring peace in the time allotted—by 4 May 1999, when a Palestinian state was to have been declared—has highlighted a truth that all the duplicity in the world has not been able to hide, and wherein lies the potential for the "Arab/U.S. crisis." This truth is the role played by Israel itself as an aggressor, as the destroyer of a peace process that key Arab states had found they could accommodate despite popular domestic opposition.

Whereas for the United States the villain had to be an Arab, the real villain in the region after his election in 1996 has been Benjamin Netanyahu, the right-wing Israeli prime minister ousted in May 1999.[21] No regional leader since the end of the Gulf War that ousted Saddam Hussein's forces from Kuwait had been as destabilizing to the region as Netanyahu. No leader had so steadfastly insisted upon using the term "the Arabs" as frequently as Netanyahu, purely as a term of abuse, as a means of conjuring up fears drawn upon racist stereotypes. As significant, no regional leader had done so much to undermine the credibility of U.S. policy in the region, only to find that his every destructive move brought barely a murmur of disapproval from Washington, despite the occasional chiding of the U.S. State Department, which both Israel and the United States knew meant nothing and would have no meaningful consequence.

Certainly, from the U.S. perspective, this relationship with Netanyahu did not amount to "clumsiness and failures," as Said claims. Steadfast U.S. support for Israel is guaranteed. And therein lies the potential for an "Arab/U.S. crisis," because ultimately, when the promised comprehensive peace does not materialize, the value to the Arab states of continuing to pander to a pro-Israel U.S. policy will unravel. More than twenty years ago, David Hirst, the most widely respected and incisive foreign correspondent writing on the Middle East, wrote:

> [The] Arabs will not remain in such disarray forever; a new order will eventually emerge which is better able and—in the absence of a peaceful settlement—more determined to mobilize the vast potential at its disposal.
>
> The olive branch will never replace the gun unless the outside world does save Israel from itself. . . . Without that salvation the last act of violence in the Middle East will be nuclear; the fatal Zionist propensity for the extreme solution, which we have seen in action at every stage of this history, all but guarantees it. Israel has not signed the Non-proliferation Treaty, it possesses the Bomb, and the further development of its nuclear capability is the only way it can match its enemies' ever-growing conventional strength.[22]

These words are as true now as they were when Hirst wrote them. The double standard that lies at the heart of U.S. Middle East policy cannot be tolerated forever. Increasingly, the parameters of the peace process will come to be exposed for what they really are—an attempt by the United States to ensure that its own interests are served by the outcome, through protection of its local ally. At no point can it be said that the process has established any lasting depth beyond that with which the United States has endowed it. The fact that it is not a process that could be sustained without a U.S. role is one of its the most dangerous aspects.

The election of Ehud Barak to the Israeli premiership was met with dutiful expressions of hope by Arab leaders, but against a background of weariness, skepticism, and a lengthening history of broken Israeli promises. As most Israeli political commentators said on election night, a major reason for Netanyahu's defeat was that he was loathed personally. "Netanyahu was not merely deposed, shamefaced, without finishing even one term in office, Netanyahu was vomited out from inside us, expelled," wrote Doron Rosenblum in *Ha'aretz*, an Israeli daily newspaper, the day after the election.[23] "Israel has awakened as from a nightmare, or from an operation for the removal of an abscess after endlessly putting it off and ducking it."

The strong element played by character had long affected Netanyahu's relations with regional leaders, whatever his policies. President Mubarak made it clear on more than one occasion that he did not trust Netanyahu. When it became clear that Netanyahu was not going to abide by the agreement on troop redeployment he had signed at the Wye River conference, Arab expectations concentrated entirely on the desperate hope that Netanyahu would lose the election.

With Barak's election the readiness to reopen discussions on all sides has undoubtedly intensified. Both his commitment to reopening negotiations with Syria with a view to meeting Syrian demands for an end to the Israeli occupation of the Golan Heights, and his promise to withdraw Israeli troops from southern Lebanon within one year of his election are big promises. Arab leaders will await action with interest. More important will be the restarting of the program agreed to by Israel and the Palestinians at Oslo and subsequently at Wye River. But it should be remembered that Mr. Barak has not made absolutely clear how he envisages the shape of a Palestinian state, nor how much land it will incorporate, nor whether he will abide by the agreement signed by Israel regarding the negotiations on the Palestinian demand that East Jerusalem will be the capital of that Palestinian state.

The silence of the Islamist extremists, in particular Hamas, during the Israeli election did much to facilitate the end of Netanyahu's catastrophic period in office. One bomb could have catapulted the Likud leader back into the premiership by unnerving the Israeli public and reigniting calls for security measures of the kind the right-wing government had practiced. Even so, the continued resistance to Israel from Hamas, Lebanese Hizbollah, and further afield will not diminish in light of a new government in Israel. Barak is a moderate relative to Netanyahu and is likely to improve ties with Egypt and Jordan, ties that had suffered under Likud. But his government still occupies Arab land, and the outcome of the election will not alter the fundamental perception in the region that Israel is an occupying force that operates a vicious policy of *apartheid* against Arabs within its territory, and that initiates violence against its opponents outside that territory. Nor is Ehud Barak likely to change this perception. Consequently, although the election may bring the peace process back on track, it will not win new supporters of that process on the Arab side. Israel will continue to be seen within the region as a threat—real, imaginary, or potential.

U.S. policy will continue to require, therefore, that the Middle East be rid of all leaders capable of opposing Israel. This opposition has shifted from being purely military to incorporating a wider variety of oppositions—military, political, and economic. Only when the potential military threat to Israel has disappeared will there no longer be any use for bogeymen like Saddam Hussein. That moment is a long way off. But to speed its arrival, U.S. policy has shifted from the policy of "containment" to the strategy of overthrow, called "rollback" by policy makers. It was with the announcement of this policy—with the passing of the Iraq Liberation Act by the U.S. Congress in October 1998 and the allocation of $97 million for military supplies to the Iraqi opposition—that the wedge between the United States and its Arab interlocutors in the region was driven deeper.

The impact of the sanctions imposed on Iraq at the end of the Gulf War has been to strengthen the political status quo rather than to achieve the U.S. intention of delegitimizing President Hussein. The sanctions have also isolated the majority of Iraqis from both the regime that oppressed them and the Western powers whose strategy failed to ease their condition. "There were originally many Iraqis who agreed with Western policy," said a senior Iraqi relief official opposed to the regime.[24] "Now, there's a silent majority who feel they have no chance to decide their fate. And they feel misled by both sides."

Meanwhile, the spurious U.S. aim of protecting its allies in the Gulf has been exposed as such by adoption of a policy to which no Arab leaders have subscribed. Although many leaders in the region—most, in fact—regard Saddam Hussein as a menace whom they would rather be without, the practice of "rollback" is one that they cannot justify to their own populations and would therefore not like to see. "I told Albright: please don't make the attack now. We have to deal with Arab public opinion. If the people aren't prepared, we will face a whole lot of problems. Give room for a diplomatic solution," President Mubarak of Egypt said in an interview as the Iraq crisis loomed in February 1998.[25] "The double standard [on the issue of weapons of mass destruction], of Israel versus Iraq—we feel it. And I am very sincere. There are extremists who are ready to act. You will not find any leader who will say they are in favor of the air strikes," he said.

During its preparations for the bombing of Iraq in February 1998—a bombing campaign eventually prevented by the successful intervention of Kofi Annan, the UN secretary general, on 23 February—it became clear how dangerous U.S. policy in the region had become. A public relations exercise intended to pacify Arab public opinion was launched. The U.S. State Department dispatched Ambassador David Newton, a retired diplomat, to the region to face a growing welter of criticism, which can have left him in no doubt as to how unpopular the U.S. threat against Iraq had become.

When Newton was asked at a press conference in Cairo why the United States insisted on going ahead with a strategy for which it had not received any public support in the region, his response was as disdainful as U.S. policy had always been: "There is in some countries a difference between public and private support. This is a part of the world where people are cautious about getting involved," he said, adding that, on the issue of U.S. acceptance of Israel's nuclear capability seen against its determination to deprive Saddam Hussein of his weapons of mass destruction, "there is a double standard."[26] The United States was pursuing a policy that no leaders in the region could support, that public opinion vehemently opposed, and that was a precursor to a longer-term policy of "rollback," which neither found support in the region nor even informed support in the United States. "To divide Iraq is not in the interests of peace in this region," said President Mubarak.[27] "A good leadership and the country could be divided. If there was a division of Iraq, part of it might join Iran. That would create another big problem. If Saddam is removed, whoever leads the country would be worse."

Kofi Annan's determined diplomacy in the face of intense hostility from the United States, and from Madeleine Albright in particular, denied the United States and its British allies the chance to bomb Iraq. President Hussein agreed to open up presidential sites to inspection by teams from the UNSCOM operation charged with finding and destroying Iraq's arsenal of weapons of mass destruction.[28] But it was not long before the chief weapons inspector, Richard Butler, identified alleged infringements of the agreement made with Annan. Determined not to be subject to the diplomatic delays that had thwarted the launch of their campaign the previous February, the U.S. and British military machines were gearing up within hours of when Iraq, on 31 October 1998, denied UNSCOM the right to carry out spot inspections of its military sites until the UN lifted the embargo on oil sales imposed after the Gulf War.

During the buildup to the 1991 Gulf War, the potential for a negotiated Iraqi withdrawal from Kuwait had been quashed by the United States. The "diplomatic track" as Noam Chomsky notes, "was too dangerous, given Washington's fears that it might lead to Iraqi withdrawal, undermining the opportunity to smash a defenceless country to bits and teach a few lessons about obedience."[29] Chomsky's damning critique of the motives behind U.S. action in Iraq leads ultimately to the frightening conclusion that the end of the Cold War has created a logic in which, rather than creating greater opportunities for peace, U.S. supremacy has reduced the inhibitions that have prevented war. The United States sought to avoid discussion of solutions during

George Bush's tenure in the White House, just as Madeleine Albright gave a frosty and dismissive response to the potential for a UN diplomatic success when Kofi Annan went to Iraq in 1998. The United States has always sought the excuse to bomb Iraq. "The most interesting feature of the debate over the Iraq crisis is that it [the debate] never took place. True, many words flowed, and there was dispute about how to proceed. But discussions kept within rigid bounds that excluded the obvious answer: the United States and Britain should act in accord with their laws and treaty obligations," Chomsky writes.[30]

As air strikes erupted in November 1998, Palestinians burned the American flags that just a day earlier had decorated their streets to mark the visit of Bill Clinton to the Gaza Strip. Although Palestinian Authority leaders did not say they supported the Iraqi regime, they, like other Arab leaders, highlighted the impact of the bombing on Iraqi civilians. For the Palestinians, as for states directly involved in the Middle East peace process, the strikes that the United States says were intended to destroy Iraqi weapons of mass destruction sent a different message, centering on the U.S. acceptance of Israel's retention of similarly powerful weapons and on the double standard this implied. Most Arab states rejected the view that disarming Saddam Hussein's regime in such a manner would bring regional security. President Mubarak issued a statement on 17 December that blamed Richard Butler, the UN chief weapons inspector, for having "pushed the situation to the current crisis."[31] Even though few accepted that air strikes were a solution, most Arab states, including Syria, nevertheless retained the position that as long as Iraq refused to comply with UN resolutions, it would have only itself to blame for military strikes. Meanwhile, the legality of the strikes was raised in a statement issued by the Organization of the Islamic Conference (OIC), which asserted: "Iraq is target again to military strikes, carried out in vague circumstances and with unknown intentions."[32]

The Iraqi regime, however, became isolated by other Arab states and failed to attract support for its case. President Mubarak announced that Iraq's "ruling regime . . . is the cause of all problems. Egypt, of course, does not support that regime."[33] While rejecting U.S. and U.K. strategies to precipitate the overthrow of President Hussein, Mr. Mubarak said: "It is high time the Iraqi regime took responsibility for the suffering it has brought Iraqis." Egypt's major concern was with its own regional prestige, which it saw as undermined because of its close ties with the United States.

Iraq further polarized Arab opinion by denouncing countries that refused to condemn the air strikes and by threatening to launch attacks inside Kuwait and Saudi Arabia. Saudi Arabia's offer to propose to the

UN that sanctions on imports of food and medical supplies to Iraq be eased was rejected by Baghdad on the grounds that it closely resembled British proposals. The estrangement of the Iraqi leadership from regional states was cemented when Arab leaders sought to prevent Iraqi participation in Arab League discussions on the crisis, believing Baghdad would seek to divide Arab opinion.

Intending to clarify the distinction between Iraq's government and the Iraqi population, whose suffering had inflamed public opinion throughout the region, foreign ministers from Egypt, Syria, Saudi Arabia, Yemen, and Oman met on 14 January 1999 to prepare a common strategy in advance of an Arab League foreign ministers meeting in Cairo on 24 January. "Saddam misjudged Arab opinion when there were protests against the bombing of Baghdad in December," was how one senior Egyptian official dismissed Iraq's strategy.[34] "He thought Arabs were supporting him. But in fact they were just supporting the Iraqi people." In response to this growing isolation, Mohammed Saeed al-Sahaf, Iraq's foreign minister, denounced the five-nation consultations in Egypt, which he said "can only be described as the insistence of some states not to follow a sound Arab course in the framework of the Arab League, and to continue a policy of creating axes and blocs."[35] In response, an editorial issued by Saudi Arabia's official news agency described President Saddam Hussein as a "disease that should be removed, so peace and security can return to Iraq and its people. The holding of an Arab summit or a ministerial meeting in which Saddam Hussein and his gang take part will not be successful under the circumstances."[36]

Arab League determination not to allow divisions to emerge within its ranks on the Iraqi issue ultimately succeeded—by preventing the forums from being convened at which such divisions could be created. On 24 January 1999, Iraqi delegates stormed out of a meeting of Arab League foreign ministers in Cairo, in protest at the ministers' refusal to condemn the air strikes and at their call for an end to Iraqi threats against Kuwait. Thus was the U.S. military action against Iraq allowed to seep into the Arab popular memory as a devastating show of military force in the face of which Arab leaders could only watch from the sidelines, refusing to support it, unable to prevent it, and ultimately incapable of resolving the conflict through negotiation.

Despite Saddam Hussein's undoubted unpopularity across the region, as well as in Iraq itself, owing in large part to his betrayal of the Arab cause by his dishonesty in dealings with other Arab leaders, nobody was strengthened by the U.S. and British military action. Nobody ultimately drew comfort. The Arab world was left simply wondering where its real interests lay. Meanwhile, the United States could not claim to have helped its allies. Its campaign was one carried out in total defiance of what those very allies had, at least publicly, called upon it to do. Meanwhile, as the world's attention turned to the Balkans in early and mid-1999, it went almost unnoticed that U.S. and British bombing raids continued against Iraq on a weekly and occasionally daily basis.

The ambiguities dominating U.S. relations with the Arab world have hindered the establishment of a relationship with depth. The divisiveness of U.S. policy towards the region in the early 1970s, during Henry Kissinger's tenure as U.S. secretary of state, first cemented Israel's central role in Arab strategic thinking. Kissinger turned what was initially an Israeli disaster into a major Israeli success and thus added to the humiliation of the 1967 war the painful realization that what to this day is claimed in Egypt as having been the Egyptian–Syrian "victory" of 1973 was an illusion.

> Into this context Kissinger appeared like a *diabolus ex machina*, enjoying unfettered scope because Nixon's last year and Ford's first were a time of unusual presidential weakness. Devoted to the Israeli cause and endowed through charm, quick wits and tactical skill with extraordinary personal authority, he was able to sweep aside dissenting views whether from the Pentagon, from leading figures of the foreign policy establishment, prominent academics or American ambassadors to key Arab countries. Kissinger even managed to steer two presidents away from the global [Middle East] settlement both appeared to want.
>
> There was perhaps a more particular reason why the opportunity for peace was missed in 1973–5, and this was the manipulative attitude toward the region which Israel had long had but which took root in Washington also as the two countries embarked on their strategic relationship from 1970 onward.[37]

U.S. manipulation had worked in Israel's favor. In the wake of the 1973 war, President Sadat of Egypt had capitulated entirely to Kissinger's determined policy of first splitting the already vulnerable Syrian–Egyptian wartime alliance and then using the threat of ongoing Israeli military activity against Egypt to convince Sadat that Egypt ought to desert its Syrian ally entirely and seek a separate peace with Israel over the Sinai, thereby securing Israeli occupation of the desert. Sadat's vanity, weakness, and dishonesty in his dealings with Hafez al-Asad, the Syrian president with whom he had gone to war with Israel, laid the foundation for the Islamist backlash that would, in 1981, lead to his assassination. The United States effectively sacrificed one of its closest allies in the region by failing to see how far its interests had driven a wedge between Sadat and the sentiments of those he ruled.

This scenario has been repeated throughout the region. The emergence of militant Islamist groups in the region in the mid-1970s—on the campuses of Egyptian universities, among Palestinian refugees, in West Beirut, and culminating in the Iranian revolution of 1979—were all, to varying degrees, the consequence of U.S. alliances with regimes, militias, and dictators to which the United States allied itself in the hope of installing powers that would allow it to redraw the map of the region in Israel's favor. Most striking has been the fact that Islamists have capitalized on the friction between the United States and its opponents in the region, even where those opponents are avowedly anti-Islamist. Of the leaders of the region's "rogue states," neither Col. Muammar Gadaffi of Libya nor Saddam Hussein have any tolerance for the Islamists, who rightly regard the two dictators as modernizers.[38] Gadaffi has reportedly been the target of at least one assassination attempt in which Islamists are thought to have been implicated.

These complexities are apparently lost on U.S. strategic planners, whose preference for scientific assessments of U.S. needs and strategy reveals a major tendency to ignore the cultural, historical, and religious history of the region, as if, ultimately, it simply does not impinge on politics. One such misconception is reflected in the most comprehensive recent study of U.S. foreign policy, *The Pivotal States: A New Framework for U.S. Policy in the Developing World*, in which it was asserted: "The [U.S.] commitment to Israel has spilled over to buttress Egypt's position, for the Israeli-Egyptian accommodation has led the United States to see Egypt as a 'cornerstone of the American-led effort to achieve a comprehensive Middle East peace.'"[39] Such interpretations are at best naive, at worst propaganda. The benefits to Egypt of involvement in the peace process have become increasingly uncertain, due in large part to Israel's refusal to abide by its signed commitments during the premiership of Benjamin Netanyahu, coupled with the pro-Israeli bias of the United States, which is a major humiliation to the Egyptian leadership.

As important, the absence of real depth to the Egyptian-Israeli relationship was revealed in 1997, when Egypt attempted to use its eighteen-year-old diplomatic ties with Israel to revive the Israeli-Palestinian dialogue. This dialogue had collapsed on 18 March that year, when Israel began construction of a new Israeli settlement on Arab land outside Jerusalem, at Jebel Abu Ghneim. The construction broke Israel's commitment not to change "facts on the ground" with regard to the topology of Jerusalem prior to the opening of the last stage of the process agreed to at Oslo, which would deal with the final status of the city. Egypt used all the diplomatic resources at its disposal to try and convince Netanyahu that the building should stop in order to save the peace process. But Egypt's weight was insufficient. Thus, the failure of a long-standing U.S. interlocutor in the region—one that had been the first to sign a peace agreement with Israel—to use its own weight to push forward a process sponsored mainly by the United States exposed the reality of U.S. policy itself. That policy was never designed to strengthen Arab interlocutors in the region for their own ends. It was always designed to keep them under control, that they could never assert any meaningful influence on a regional level without the approval of Washington. It is of small wonder, then, that when Arab states object en masse to the bombing of Iraq, they are ignored.

Although U.S. policy toward the Arabs is founded on the three-way U.S.-Israel-Arab relationship, the U.S. relationship with the Arab nations will see little change. U.S. policy toward Iraq is therefore likely to continue to draw upon analyses and counter-analyses emerging from Washington, with little heed paid to U.S. interlocutors in the Arab world, who have made plain all along their general acceptance of the view that has, separately and for wholly different reasons, recently been voiced in Washington. For example, an article in *Foreign Affairs* concluded: "Since the United States can neither engineer Saddam's fall nor accept him back into the international community, it really has only one option left—the much-maligned policy of containment."[40] Having concluded that the overthrow of Saddam was untenable in large part due to the military weakness of the opposition Iraqi National Congress, the article went on: "The real and pressing challenge the United States faces in Iraq is therefore not whether to abandon containment for a better alternative—there is none—but rather how to shore it up."[41]

Containment has generally found acceptance among Iraq's neighbors, whereas an overthrow or, worse, a full-scale civil war has not. With Iraq crippled by sanctions, its children dying, it is impossible to ignore the fact that the measures taken by Western powers to cripple the Iraqi regime have failed. Pressure for shoring up containment has risen in the United States, as the alternative policies have proven inhumane and ineffective:

> With or without the help of sanctions, containment and deterrence have rather good track records as policies for dealing with menaces far more significant that that posed by contemporary Iraq, with its demoralized and potentially mutinous army. There is little reason to believe they would not work in this case as well. An Iraqi attack or major provocation—certainly any involving chemical, biological or nuclear weapons—would be suicidal. And survival, not suicide, seems to be Saddam's chief goal.[42]

For now, President Saddam Hussein's is the only face that smiles on the streets of Baghdad: Saddam with a child on his knee, Saddam wearing a fishing hat, Saddam making policy at a table, Saddam greeting a crowd. Everywhere, the image of the Iraqi leader smiles out from high upon walls, pillars, pedestals, and statues. But the power behind the smile, and the Iraqi assumption that with the eventual lifting of UN sanctions the country will reassert its role within the Middle East, remain focused on ensuring that the current leadership retains power. "The regime is highly unpopular. But this is coupled with a sense of total helplessness about being able to do anything about it, which has meant that nobody will do anything about it," an Iraqi academic said in Baghdad.[43] "Anybody who thinks he can take an organized action against Saddam is a fool. Saddam is our safety valve. However awful he is, he keeps the country together, and if he goes it would be the end of Iraq. If he goes nobody would be able to assert any sort of control over the country." This view is reflected by dissenting voices from outside the region, who generally regard the regime as secure and therefore regard any future strategy as necessarily taking into account its probable durability. "Air strikes wouldn't have dislodged it, and anyway it is more collective than one thinks," said a senior diplomat in Baghdad, after the crisis of February 1998 but before that of December. "The contacts with Arab states will continue. Saddam Hussein is now dealing with everybody. There will be the reestablishment of diplomatic relations, though now is too early," he predicted—an analysis still to be proven correct.[44]

The regime has sought to improve relations with its neighbors but has generally misread the regional mood. In its isolation Iraq has assumed that the region is as obsessed by Iraq as Iraq is by itself. "Regional states have been waiting for a moment at which they could say "enough," said Riyadh al-Qaysi, Iraq's deputy foreign minister.[45] "Iraq will not [again] invade Kuwait. You learn from your mistakes. We have turned a page. What other choice do we have? If you lift the external pressure immediately, the Arabs will put aside their differences. They will see that the danger does not come from Iraq," he said. Having survived war, sanctions, international opprobrium, and the failure of attempts to unseat him, Saddam Hussein is now viewed domestically and regionally as likely to continue smiling on the streets of Baghdad. But his intentions, denied the weapons capability built-up over fifteen years, still remain unclear. "President Saddam hasn't changed," said Mr. al-Qaysi, a member of Iraq's inner circle of decision makers. "I don't think that he has ever lost the conviction that he was right. The man is the same man. The qualities are the same qualities. The ideas are the same ideas."

The Islamists' Twilight

"What Khatami has done is change the language of politics. And he has changed the foreign policy by changing the image. And 80 per cent of foreign policy is image."[46] September in Tehran brings with it a silvery light, which, in the afternoons, throws the spindly trees of the city into stark relief against the sky and the Elburz Mountains, which rise above the city to the north. The wide boulevards appear to have remained unchanged since the days before the revolution that shaped the non-Muslim world's image of Islam and that left U.S. policy in the Middle East deprived of one of its "deputy sheriffs," as Said Aburish describes the Shah before his overthrow in 1979.[47] The revolution also led to the U.S. policy of "containment" of Iran's new Islamist regime:

> Until the late-1970s Saudi Arabia, Iran and Israel were the deputy sheriffs that promoted and implemented U.S. policy in the Middle East. A hangover for the anti-colonial ideology, which rejected direct intervention in countries' affairs, the Americans' reliance on indirect control allocated different tasks to each deputy sheriff. Israel's role consisted in being available to render military help to protect the region against communist encroachment and it came to an end with the collapse of the USSR. Iran under the Shah was the pro-West country charged with keeping the Gulf stable, and this ended with the downfall of the Shah. Saudi Arabia, though no longer threatened by communism or countries allied to the communist camp, is the one remaining country whose duties haven't changed, and the containment of Iran and Iraq has replaced the threat of communism as a reason for its strategic importance.[48]

The dramatic changes that have taken place in Iran since the election of President Mohamed Khatami on 23 May 1997 mirror much that has been taking place in its fellow Islamic state, Sudan. Fundamentally, the two countries have, at more or less the same time, been forced to accept a broadening of the political power base as the key vehicle to ensuring that the leaders do not become alienated from the concerns of the led. In Iran, revolutionary ideals have taken root but are now in great need of new energy. Consequently, the new leaders are, not necessarily uniformly, both of a generally younger generation than that of the revolutionary leaders and representative of social groups that have been able to regard the ideals of the revolution from a distance while contemplating the potential for these ideals to endure.

There are, however, major differences between the Iranian Mullahs who swept to power on the overthrow of the Shah in 1979 and the alliance of military officers and Islamists who forged Sudan's Islamic agenda after 1991. Whereas Ayatollah Ruhollah Khomeni, the spiritual leader of Iran's Islamic revolution, remained an essentially religious figure with a strong political agenda, Hassan al-Tourabi, the Sudanese regime's main ideologue, is essentially a political figure with a strong religious agenda. In both countries, domestic pressures have essentially dictated the changes that have taken place at the end of the 1990s. Although Khatami may have "changed foreign policy by changing the image," the question remains as to whether the substance behind the image has also changed. What seems increasingly clear is that it has changed profoundly in the past two years and will continue to do so.

Since his election, Khatami has been faced with a bruising battle—which has occasionally led to assassinations—with right-wingers within the various arms of the sprawling government. Although those surrounding the reformist president insist that he has cordial personal relations with the religious leadership, including the country's supreme leader, Ayatollah Ali Khamenei, the pursuit of reform has created a political conflict between the reformist camp led by Khatami and the conservative camp surrounding the religious leadership. In Sudan, the split, though similarly stark, amounts largely to a shift in alliances within the ruling group (rather than to an injection of new blood from outside it), with the power of Hassan al-Tourabi receding as that of President Omar Hassan el-Bashir expands.

The nature of the clash between the past and present leaders has thrown into stark relief the credibility of the revolutions themselves. The increasing bitterness of the battle in Iran exposes the extent to which the old guard has entrenched its power, despite having become unpopular and deemed responsible for Iran's enormous economic problems. Increasingly, the key question in Iran is not whether the old guard is the true guardian of the revolutionary ideals. Instead, those jealously guarding their power against encroachment by reformers are increasingly regarded as having failed to adapt theocratic ideals to the political reality. The need to adapt the power structure itself to the pressing needs of Iranian society is essentially the task facing President Khatami.

A very similar process is taking place in Sudan. But whereas in Iran the Mullahs exercise hands-on political power through a government and judicial structure that was designed to reflect the religious ideals of the country, in Sudan the lack of clarity over the role of the religious leadership in government has forced a review. In Iran, the judicial bodies charged with safeguarding the revolutionary ideals have remained. Khatami has simply tried, with increasing success, to appoint his own people to lead them. In Sudan, Hassan al-Tourabi's Pan-Arab and Islamic Conference (PAIC)—the body through which he exercised his behind-the-scenes political power—is now all but defunct. Al-Tourabi has taken on a purely political role, as secretary general of the National Congress, a political party. Thus, there has been a major review of the form of the institutions of Sudan's Islamic state. In Iran, meanwhile, the institutions remain but have become subject to internal reform.

Vital to developing an appropriate response to the changes within the Islamic states is an understanding of the domestic considerations that have led to these changes. In Sudan, pressure for change emerged as the personalities controlling the political life of the country found that the accommodation that had sustained their military-political alliance had not produced solutions to the pressing problems facing the country: the devastating war in the south; the armed opposition of northerners based in Eritrea; the isolation of Sudan from African, Arab, and Western countries; the pursuit of modernization in the political sphere by way of curtailing the influence and legacy of the political-religious sects—the Ansar and the Khatmiyya—whose ties to the establishment remained a thorn in the flesh of the new order. The strains within Sudan's ruling group had intensified the disaffection among natural supporters of al-Tourabi from within the Islamic Movement, many of whom had remained passive during the early years of the regime but had then joined the chorus of voices critical of both the evolving style of government and the poor results. "Since the last election, which made him president, Bashir has distanced himself from Dr. Tourabi," said Osman Khalid Mudawi, a Khartoum lawyer and founding member of the National Islamic Front (NIF). He continued:

> Tourabi had great influence in the early years. He was practically the only voice. But he has used up his political capital. Over the years he has antagonized his political base. Now he has very little influence on decisions. There is a preponderance of evidence that Bashir is firmly in power and is calling the shots. People learn from their mistakes. Tourabi unnecessarily antagonized people by making them afraid of nonexistent dangers, making threats that weren't there. He didn't project the right image. He has a love affair with the media. The Tourabi I knew in the past was a very different person. Why this change? I have no answer. Tourabi is no longer an asset, but is the greatest liability to Sudan, and I think the president knows it.[49]

Mr. Mudawi was clear that the evolving situation had manifested itself in growing tension between al-Tourabi and President el-Bashir, which had left the two men on nonspeaking terms on several occasions. It has since manifested itself in the political conflict over the role of the National Congress (NC), the political party al-Tourabi established when a new constitution was passed that allowed the creation of opposition political parties for the first time since the army seized power in 1989. It had been asserted that all ministers must be members of the party and that the NC should have the power to dismiss ministers who performed badly. These claims to power were rejected, and even its leading members rejected the idea of the NC becoming essentially the party of the state. "Sudan is trapped. The agenda is concentrated on survival strategies not long-term policies," said Hassan Maki Muhammed, an influential university professor and member of the consultative council of the National Congress:

> To make long-term policies we would have to have a stronger position and build institutions. For the past six to seven years this government has just passed from crisis to crisis. From pressure to pressure. From test to test. These people in government, after ten years, have discovered that the survival of Sudan itself depends upon [them] changing [their] policies.
>
> I think that the role of Tourabi is diminishing because there are only twenty-four hours in the day. He is fed up and has started to withdraw. He has many many problems from the government, from insiders and outsiders. I think Tourabi himself talks about the failures. He has the courage to admit them.
>
> The war in the south is the main cause of the change in the government's direction. If it hadn't been for the religious propaganda of *jihad*, the government wouldn't have lasted the ten years it has been in power. In fact it's been a success in keeping them in power. It's an unwinnable war, but it's working.[50]

The momentum of this political shift was frozen when, on 20 August 1998, the United States launched a cruise missile attack on the al-Shifa pharmaceutical factory on the outskirts of Khartoum. The United States claimed the factory was associated with Osama Bin Laden and that it was being used to produce precursors for the manufacture of chemical weapons. The attack took place simultaneously with an even more dramatic bombardment of Bin Laden's base at Khowst in Afghanistan, which was struck by seventy cruise missiles. Both attacks were the U.S. response to allegations that Bin Laden had masterminded the devastating bombings of U.S. embassies in Nairobi and Dar es Salaam on 7 August 1998, in which 263 people, most of them Kenyans and Tanzanians, were killed. The embassy bombings marked the long-expected escalation in activity by the Afghanistan-based militants, as had been threatened in the declaration of *jihad*.[51] The bombing of his base at Khowst was the direct U.S. retaliation for Bin Laden's alleged involvement in the embassy bombings. The attack on the al-Shifa pharmaceutical factory reflected, more than anything else, the U.S. military planners' desire for revenge. Two embassies had been attacked, so two targets had to be hit in response.

Within three weeks of the embassy bombings, four people had been arrested and accused of responsibility. Two people, a Saudi and a Sudanese, were arrested at Torkum—the Pakistan-Afghan border post at the western end of the Khyber Pass—by Pakistani police on 29 August 1998. The two principal suspects, Mohammed Sadiq Odeh and Khalid Salim, had been flown to the United States from Pakistan the week before, after being captured by Pakistani authorities. Mohammed Odeh had identified Bin Laden as the mastermind of the bombings when he had appeared in court in New York the previous day and had named Bin Laden's al-Qaeda organization as having arranged the bombings. In London, Khaled al-Fauwaz, the spokesman for the Advice and Reformation Committee that had declared its disassociation from Bin Laden and his call for *jihad*, was arrested, released, and rearrested in connection with the bombing after a request had been made for his extradition to the United States.

With the alleged bombers in the United States for trial, the reality of conflict between the United States and militant Islam was suddenly brought very much closer, after two or three decades. The declaration issued by Bin Laden a year beforehand suddenly meant something tangible. The issues for which Bin Laden's followers were prepared to launch suicide bomb attacks were aired in a New York courtroom. Equally important was the extent to which a trial exposed the direct links that the Saudi elite retained with Bin Laden and his cause of expelling the United States from Saudi Arabia, as was suggested at the time:

> Among the more vociferous critics of the U.S. presence is none other than Crown Prince Abdullah. No, [Bin Laden] doesn't lead 'Terror Inc'. Nor does the Saudi government. They don't need to. For Saudi Arabia is metamorphosing into an anti-American nation in front of our eyes. Of course, we're not told about that. Which is why, for most of the world, the bombing of the U.S. embassies last week was represented as an assault by Muslim 'madmen'. Arrest the usual suspects.[52]

Following the U.S. attack, a crowd in Khartoum attacked the British embassy, leaving gashes and holes in the fine brickwork and extra thick security glass of the windows. A few days later, the foreign staff of the embassy was evacuated. Great Britain, the United States' close ally, had not been given advance warning of the attack on the factory, though they pretended they had known.[53] The cruise missiles that struck the factory had been undetected by Sudanese radar because of a power cut at Khartoum airport, site of the only radar in the country.[54] Other European diplomats who knew the al-Shifa factory quickly condemned the attack itself. "On the basis of what we know of the factory and the evidence we have been given by the U.S. so far, there is no reason to believe that the U.S. knew what was going on inside that factory, other than with regard to its function as a major supplier of pharmaceuticals," one European diplomat told me. "Nor is there any evidence that the factory had links with Bin Laden. This robust support by other governments for the U.S. action was frankly very stupid," he said, clearly referring to the U.K. government and in particular to the prime minister, Tony Blair.[55] Meanwhile, U.S. State Department officials claimed to have soil samples collected from the factory before the attack that showed evidence of precursors for the production of VX nerve gas, but the department did not offer to reveal its evidence at the time and has not done so since.

Diplomats in Khartoum took seriously the Sudanese sense of grievance at the attack, largely because there was a strong sense at the time—and subsequently—that Sudan was changing its political direction and may have been diverted from this shift by the U.S. aggression. The attack was viewed by both Sudanese officials and diplomats as having been directed at Sudan itself, rather than at Bin Laden. "The U.S. says it has destroyed Bin Laden's infrastructure. The fact is that the aggression has destroyed only the infrastructure of Sudan," said Ghazi Salah Eddin, who had become the government spokesman by the time of the attack.[56] "The factory is a private facility owned by people who have links to Gulf countries who have problems with Bin Laden," he said, implying that the factory owners were not sympathetic to Bin Laden's campaign against U.S. influence in the Islamic world.

The factory was owned by Salah Idris, a Saudi Arabia-based Sudanese, whose family had close ties with the Khatmiyya sect vehemently opposed to Sudan's Islamist government—by implication an unlikely business partner for Bin Laden. Arab states only condemned the attack on Sudan four days after it had happened, such was their ongoing suspicion of the Sudanese government and their keenness to prevent Sudan from using anti-U.S. public opinion as a lever by which to diminish its own isolation from other Arab states. "Should we approve or should we reject it?" the Egyptian foreign minister Amr Moussa said in the immediate aftermath of the attacks.[57] "Why should we? Why should we use this language of black and white? We are absolutely against terrorism. We called for the [UN] Security Council to take the necessary steps and meet for an international summit [against terrorism]. So our position is very clear."

Nothing was really clear, however, least of all how the UN Security Council could allow the attack on Sudan without insisting on seeing and making public the evidence to justify it. President Khatami of Iran telephoned President el-Bashir to offer his support and sympathy after the bombing.[58] The two Islamic states could only support each other. But for Sudan the bombing failed to become an issue that it could use as a lever to force its way back onto the world stage. Ultimately, concerns that the bombing might cause a backlash away from the moderation allowed by Hassan al-Tourabi's steady withdrawal from center stage did not materialize. Within a few days Sudan returned to what it had been before the United States targeted it, a fact that highlighted its weakness. Al-Tourabi appeared not to have the energy to capitalize on such a blatant and apparently unjustifiable attack by his movement's archenemy. Speaking in his house near Khartoum airport late one evening, he seemed almost resigned to his eclipse when he said with obvious bitterness:

> I don't mean much myself, personally. If religious values are spreading I don't have to be in government. People are haunted sometimes by ghosts. There's a renaissance of the Islamic spirit. People don't know much about Islam. In Islam we don't believe in the concentration of religious power. That's why I supported Omar Bashir. Islam cannot come to power except by force, because the West wouldn't allow it. All things being equal, they hate me because I'm a Muslim.[59]

Whereas the Sudanese government's Islamic identity faces increasing strains as it seeks to break the cycle of war, poverty, and political instability that have merely worsened under its tenure, the government of Iran seems to be successfully redirecting Islamic values in an effort to tailor these values to new realities without a major shift in ideology. Sudan must abandon the *jihad* in the south in order to avoid its own disintegration, but "Iranian society appears to be back where it started—debating basic political and social issues in an atmosphere reminiscent of the free-wheeling days of 1979."[60]

"It's not a new Iran, but it's not the same as it was ten years ago. There are elements of continuity and change," said Gholam Ali Koshroo—who, as a senior advisor to Kamal Kharazi, the Iranian foreign minister, had been at the center of the image change that Iran's government had undertaken since the election of Khatami.[61] He continued:

> One should consider continuity and change together. The main slogans of the revolution were independence, freedom, and the Islamic republic. During the Iraq war the issue of independence was much more salient.

After that, freedom became most important. In each context, one of these elements came to the forefront. Now we are concentrating on civil society. This should not be interpreted as opposed to the revolution itself. It's not correct that the revolution isn't ongoing. Our situation has changed. And if a war with Afghanistan takes place, the situation will change again. The constitution is that of an Islamic republic. These are two notions. Neither should work against the other. Although the content of the revolution is Islamic, the people should choose these elements: Islamic, republic/popular participation, independence, freedom, justice, development.[62]

The officials surrounding President Khatami regard the change within government as reflective of changes that had already taken place within society. Twenty years after the Islamic revolution, Iran had evolved and new needs had developed. The clamor for greater popular participation together with a major effort to confront official corruption and measures to stem the spiraling decline in the economy required a major shift in emphasis. As part of this shift, Iran needed to reassess relations with its immediate neighbors, in particular the Gulf Arab states and the other countries of the Middle East, as well as with the United States. Investment in the oil and gas industries was vital and increased the urgency with which the sanctions imposed by the United States needed to be overcome. The question facing Iran's political establishment was how such a change—even the apparently insubstantial change of image in the eyes of the outside world—would affect domestic popular perceptions of the political structure. "It's clear to the clerics that if there were going to be normal relations with the United States, that over time there was not going to be any need for a clerical influence in the system of government," said a leading academic at Tehran National University.[63] He continued:

It would raise the question of: Why do you need clergymen in parliament? It's a question of revolutionary vitality for the clerics to maintain a distance between the U.S. and Iran. The U.S. does have a very strong and penetrating propaganda machine. There are enough groups, individuals, and elements of public opinion inside Iran to promote those policies. The clergy are aware of that. And they want control. But if this country really moves in the direction of modernization, then the clerics have to be reduced to their role of preaching.

The success of Khatami's drive toward a more open society in Iran has depended in large part on the failure of successive conservative campaigns to divert him and his supporters. Right wingers have used the police, the revolutionary courts, and the intelligence and security services to harass, undermine, discredit, and occasionally murder the reformers. These attempts have largely failed, in part due to the fact of Khatami's massive popular support, and in part because the conservatives have been wrong-footed and outwitted by the reformers. Also significant is the fact that Iran's supreme leader, Ayatollah Ali Khamenei, has drawn closer to President Khatami on key issues, lending clerical support for the reformist drive, or at least diminishing the extent of clerical obstruction. "The right simply had no idea that the result would turn out as it did. They made a fundamental error of judgment during the election, by attacking Khatami personally," said Sadeq Zibakalem, one of Iran's most outspoken political commentators and a columnist on the newspaper *Toos*, which was banned by the conservative-dominated courts in 1998.[64] Referring to the physical attacks on Atoallah Mohajerani, the reformist Minister of Culture and Islamic Guidance, and on Vice President Abdoallah Nuri, he continued:

> Then people became more aware that the election was genuine. The more the right attacked Khatami, the more they began to believe in Khatami. It took the right months to begin to consider a strategy after the election. And it was the period after the election and before that strategy had been agreed that we saw the greatest degree of freedom. There were opposing views within the right about what to do about Khatami. Now it seems that the extreme right faction is winning the upper hand.

The view among reformers is that Ayatollah Khamenei has reached the point where he believes that Khatami should be "controlled and should stay in power," and this will assist Khatami in his reform program.

> How far the right is prepared to go very much depends on how far Khatami is prepared to support the things he has promoted. It's possible that he will stand strongly behind the press freedom. The media was the most important issue that was bothering and troubling the right. The radio and television belong to them. For them the media was the most important hill to capture. It's also the biggest blow to Khatami. In Iran we don't have political parties. So political freedom is concentrated solely within the media. An attack on the media is an attack on political freedom in the most fundamental and severe way.

Khatami's forthright strategy of seizing control of the levers of power, which will reach their high point in the elections for the *majlis*, or parliament, in January 2000, has reshaped the Middle East in profound ways. Iran's assertiveness now is as significant as the Islamic revolution it experienced in 1979. The networks of regional states divided by domestic agendas, the progress of the Middle East peace process, the political direction of Israel, and the interests of the United States will be reshaped by what takes place in Iran. As President Khatami seeks to improve ties with the Arab states with which Iran has had poor relations—in particular Saudi Arabia—so the political complexion of the region will be redrawn. The Arab fear of non-Arab neighbors—Iran and Turkey—will perhaps at least in part be assuaged. Out of Iran's relative moderation is likely to emerge a stronger cultural identity within the broader Islamic world, at least within the geographical area of the Middle East.

Iran's isolation from its Arab neighbors, who largely supported Iraq during its eight-year war with Iran, is no longer prevalent, Saddam Hussein having isolated himself from those same regimes. The Arab cause is no longer so strictly defined in relations with other Muslims. Some newfound degree of homogeneity among Muslim states will heighten expectations of Israel to reverse its policy of reneging on agreements it has signed and to end its dishonest, disdainful, and provocative attitude toward the Palestinians. In Tehran in 1998, Yasser Arafat attended the meeting of the Organization of the Islamic Conference for the first time, after a long period of cool relations with Iran. Although there is a shift toward political reform within Iran, there is certainly no letup on the issue of Iran's nonrecognition of Israel, and no political tendencies within Iran are calling for any change in this policy.

President Khatami has sought a "dialogue of civilizations" with the West. The phrase is the positive echo of Huntington's highly negative theory of the "clash of civilizations," a phrase directed implicitly at the Islamic world. The very idea of dialogue has yet to really take root. On the political issues, the question of Israel is clearly the most potent. Successive Israeli governments have secured most of what they want from negotiations with their Palestinian adversaries by steamrollering the emergent Arafat, rather than by engaging in a dialogue that will create the stable Palestinian state that is the only guarantee of Israeli security. Uri Savir's account of his experience as Israel's chief negotiator at the Oslo talks reveals in great detail the ineptitude of the Palestinian leader as a negotiator, subjected to the manipulations of better-briefed Israeli officials and to the shortcomings of his own Palestinian team.[65]

Said Aburish describes the result of the signing of the Declaration of Principles: "What had been achieved was mutual recognition and a commitment to end the conflict through diplomatic means. Everything else depended on Israeli and PLO goodwill."[66] With the election in 1996 of Benjamin Netanyahu and the disappearance of Israeli "goodwill" to abide by obligations it had signed with the Palestinians, the process collapsed. There was no dialogue, and what emerged was the fact that in many areas there had never been a dialogue, except between the individuals who had sat across from each other at the negotiating tables and hammered out the agreements. On the part of Netanyahu's Likud-led coalition government, there was no dialogue based on respect of rights. Israeli settlement building at Jebel Abu Ghneim proved as much.

The civilizational aspects of an Israeli–PLO dialogue—aspects like those present in the dialogue between successive Israeli governments and the late King Hussein of Jordan, or between Israel and Egypt under Sadat and Mubarak—have not taken any meaningful root. And yet such a dialogue, and an accommodation resulting from it, is the only guarantee of peaceful coexistence in the Middle East. The Israeli–Palestinian relationship is one important aspect of this peace. If one accepts that religious and cultural issues lie at the heart not only of the "civilizational" conflict but also of the immediate political conflict, then there is clearly an urgent need across the region for the kind of dialogue President Khatami has been promoting in Iran.

Such dialogue has yet to be seen. U.S. foreign policy has yet to respond to the relatively rapid evolution now taking place within the Islamic world. The policy of "dual containment" in the 1980s was reliant upon the existence of a divided Muslim world in the Middle East. Since then, the U.S. support for Israel, the U.S. manipulation of Arab allies, and the connivance of the Western media in strengthening the racist stereotype of the Arab world and its relations with and attitude toward Israel have been made possible by the atmosphere of turmoil—which itself is the result of Israeli military superiority, U.S. impunity in its policing of the "rogue states" of the Middle East, and the illegitimacy of all Arab leaders.

Now, political Islam has done some of its work. The states of Islam are likely to emerge from this period of turmoil with a clearer sense of how best to marry their cultural history with political necessity. The test for the United States is as great as it is for these states themselves. With Iran, in the eyes of Arab states, no longer the threat it once was on the eastern flank of the Middle East, and with Sudan no longer occupying a similar though clearly much weaker position along the southern flank, there has been a significant shift in the geopolitics of the Middle East. With such changes now taking place, the double standard that lies at the heart of U.S. policy will have to change if it is to meet the challenge of a dialogue rather than to continue to foster the dangers of a clash.

Conclusion

THE LATE 1990S HAVE BEEN DOMINATED by the shattering of unity within the Islamist movements, which began the decade with the conviction that it was only a matter of time before their demands would be met. The bloody first days of 1998 saw calls by the Algerian Islamic Salvation Front for a negotiated settlement to the Algerian crisis, while the rival Armed Islamic Group (GIA) continued to slaughter; demands by the imprisoned leaders of the Egyptian Gama'a al-Islamiyya for a resumption of the cease-fire they had called for in 1997, while its radical militants rejected calls for moderation; a softening of the Islamist policies, at least in foreign affairs, of the Sudanese government, while hard-liners continued the onslaught against southern rebels.

The disarray within the most active Islamist movements during 1997–1998 has now, in 1999, evolved further, resulting in what appear to be significant steps toward a reassessment of their future strategies. On 25 March 1999, the jailed leaders of Egypt's al-Gama'a al-Islamiyya, in concert with its leaders in exile, declared a further cease-fire in their conflict with the government. The cease-fire was the result of a year of discussions between the two leaderships. It was the breakdown of communication between them that had led to the killing of fifty-eight foreign tourists and six Egyptians at Luxor on 17 November 1997. Whereas the jailed leaders had already called for a cease-fire, the exiled leaders had not been party to the decision, and the six gunmen who slaughtered the tourists were taking their orders from outside Egypt. By 1999 the confusion within the organization appeared to have been overcome, with the recognition that the armed campaign was going nowhere, as Muntassir al-Zayat, the organization's lawyer and the man who liaised between the two leaderships, acknowledged:

> There's an official feeling that the government has won. We want to create a peaceful climate so that we can take our time and think about what should happen next. Fighting is not an aim in itself. It's a means. If that means proves a failure we should find another way. Within two years we

will begin to see some fruit. What is clear now is that the Gama'a has grown up, based on the experience of the past ten years. We will still op-pose the government. Strongly oppose the government. But it will be peaceful.[1]

The Gama'a al-Islamiyya's shift in strategy is also now being re-garded by some as reflective of a significant change in the political role of militant organizations across the Islamic world. As with the Islamic Salvation Front (FIS) in Algeria—which has sought and so far failed to launch a dialogue with the government despite abandoning its armed campaign (versus the extremist Armed Islamic Group—GIA—which has continued to fight)—the al-Gama'a al-Islamiyya cease-fire is in contrast to the ongoing strategy of Jihad, the smaller Egyptian group. Increasingly, the trend within Islamic organizations has become de-fined by their response to the call in 1998 by Osama Bin Laden for a global assault on U.S. interests. Whereas Jihad and its Afghanistan-based leader, Ayman Zoheiri, have allied themselves with Bin Laden, Gama'a al-Islamiyya rejected the alliance. Although three Gama'a leaders are known to be in Afghanistan, they are not with Bin Laden. "They saw no urgency in declaring the war against America. The Gama'a says that its problem is with the Egyptian government. It's not wise to win extra enemies," Mr. al-Zayat said.

The same approach remains largely true in Algeria, where the diminution of the violence in the past year has exposed a fatigue on the part of the guerrillas, rather than any success in bringing the crisis to an end. The 15 April 1999 election, which saw the former foreign minister, Abdelaziz Bouteflika, win the presidency, does not represent any con-clusion to the political impasse, despite the violence being at a low ebb. Bouteflika, the army's approved candidate, won a flawed poll from which the six opposing candidates withdrew after identifying serious fraud in the electoral process. The key division within Algerian society remains that between the army, the political class, and the Islamists. Despite the path to democracy now being long-trodden, the army is still pulling the strings, using the FIS's armed wing, the AIS, to fight the GIA, even while the FIS's leader, Abbasi Madani, remains under house arrest. Opposition politicians regard the army influence on Bouteflika as unlikely to lead to a reconciliation with the armed extremists, and thus as unlikely to bring a rapid end to the ongoing violence.

What does this evolution mean for political Islam? Has the core of its violent manifestations been quashed, leaving only an extremist fringe, which stands increasingly isolated from the more moderate Is-lamist politicians who themselves have been left wondering what their future role really is?

For each of these countries, movements, and experiences, the prospects are different. The "social movement" of Islamism is deeply rooted in all the societies in which it has manifested itself. History has conspired for it to be so. The history of the Islamist movements, which I have attempted to trace over the past decades and to detail in their current forms, is one chapter in the history of Islam. As the Sudanese politician John Garang made clear, for him the National Islamic Front (NIF) in Sudan is the apex of the Islamist phenomenon. After the NIF, nothing could be worse, and it is unlikely to be replaced by anything as radical. Perhaps. The history of Sudan reveals the constant presence of the religious establishment in all areas of political life. From the days of the early Sufi orders, religion has wielded an important political role. The *Mahdiyya* was one of the most dynamic efforts in history to create an Islamic state. A hundred years later, a reformist theocracy with its own interpretation of how religious belief should be transposed into the political arena has experimented with these same issues, against significant odds, many of the obstacles of its own making.

Garang's perspective is revealing. One historical phase, he is suggesting, is coming to an end. The evolution of Islamism over the past century has reached its climax, and its opponents have successfully confronted it. The beleaguered condition of the Sudanese government does much to testify to the validity of his viewpoint. If, as one British prime minister once said, politics is the art of the possible, then the Sudanese government cannot be said to have successfully practiced its politics. Its ideas have been imposed. Its experiment has relied upon repression. There is no debate. But history explains why this is the case. There is no doubt that failure has been a more omnipresent quality of Sudanese political practice than success. Why then should there not have been a backlash, a radical alternative like the Islamist experiment of the past nine years—something truly different from all the inept and ill-conceived experiments that have kept the country well below the poverty line and that have failed to resolve its problems?

Some of the answers, I hope, emerge from the views of those who are the key characters of this book. The success of Islamism has been in expressing the outlook and articulating the perspective of believers in and practitioners of a social and philosophical experiment that is rooted in the reality of the countries in which it has emerged. Sadiq al-Mahdi was not a successful democratic prime minister. His traditional power base was, in itself, symbolic of the stagnation of the Sudanese political scene. He, and other critics of Islamism, have much to answer for and little to suggest as alternatives. Meanwhile, the only indigenous political philosophy to have emerged from the land of Islam is Islamism, in all its guises. Nationalism was imitative. Democracy has not emerged as a credible alternative, as it has time and again proved too susceptible to corruption, abuse, and the whims of those wielding military power. Strong democracy can only evolve if it reflects popular sentiment. As was explained in Chapter 1, democracy was rejected by the Islamists who gathered in Afghanistan and formed the Islamist army that has made such a strong impression on the Islamic world in the 1990s. Why was it rejected? Essentially because its intrinsic value was not apparent. But also because democracy is associated with the West, and the West has become an opponent of Islamism.

Increasingly, the usefulness of political polarities is becoming less rather than more clear. The end of the Cold War has changed little in the Islamic world. Unlike in sub-Saharan Africa, the same regimes remain in power. The relative immunity of the Islamic world to the ebb and flow of global trends has become more stark. When the short-serving secretary general of the North Atlantic Treaty Organization (NATO), Willy Claes, deemed Islam the new global threat replacing communism, he was wrong on many counts. The most important was the fact that the evaluation and reevaluation that takes place within the Islamic world does not draw upon the same roots that communism did. Essentially, Islam is about belief. Communism was about political power. There is now sufficient evidence to prove that even the most ambitious Islamist is not seeking to emulate the ambitions of communism. Power within the state rather than global domination is the relatively modest ambition of the Islamist. A few short years after it embarked upon its policy of training Islamist military units from abroad, Sudan has been forced to largely abandon this program. The intention was there. But the program failed, and that is really all that matters. It did not work.

The Islamist who wants to run his own country has a clear idea of the obstacles that are likely to be placed in front of him. The military power of the secular state, in league with its Western allies, is the most formidable. Islamism is not imperialism, and the evolution of Islamist thought over the past hundred years has shown this to be the case. The political disunity of the *umma* has been recognized; the Turks, the former leaders of the caliphate, now hold joint military maneuvers with Israel in the eastern Mediterranean. Such an alliance perhaps cements Arab disappointment with the former would-be rulers of the Islamic world. So, the Islamist turns to his own country and hopes to reform it by using political pressure. When this fails, he becomes frustrated. The consequences are multifarious.

"The youth here are lost. You can have intelligence, physical strength, and determination. But there's no hope of finding work."

Zen Arab was not the real name of the young Moroccan Islamist who sat staring out to sea as we talked at a deserted café on the beach. The Atlantic Ocean pounded the coastline just below the Old Mountain of Tangier, on Morocco's northwestern tip. "We are living in a repressive time, when it's very difficult to express the things we are thinking and believing in. There are lots of people who aren't part of the left-right political spectrum, but who are instead waiting to find a role. And Islam is providing that role." Four times in his early twenties he had attempted to illegally cross the Straits of Gibraltar, which divide Morocco from Spain. To reach Europe was the goal. That was where a golden future lay. Then one day he decided he would not try again. He realized that the promise of Europe was an illusion. The truth lay closer to home. "But even now," he said, staring out to sea, "in terms of real change, I don't see anything on the horizon."

Notes

Introduction

1. Samuel P. Huntington, *The Clash of Civilizations and the Remaking of World Order* (New York: Simon and Schuster, 1996), p. 264.

Chapter One

1. At least two hundred former Arab Afghan fighters are thought to be living in the New York and New Jersey areas. James Bruce, "Arab Veterans of the Afghan War," *Jane's Intelligence Review* 7, no. 4 (April 1995):175–179.

2. The Mujahideen are those who fight jihad or holy war.

3. Karim Omar, interview by author, London, 15–16 January 1997.

4. Azzam, a member of the Muslim Brotherhood, was killed by a car bomb in Peshawar in November 1989, in as yet unexplained circumstances.

5. The Muslim Brotherhood was founded in 1928 by the Egyptian Hassan al-Banna and remains the single most influential Islamist organization. Its broad following, political importance especially in the Middle East, and intellectual force have ensured the brotherhood's primacy among Islamist organizations despite attempts particularly by Arab governments to destroy it. Its emergence and impact is examined in Chapter 4.

6. Gulbeddin Hekmatyar, Burhanuddin Rabbani, and Mawlawi Younes Khales are three Afghan Mujahideen leaders.

7. In June 1996, Bin Laden was forced to leave Sudan, where he had been based after leaving Afghanistan in the early 1990s. He returned to Afghanistan, first to Nanghahar province and then to the southern province of Kandahar.

8. The *sharia* literally means the "path" or "way," and in this context refers to Islamic law as defined and explained in the holy book of Islam, the Koran.

9. Asta Olesen, *Islam and Politics in Afghanistan*, Nordic Institute of Asian Studies, Monograph Series no. 67 (Richmond, Surrey, England: Curzon Press, 1995), p. 256.

10. Ibid.

11. For a more detailed discussion of the different schools of thought within Islam, see Chapter 4.

12. Olivier Roy, *The Failure of Political Islam* (London: I. B. Tauris, 1994), p. 150.

13. Olesen, op. cit., p. 267.

14. The Mujahideen, based at that time in Peshawar, declared jihad against the Kabul government on 27 November 1979, before the Soviet invasion, which took place the following month.

15. Dilip Hiro says: "Muhammad realised that the best way to ensure the survival of the Islamic umma was by inculcating the new converts with a sense of solidarity which transcended traditional loyalties, and which was so ritualised that it impinged on everyday life. Out of this emerged the five pillars of Islam [*shahada*, or religious witness; *salat*, or prayer; *zakat*, or charity; *sawm*, or feast; and *hadj*, or pilgrimage]." Dilip Hiro, *Islamic Fundamentalism*, rev. ed. (London: Paladin, 1989), p. 11.

16. Barnett R. Rubin, *The Search for Peace in Afghanistan: From Buffer State to Failed State* (New Haven and London: Yale University Press, 1995), pp. 28–29.

17. Ibid., p. 29.

18. In 1990, the Soviet Union continued to provide military supplies to Kabul, providing in that year alone 54 military aircraft, 865 armored personnel carriers, 680 antiaircraft guns, 150 R-17 rocket launchers, about 500 Scud missiles (each costing $1 million), and large quantities of fuel. *Washington Post*, 16 November 1992.

19. As Rubin writes: "The Islamists in their Pakistani exile declared jihad against the communists. They were soon joined by representatives of the conservative clergy and the elites of the old [pre-PDPA] regime, although most former high state officials, rather than joining the struggle, made their way to the West, where they had often been educated. Dozens of exiled leaders competed to form resistance organizations in Peshawar. One of the legacies of the old regime was a fragmented polity without any civil society or political parties, so the Islamists aided by Pakistan were the only organizations ready to take to the field." Rubin, op. cit., p. 28.

20. Ibid., p. 30.

21. Mohammad Yousaf and Mark Adkin, *The Bear Trap: Afghanistan's Untold Story* (London: Leo Cooper, 1992), p. 81. Between 1983 and 1987, Brigadier Yousaf was director of the ISI's Afghan bureau and Pakistan's primary liaison with the Mujahideen, providing military advice as well as organizing the distribution of weapons procured by the CIA to the Afghan factions.

22. Ibid., p. 83

23. As Yousaf and Adkin write: "To admit Americans directly into the system of supply and training would not only have led to chaos but would have proved the communist propaganda correct. All along, the Soviets, and their Afghan agents in the KHAD (the Afghan secret police, which was trained and advised by the KGB), endeavored to subvert the Mujahideen supporters and their families by claiming they were not fighting Jihad, but merely doing the dirty work of, and dying for, the US. Their assertion that the Afghans had no real quarrel with each other but were pawns in a superpower conflict would have been impossible to refute if Americans became overtly involved inside [Afghanistan]" (Ibid., p. 81).

24. As Yousaf and Adkin write: "This view was similarly prevalent among CIA officers including, particularly, the Director, William Casey. I could see they were deeply resentful of their failure to win in Vietnam, which had been a major military defeat for the world's leading superpower. To me, getting their own back seems to be the primary reason for the US backing the [Afghan] war with so much money" (Ibid., p. 63). Yousaf and Adkin quote U.S. Congressman Charles Wilson, for whom Yousaf arranged a secret visit to Afghanistan in 1987, as saying: "There were 58,000 [U.S.] dead in Vietnam and we owe the Russians one. . . . I have a slight obsession with it because of Vietnam. I thought the Soviets ought to have a dose of it." *Daily Telegraph,* 14 January 1985; quoted in Yousaf and Adkin, op. cit., p. 62.

25. *Los Angeles Times,* 4 August 1996.

26. See Chapter 3.

27. Bruce, op. cit.

28. Ibid.

29. See Chapter 7.

30. Dudayev acknowledged that this had taken place in an interview with the *Los Angeles Times* (4 August 1996).

31. Omar, op. cit.

32. Amid Khan Motaqi, interview by author, Kabul, 4 December 1996.

33. Such a view is common among both radical Islamists and scholars well acquainted with the militarism of the Prophet Mohammed and his immediate successors. Dilip Hiro writes: "The sustained expansion of the Dar al Islam through the waging of jihad, holy war, helped Umar to hold together the coalition of Arabian tribes under his leadership. . . . He intensified the holy struggle while strengthening the ideological basis of Islam." Hiro is referring to Umar ibn Khattab, one of the early caliphs in the years following the death of the Prophet Mohammed. Hiro, op. cit., p. 13.

34. "Only if we deviate from Islam will we start losing. . . . The time for a negotiated settlement is running out fast. We feel a military solution has better prospects right now," Sheikh Omar said in a rare interview. *Time,* 31 March 1997, p. 33.

35. Mawlawi Abdarab Akhunzada, interview by author, Kabul, 4 December 1996.

36. Amir Hassanyar, interview by author, Kabul, 6 December 1996.

37. "I shall go far and far into the North, playing the Great Game." Rudyard Kipling, *Kim,* 1901.

38. Nikolai Sherchenko, interview by author, Termez, Uzbekistan, 9 December 1996.

39. See Olivier Roy, op. cit., chap. 9. Roy argues convincingly that the war fought by the Afghan Mujahideen remained rooted in the traditional practices of war, which had evolved over two centuries. The only real innovation during the 1980s was the insertion of external resources—money, arms, and international aid—which gave the factional leaders access to assets that had not been seized from the local population and that therefore did not play the role that the seizure of "booty" traditionally played in establishing the supremacy of the strong over the weak. This allowed Mujahideen leaders who were not tra-

ditional tribal chiefs, and who had not had such access before external aid began to flood in, to distribute patronage and to partially reshape the system of
wealth distribution as well as the local, tribal power structure.

40. Ibid., p. 157.

41. Ibid.

42. Ibid.

43. Ibid., pp. 152–154.

44. Senior Pakistani military officer, interview by author, Kabul, 4 December 1996.

Chapter Two

1. *Qat* is a leaf chewed as a mild stimulant in Somalia.

2. North Mogadishu, 11 February 1995.

3. See Malise Ruthven, *Islam in the World*, rev. ed. (Harmondsworth, England: Penguin Books, 1991), chap. 2.

4. This date is that given by Ruthven, op. cit.

5. Maududi died in 1979

6. Sayyid Abul A'la Maududi, *Towards Understanding Islam*, trans. Khur-
shid Ahmad (Lahore: International Islamic Federation of Student Organisa-
tions, 1960), p. 40. Originally published as *Risala-e-Diniyat*.

7. Ibid., p. 43.

8. Sayyid Qutb, *The Islamic Concept and Its Characteristics* (Indianapolis:
American Trust Publications, 1991), p. 17.

9. Ibid.

10. Ibid., p. 18.

11. Maxime Rodinson, *Muhammad*, trans. Anne Carter, 2nd English-
language ed. (Harmondsworth, England: Penguin Books, 1996).

12. Rodinson quotes a letter from a Persian emperor, in reference to the
Byzantine and Persian Empires: "By these two great empires, turbulent and
warlike nations are controlled and the lives of men in general set in order and
governed." Theophylact Simocatta, *Historiae*, IV, 11, ed. C. de Boor (Leipzig:
Teubner, 1887), p. 169.

13. Rodinson, op. cit., p. 14.

14. Ibid., p. 18.

15. William Montgomery Watt, *A Short History of Islam* (Oxford:
Oneworld Publications, 1996), pp. 9–10.

16. Islamic *sharia* law has been introduced in North Mogadishu as well as
in the southern towns of Baidoa and Lugh.

17. The division of Islam into Sunni and Shia has its roots in the political
rather than theological differences among the followers of the Prophet Mohammed in the years immediately after his death in A.D. 632. Mohammed was
succeeded as caliph of the Muslim community in Medina not by the man
viewed by the Shia as his designated successor—his cousin and son-in-law
Ali—but by another follower, Abu Bakr. He was in turn succeeded by Umar,

who was followed by Uthman. Personal rivalries between Ali and the successors to the caliphate culminated in Ali's assassination in 661. In the intervening years, Ali had denounced the political innovations instituted by Abu Bakr and Umar. Ali argued that ascent to the position of caliph should not be limited to those of a particular class. Subsequently, the Shia—an abbreviation of *shia A'li*, or followers of the path of Ali—have sought the true nature of their religion in the practice—the *sunna*—of the Prophet, as revealed in the hadith, or sayings of the Prophet. Shias reject the Sunni claim that the caliphs were the spiritual leaders of Islam, claiming that only the direct descendants of Mohammed could become caliph. The practice of the Sunni originally drew upon a much wider body of thought, evolving through the caliphates during which the word of Allah was clarified in the hadith.

18. As Dilip Hiro writes: "But Muhammad knew that this unity was tenuous, and that the only means by which he could ensure the survival of the Medinese nucleus of the Dar al Islam after his death was by keeping up an expansionary drive—a strategy which also appealed to his beduin followers eager to appropriate the [legitimate] booty from his successful campaigns." Dilip Hiro, *Islamic Fundamentalism*, rev. ed. (London: Paladin, 1989), p. 11.

19. François Burgat, *L'Islamisme en Face* (Paris: La Decouverte, 1995), p. 24. My translation.

20. As von Grunebaum writes: "Salvation by sameness, the implied belief that what worked once will always work, and the unconcerned readiness to forego the wider horizons that have been opened by man, and, for the most part, by Western man, during the last centuries—one cannot help feeling both frightened and concerned and depressed by the appeal that Nadwi's message appears to have for certain Muslim circles. The ultimate impenetrability of one civilization by another is demonstrated, unintentionally it is true, but, for all that, all the more convincingly." Gustave von Grunebaum, *Modern Islam* (Westport, Conn.: Greenwood Press, 1962), p. 188.

21. Ibid., p. 189.

22. Hiro, op. cit., p. 6.

23. Ibid., p. 5.

24. Referring to the decline of Islamic values in the Caliphate during the eighth century, Khaled al-Fauwaz, the London representative of the exiled Saudi Arabian Islamist Advice and Reformation Committee, says: "People started to base their behavior on their own ideas, not on the *sharia*. The dangerous part was when they put a boundary between the religion and human life, and were dealing with religion as a spiritual behavior." Khaled al-Fauwaz, interview by author, London, 30 October 1996.

25. Maududi, op. cit., p. 39.

26. Mohamed Moalim Hassan, interview by author, Mogadishu, 2 March 1993.

27. The OIC is the main inter-governmental pan-Islamic organization, meeting at head of state level every two years to discuss issues facing the Islamic world.

28. Baha al-Din Hanafi, interview by author, Khartoum, 13 December 1993.

29. Ahmed Jili'ow, interview by author, Mogadishu, 23 September 1992.

30. As General Aideed told me: "An Islamic group known as al-Itihad is in the town of Merka, and they are equipping themselves to take over the country. They have a connection with outside countries, and they are receiving money and military equipment and buying weapons." Mohamed Farah Aideed, interview by author, Bardera, Somalia, 20 September 1992.

31. Aideed was the leader of the Somali National Alliance–United Somali Congress faction, which controlled South Mogadishu and areas outside the city. He was killed in a gun battle in Mogadishu in June 1996.

32. Osama Bin Laden, interview by Abdelbari Atwan, *Al-Quds Al-Arabi,* 27 November 1996.

33. Osama Bin Laden, "Declaration of Jihad on the Americans Occupying the Country of the Two Sacred Places," Khurasan, Afghanistan, 23 August 1996 (unpublished).

34. Statement by Madeleine Albright, issued by the U.S. State Department, 7 October 1993.

35. Abdi Ali Alasow, interview by author. Mogadishu, 9 February 1995.

36. As one clan chief told me: "We don't feel that we will get a government soon, and *sharia* is the solution to the problem of law and order. The prewar constitution that we have has some elements of the *sharia,* and the Muslim Brotherhood is drawing up the *sharia* code for the court. But the [clan] elders and the fundamentalists are in opposition, as it is not possible to have two courts." Malak Moktar Hassan, chief of the Rahanweyn clan, interview by author, Baidoa, Somalia, 16 February 1995.

37. As a Somali police officer told me: "I'm not saying we should bring *sharia* because it will bring the Somali factions together. It's because we are Muslims that we should use *sharia.* But there's conflict between the fundamentalists and the moderates. The fundamentalists are against the former constitution of the country." Lieutenant Yusuf Mohamed Ali, police chief in Baidoa, interview by author, Baidoa, Somalia, 10 February 1995.

38. The Horn of Africa consists of Eritrea, Ethiopia, Djibouti, and Somalia, though Sudan and Kenya are often considered politically linked to what is essentially a geographical grouping.

39. I shall examine this political program in more detail in Chapter 7.

40. Maududi, op. cit., pp. 40–42.

41. In an interview with the author, Sudan's justice minister, Abdelaziz Shiddo, said: "Sudan would have become the first Somalia had it not been for the 1989 takeover. There was complete breakdown of authority. I believe that this government was capable of confronting the major problems confronting Sudan. It would have succeeded completely if there had been international assistance. But the isolation imposed by the international community has hindered it." Abdelaziz Shiddo, interview by author, Khartoum, 13 December 1993. However, critics of the NIF among Sudan's conservative Muslim population point to the continuing potential for disintegration in Sudan. I shall look more closely at this in Chapter 7.

42. This was explained to me clearly by, among others, Khaled al-Fauwaz, of the Saudi Arabian Advice and Reformation Committee, who said: "One of the problems for the Islamic scholars is that in *sharia* we always find general

rules. But these general rules are useless unless they are applied in practical ways. You can't talk about theoretical things. Islam is a way of life for people. You have to practice these rules. We have scholars who are very good at issuing fatwas, but when you ask them about practical things, they are useless. The question is: What is wrong with applying these rules. In general [the scholars] can give volumes of knowledge. But they fail to apply it in real life." Al-Fauwaz, op. cit.

Chapter Three

1. Sufism is a branch of Islam that, unlike the more orthodox schools of thought, emphasizes the mystical experiences of individual Muslims and venerates their experiences, in a way similar to the veneration of saints in Christianity. Orthodox Muslims, and in particular those viewed as fundamentalists, reject, often violently, the Sufi practices, which they view as contrary to the Islamic notion that no individuals other than Allah are worthy of veneration. Sufis, who are organized into brotherhoods and sects, have often been criticized for their practice of celebrating, with music and dance—practices that are themselves rejected by more orthodox Muslims—the lives of Muslim saints, whose tombs have become meeting places for their followers. The word "Sufi" stems from the Arabic word for wool—*suf*—a coat of which the early Sufis wore between the seventh and eleventh centuries, after which this material was replaced by a patched cotton coat.

2. Bentounes Kelim Mourad, interview by author, Mostaganem, Algeria, 8 November 1995.

3. Between 1832 and 1871, a number of religious leaders emerged to head armed opposition against the French colonial power that had established its rule in Algeria in 1830. Most prominent among these leaders was the Sufi Emir Abd al-Qadir, who was the elected leader of Algeria's western tribes. Between 1832 and 1847 he prevented French rule from taking root in the western areas around Oran, organizing a state based on Islamic principles and stressing the religious nature of his struggle against the non-Muslim French. His revolt collapsed in 1847 but was followed by others, all of them motivated by religion. Only in 1871 was France able to impose its rule throughout the territory. I shall look in greater detail at the historical roots of the modern Islamist movements in Chapter 6.

4. Ernest Renan, *L'Islamisme et la science* (Paris: n.p., 1883), pp. 2–3; quoted in Albert Hourani, *Arabic Thought in the Liberal Age, 1798–1939* (Cambridge: Cambridge University Press, 1983), p. 120.

5. See note 1 above.

6. A marabout is a holy man invested with the power to heal, predict the future, and, in many areas of Africa, perform magic. In Muslim countries, the marabout is viewed as a living saint, invested with the authority to pronounce on religious matters with an authority derived from an exemplary lifestyle.

7. Michael Willis, *The Islamist Challenge in Algeria: A Political History* (Reading, England: Ithaca Press, 1996), p. 2.

8. The acronym stems from the organization's French name, the Association d'Ulama Musulman Algérien.

9. Willis, op. cit., p. 15.

10. Abd al-Hamid Ibn Badis, quoted in Willis, op. cit., p. 18.

11. Willis, op. cit., p. 23.

12. Edward Said, *Orientalism: Western Conceptions of the Orient* (Harmondsworth, England: Penguin Books, 1991), p. 60.

13. "The Orient" can be considered the countries with which in large part this book deals, stretching from North Africa through the Middle East and into central Asia as far east as Afghanistan.

14. Mohammedans are followers of Mohammed, the Muslim Prophet.

15. James Boswell, *Life of Samuel Johnson*, ed. G. Birkbeck Hill, rev. ed., vol. 4 (Oxford: L. F. Powell, 1934), p. 199.

16. Albert Hourani, "Islam in European Thought," in *Islam in European Thought* (Cambridge: Cambridge University Press, 1991), p. 15.

17. Ibid., p. 57.

18. Said, op. cit., p. 307.

19. Albert Hourani, "Wednesday Afternoons Remembered," in *Islam in European Thought* (Cambridge: Cambridge University Press, 1991), p. 63.

20. Fred Halliday, *Islam and the Myth of Confrontation: Religion and Politics in the Middle East* (London: I. B. Tauris, 1996), p. 179.

21. Ibid., p. 210.

22. Ibid., p. 211.

23. The Arab conquests of the Balkans during the fourteenth and fifteenth centuries were followed by a period of reasonably successful Christian-Muslim coexistence, which lasted until the nineteenth and early twentieth centuries. But with the outbreak of the Bosnian war in the former Yugoslavia, the Serbian leadership was able to revitalize fears of the Muslim hordes among Serb communities in Bosnia-Herzegovina. The growing influence of Turkey in western Asia, the Balkans, and the Middle East has aroused similar feelings among Greeks, Halliday claims, with suspicion among Greeks of a Turkish conspiracy to seize Greek land in eastern Thrace. In Bulgaria, too, rising nationalism has found its voice in anti-Islamic sentiment, evoking past resentments of the Ottoman invasions. Halliday, op. cit., pp. 166–177.

24. Said, op. cit., p. 26.

25. *Ijtihad* is translated as "individual reflection," implying personal reflection on religious concepts as opposed to the unquestioning acceptance of mainstream or conservative religious interpretations.

26. Dilip Hiro, *Islamic Fundamentalism*, rev. ed. (London: Paladin, 1989), p. 45.

27. Ibid., p. 43.

28. I shall look more closely in Chapter 4 at the Islamist scholars whose work has contributed to the agendas of the twentieth-century Islamist movements.

29. François Burgat, *L'Islamisme en Face* (Paris: La Decouverte, 1995), p. 70. My translation.

30. Willis, op. cit., p. 30.

31. John P. Entelis, *Algeria: The Revolution Institutionalized* (Boulder: Westview Press, 1986), p. 42.

32. Anwar Haddam, exiled leader of the Islamic Salvation Front parliamentarians, telephone interview by author, 17 August 1995.

33. FIS is the French acronym for the Front Islamique de Salut or Islamic Salvation Front.

34. The FIS won 4,332,472 votes (54.25 percent of the votes cast and 33.73 percent of the registered votes) in the local elections. *Monde Arabe: Maghreb/Machrek*, no. 135 (January-March 1992):155.

35. The FIS won 3,260,222 votes (47.27 percent of the votes cast and 24.59 percent of the registered votes) in the first ballot. *Monde Arabe: Maghreb/Machrek*, no. 135 (January-March 1992):155.

36. Full results of the first ballot were never published, with only the results of candidates who would be contesting the second ballot being made public.

37. Keith Sutton and Ahmed Aghrout, "Multiparty Elections in Algeria: Problems and Prospects," *Bulletin of Francophone Africa*, no. 2 (Autumn 1992):76–77.

38. The High Council for Security was dominated by three military officers: the defense minister, Khaled Nazzar; the chief of the general staff, Abdelmalek Guenaizia; and the interior minister, Larbi Belkheir. It also comprised the leaders of the navy, the gendarmerie, the security services, and the commanding colonels of the military regions. See Willis, op. cit., p. 247.

39. *Middle East International*, 24 January 1993, quoted in Willis, op. cit., p. 250.

40. The HCE was intended to dilute the impression that the army takeover was a coup d'état. Alongside Boudiaf, the other members of the group were General Khaled Nazzar, the defense minister; Ali Kafi, head of the association of former veterans of the war of independence; Ali Haroun, a former human rights minister; and Tijani Haddam, the rector of the Paris mosque.

41. Willis, op. cit., p. 256.

42. The regime said that the number was 5,000. Willis, op. cit., p. 257.

43. *Jeune Afrique*, 26 November 1986 and 3 December 1986, quoted in Willis, op. cit., p. 99.

44. Mahfoud Benoune, *The Making of Contemporary Algeria: 1830–1987* (Cambridge: Cambridge University Press, 1988), p. 286.

45. Meriem Verges, "Genesis of Mobilization: The Young Activists of Algeria's Islamic Salvation Front," in *Political Islam: Essays from Middle East Report*, ed. Joel Beinin and Joe Stork (London: I. B. Tauris, 1997), p. 293.

46. Ibid.

47. Ibid., p. 302.

48. Burgat, op. cit., p. 163.

49. Karim Omar, interview by author, London, 15–16 January 1997.

50. In English, the Armed Islamic Movement.

51. The acronym stems from the group's French name, Group Islamique Armée.

52. Abdelhamid Mehri, telephone interview by author, 13 August 1995.

53. See Willis, op. cit., pp. 263–266.

54. The Rome meetings, organized by the Catholic St. Egidio Community, brought the FIS, the FLN, the legal Hamas Islamic Party, the Socialist Forces Front (FFS), the Algerian Democratic Movement (MDA), and several other parties together. Their final communiqué—known as the Contract of Rome or the National Contract—included several concessions by the FIS, including its rejection of violence and its support for a multiparty system, the alternation of power, and religious freedom. The meetings had a line of communication to the FIS's imprisoned leader, Ali Belhadj, allowing decisions to be taken with his direct involvement, including the phrasing of the final communiqué (though Belhadj did not specifically agree to the alternation of power). The military government, which ignored an invitation to attend the meetings, deemed the discussions an interference in Algeria's internal affairs. The framework for a solution agreed upon in Rome has not since been adopted, largely due to government refusal to cooperate as well as to the continuing violence of the GIA, which was also not a participant.

55. Mahiou Mebarak, telephone interview by author, 24 August 1995.

56. Government officials had attempted direct talks with imprisoned FIS leaders; however, the contacts were terminated in November 1994 when it became clear that the discussions were getting nowhere.

57. The promotion of the army chief of staff, Mohammed Lamari, to the rank of Lieutenant General in November 1994 is regarded as a sign that the tendency within the regime that sought to "eradicate" the Islamists was in the ascendancy. Willis, op. cit., p. 347.

58. By 1997 the official figure had passed sixty.

59. *Jeune Afrique,* 27 January, 1994, quoted in Willis, op. cit.

60. Haddam, op. cit.

61. Redha Malek was appointed prime minister in August 1993 and resigned in April 1994; during his tenure the government attempted to implement a series of tough measures against the Islamists. The failure of the measures led to the appointment of a more pragmatic government headed by Mokdad Sifi.

62. Redha Malek, telephone interview by author, 28 August 1995.

63. "FIS: National Strike."

64. Interview by author, Mostaganem, Algeria, 8 November 1995.

65. The 1954–1962 war that brought independence from France.

66. Yves Lacoste, telephone interview by author, 19 October 1995.

67. Said Sadi, interview by author, Mostaganem, Algeria, 8 November 1995.

68. The meeting was to have been held at the United Nations in New York during the celebrations marking the UN's fiftieth anniversary.

69. Zeroual and Chirac were later photographed together in discussion at an impromptu meeting in New York on 22 October 1995.

70. Abdelhamid Mehri, *Al-Hayat,* 15 October 1995.

71. Sadi, op. cit.

72. Imam Mesaudi Yaya, Laghouat, 7 November 1995.

73. This rally occurred on 10 November 1995.

74. The Muslim Brotherhood will be examined more closely in Chapter 4.

75. A sheikh is a senior religious scholar.

76. Willis, op. cit., p. 358.

77. Rabia Bekkar, "Taking Up Space in Tlemcen: The Islamist Occupation of Urban Algeria, Interview with Hannah Davis Taieb," in *Political Islam: Essays from Middle East Report*, ed. Joel Beinin and Joe Stork (London: I. B. Tauris, 1997), pp. 283–291.

78. Interview by author, Tlemcen, Algeria, 11 November 1995.

79. Interview by author, Oued al-Jamaa, Algeria, 11 November 1995.

80. Omar Sadi, chief of the civilian defense force, Ammouche, eastern Algeria, interview by author, Ammouche, 15 November 1995.

81. The election was held on 16 November 1995.

82. Interviewed by author, Bab el-Oued, Algiers, 16 November 1995.

83. The final results of the election gave Zeroual 61.34 percent of the vote, Mahfoud Nahnah 25.38 percent, Said Sadi 9.29 percent, and Noureddin Boukrouh 3.9 percent. The official turnout was 75.7 percent of eligible voters.

84. Three organizations sent a total 101 election observers.

85. *The European*, 21 March 1996, quoted in Willis, op. cit., p. 363.

86. Mahfoud Nahnah, interview by author, Algiers, 18 November 1995.

87. Rabeh Kebir, letter to Liamine Zeroual, 19 November 1995.

88. Anwar Haddam, statement, 22 November 1995.

89. Abou Abderrahmane Amine, GIA, statement, 1 December 1995.

90. Founded in the 1960s, the Jazara group began as an Islamic study group with a significant intellectual basis. Mohammed Said allied the group with the FIS in 1991. In May 1994 Said and Abderazak Redjam joined the GIA.

Chapter Four

1. Mamoun al-Hodeibi, interview by author, Cairo, 24 April 1996.

2. Dilip Hiro, *Islamic Fundamentalism*, rev. ed. (London: Paladin, 1989), p. 63.

3. Edward Mortimer, *Faith and Power: The Politics of Islam* (New York: Vintage Books, 1982), p. 231.

4. Faisal, quoted in Edward Mortimer, ibid., p. 232 n.

5. Hejaz is an area in western Saudi Arabia that includes the Muslim holy sites of Mecca and Medina; it was an independent kingdom prior to the unification of most of the Arabian peninsula under Abdul-Aziz ibn Abdul-Rahman Al Sa'ud (King Abdul-Aziz) as Saudi Arabia in 1932.

6. Sayyid Qutb, quoted in Fouad Ajami, "In the Pharaoh's Shadow: Religion and Authority in Egypt," in *Islam in the Political Process*, ed. James P. Piscatori (Cambridge: Cambridge University Press, 1983), p. 25.

7. Edward William Lane, *Manners and Customs of the Modern Egyptians: Written During the Years 1833–1835* (London: Darf, 1986), p. 84.

8. Ibid., p. 94.

9. Ibid., p. 106.

10. Albert Hourani, *Arabic Thought in the Liberal Age, 1798–1939* (Cambridge: Cambridge University Press, 1983), p. 103.

11. Afghanistan, by contrast, is largely Sunni, though the country has a substantial Shia minority among the Hazara tribe in the west. Al-Afghani hoped that by asserting an Afghan rather than Persian identity, he could exert greater influence among Sunni Muslims, who form the majority—around 85 percent—of the world's Muslim population.

12. "The Firmest Bond."

13. Hourani, op. cit., p. 117.

14. Ibid., p. 125.

15. Jamal al-Din al-Afghani, *The Refutation of the Materialists* (Cairo: n.p., 1903), p. 70; quoted in Hourani, op. cit., p. 126.

16. See Chapter 3, n. 27.

17. The Koran, sura 13, verse 11, in *The Message of the Qur'an*, ed. and trans. Muhammad Asad (Gibraltar: Dar al-Andalus, 1980), p. 360.

18. Muhammad Asad, ed. and trans., *The Message of the Qur'an* (Gibraltar: Dar al-Andalus, 1980), p. 360.

19. Hourani, op. cit., p. 129.

20. Ibid., p. 139.

21. Rida describes in his own autobiography how he attended a Sufi meeting that culminated in a dervish dance, in which the devotees spin in a frenzied display. Rida stood up and accused the Sufis of making "religion a joke and a plaything" before walking out in disgust, followed by several other spectators. Rashid Rida, *al-Manar wa'l-Azhar* (Cairo: al-Manar, 1934), p. 129. As with other critics of the Sufis, Rida viewed their attachment to saints as an obstacle between the individual and God, a direct relationship that forms the essence of the religion.

22. "The Beacon" or "The Lighthouse."

23. Hourani, op. cit., p. 228.

24. Ibid., p. 229.

25. Rashid Rida, *al-Wahhabiyyun* (Cairo: al-Manar, 1925), p. 47.

26. Olivier Roy, *The Failure of Political Islam* (London: I. B. Tauris, 1994), p. 34.

27. Richard P. Mitchell, *The Society of the Muslim Brothers* (New York: Oxford University Press, 1993), pp. 4–6.

28. "Al-Mu'tamar al-khamis," bulletin issued by the Muslim Brotherhood, Cairo, 1939, pp. 14–16.

29. Mitchell, op. cit., p. 213.

30. Ibid., p. 223.

31. "Al-Mu'tamar al-khamis," op. cit., pp. 8–9.

32. Ibid., p. 24.

33. Throughout World War II, and until the coup of 23 July 1952, which overthrew the Egyptian monarchy, Egypt was ruled by King Farouq, whose policies and the complexion of whose cabinet were heavily influenced by the British government.

34. Mitchell, op. cit., p. 40.

35. "Ila ayy shay' nad'u al-nas," bulletin issued by the Muslim Brotherhood, Cairo, 1940, pp. 3–4.

36. Mitchell, op. cit., p. 235.

37. Ibid., p. 236.

38. Ibid., p. 238.

39. In 1954 four of those involved in al-Banna's assassination were tried and sentenced to prison terms. Evidence presented at the trials revealed beyond doubt that the assassination was planned and approved by the prime minister with the probable assent of the royal palace.

40. The judge, Ahmad Kamil Bey, later became a member of the Muslim Brotherhood. See Mitchell, op. cit., p. 79.

41. Sayyid Qutb, *Milestones* (Indianapolis: American Trust Publications, 1990), pp. 47–49. The same work, originally published in Arabic as *Maalim fil Tariq,* is sometimes referred to as "Signposts" or "Signposts on the Road."

42. John L. Esposito, *The Islamic Threat: Myth or Reality?* 2nd ed. (New York: Oxford University Press, 1995), p. 127.

43. "There shall be no coercion in matters of faith." The Koran, sura 2, verse 256, in Asad, op. cit., p. 57.

44. Sayyid Qutb, *The Islamic Concept and Its Characteristics,* trans. Mohammed Moinuddin Siddiqui (Indianapolis: American Trust Publications, 1991), pp. 45–48.

45. Qutb, *Milestones,* op. cit., p. 51.

46. Ibid., p. 50.

47. Sayyid Qutb, *Islam and Universal Peace* (Indianapolis: American Trust Publications, 1993), p. 10.

48. Qutb, *Milestones,* op. cit., p. 53.

49. Ibid., p. 59.

50. Ibid., p. 58.

51. "The Orientalists have painted a picture of Islam as a violent movement which imposes its belief upon people by the sword. These dishonest Orientalists know very well this is not true, but by this method they try to distort the true objectives of Islamic jihad. When some of the Muslim scholars—these defeated people—search for the rationale of 'defense' with which to refute this accusation, in their ignorance of the nature of Islam and its function, they ignore the fact that Islam has a right to take the initiative for human freedom." Ibid., p. 62.

52. Ibid.

53. This figure is the brotherhood's own estimate.

54. Qutb, *Islam and Universal Peace,* op. cit., p. 69.

55. Ibid., p. 68.

56. Roy, op. cit., pp. 36–38.

57. Al-Hodeibi, op. cit.

58. Ibid.

59. Adel Hussein, interview by author, Cairo, 25 April 1996.

60. Roy, op. cit., p. 75.

61. Ibid., p. 76.

Chapter Five

1. Nadia Yassine, interview by author, Salé, Morocco, 9 July 1996.

2. Pronounced *Sarlay,* the town is the twin of the Moroccan capital, Rabat, from which it is separated by the Bouregreg river.

3. Fathallah Arsalan, interview by author, Rabat, 8 December 1995.

4. *Makhzan*, an Arabic word with various pronunciations across the Arab world, means literally "those to whom taxes are paid." In Morocco the word is used as a general term identifying the ruling elite, at the center of which is the monarch, who holds absolute power despite the presence of opposition parties, a parliament, and a prime minister.

5. Mustapha Ramid, interview by author, Casablanca, 7 December 1995.

6. Morocco has several secular opposition parties, which have representation in parliament.

7. Mohammed Yatim, interview by author, Rabat, 10 December 1995.

8. "Movement for Rebirth and Renewal."

9. Mahdi Elmandjra, "Future Studies: Needs, Facts, and Prospects" (paper presented at the Symposium on the Future of the Islamic World, Algiers, May, 1990).

10. Ibid.

11. Taha Husayn, *The Future of Culture in Egypt*, trans. S. Glazer.

12. For the most detailed account of this period in Moroccan history, see Gilles Perrault, *Notre ami le roi* (Paris: Gallimard, 1990), pp. 45–57. The passage cited is my translation.

13. John L. Esposito, *The Islamic Threat: Myth or Reality?* 2nd ed. (New York: Oxford University Press, 1995), p. 167.

14. Ibid., p. 165.

15. Elmandjra, op. cit.; the figures are from UNESCO.

16. For a detailed account of the group's evolution, see Ammar Belhimer, "Les groupes armes de l'opposition islamique," *Les Cahiers de L'Orient*, nos. 36-37 (fourth quarter 1994–first quarter 1995):61–92.

17. This figure is probably an exaggeration. Other estimates put the GIA membership between 2,000 and 3,000 (Algerian interior ministry, quoted in *Le Monde*, 4–5 June 1995) and 8,000 (*L'Express*, 5 January 1995).

18. Djamel Zitouni, who was appointed head of the GIA's *kitaeb el-mout*, or death squad, in 1994, and became emir of the GIA later that year. He was killed during an internal feud in 1996.

19. The Algerian daily *Le Matin* claimed that Mekhloufi had at times taken refuge in Morocco, supporting the Algerian contention that Morocco was supporting the Islamists in order to strengthen its hand in the twenty-year conflict between the two countries over the disputed Western Sahara. *Le Matin*, 25 September 1994.

20. Armée Islamique de Salut (Islamic Army of Salvation), the armed wing of the FIS, which has operated with increasing independence from the FIS owing to the latter's loss of political influence and the imprisonment or departure underground or abroad of its leaders.

21. Yassine, op. cit.

22. For a detailed account of Ghannouchi's development, see François Burgat, *L'Islamisme en Face* (Paris: La Decouverte, 1995), pp. 48–60.

23. Ibid., p. 120.

24. "Tunisia's Renaissance Party provides an example of the radicalization of movements in response to government manipulation of the political sys-

tem, suppression, or violence. Increased government repression intimidates, factionalizes, and radicalizes. The result has been an escalation of confrontation and violence." Esposito, op. cit., p. 163.

25. Rached Ghannouchi, interview by author, London, 5 May 1996.

26. Gustave von Grunebaum, *Modern Islam* (Westport, Conn.: Greenwood Press, 1962).

27. Ibid.

28. For a detailed analysis of the social makeup of the Islamist movements of the Middle East, see Nazih Ayubi, *Political Islam: Religion and Politics in the Arab World* (London and New York: Routledge, 1994), pp. 70–177.

29. Hosam Issa, interview by author, Cairo, 24 April 1996.

30. Edward Mortimer, *Faith and Power: The Politics of Islam* (New York: Vintage Books, 1982), pp. 283–284.

31. Albert Hourani, *Arabic Thought in the Liberal Age, 1798–1939* (Cambridge: Cambridge University Press, 1962), pp. 193–194.

32. Ibid., p. 272.

33. Cairo's thousand-year-old Islamic university, whose sheikh is the highest legal authority in Sunni Islam.

34. Mortimer, op. cit., p. 273.

35. Adel Hussein, interview by author, Cairo, 25 April 1996.

36. Mohamed Sid Ahmed, interview by author, Cairo, 26 April 1996.

37. According to Esposito, the fallout from the defeat of 1967 was felt as acutely among the Muslim populations of Southeast Asia as it was among those of the Middle East, who had been directly involved. See Esposito, op. cit., pp. 12–15.

38. Ayubi, op. cit., p. 177.

39. Carrie Rosefsky Wickham, "Islamic Mobilization and Political Change: The Islamist Trend in Egypt's Professional Associations," in *Political Islam: Essays from Middle East Report,* ed. Joel Beinin and Joe Stork (London and New York: I. B. Tauris, 1997).

40. Islamist-oriented candidates in Egypt have scored highly in professional union elections as well as in student organizations. This is well documented in Wickham, op. cit.

41. This issue will be examined more closely in Chapter 6.

42. Seif al-Islam al-Banna, interview by author, Cairo, 27 April 1996.

43. Hussein, op. cit.

44. The Islamic Group, one of Egypt's leading militant Islamist organizations.

45. Adel Hussein, op. cit.

46. Yasser al-Sirri, interview by author, London, 17 August 1997.

47. This strategy was successfully practiced by Hassan al-Banna, the founder of the Muslim Brotherhood, during much of his life. Rejection of this strategy by the militant groups that broke away from the mainstream Muslim Brotherhood can be regarded as one aspect of these groups' general rejection of what they perceived as the brotherhood's passive approach, their exasperation with which had led to other, more militant groups being established. The distance between the Gama'a al-Islamiyya and the Muslim Brotherhood was

demonstrated when followers of the Gama'a, forced to share prison facilities with the brotherhood at various times, refused to pray alongside the latter, not believing them to be true Muslims.

48. Killings in Upper Egypt, the epicenter of the armed groups' activities during the 1992–1997 period, did continue after the cease-fire call, suggesting that the jailed leaders who had made the call did not have extensive influence over the activists.

49. Muntassir al-Zayat, interview by author, Cairo, 19 November 1997.

50. This label is used by several Islamist organizations to denote Israel.

51. Sheikh Omar Abdel Rahman.

52. "A Statement for the People," issued by Gama'a al-Islamiyya, 18 November 1997. Translated by Rania al-Razzaz.

53. Statement issued by Gama'a al-Islamiyya, 19 November 1997. Translated by Rania al-Razzaz.

54. Statement issued by Gama'a al-Islamiyya, 7 December 1997. Translated by Rania al-Razzaz.

55. Al-Sirri provided details of the discussions at a press conference in London on 23 December 1997.

56. Mohamed al-Massari, interview by author, London, 27 July 1997.

57. Khaled al-Fauwaz, interview by author, London, 30 October 1996.

58. Olivier Roy, *The Failure of Political Islam* (London: I. B. Tauris, 1994), pp. 75–88.

59. Al-Fauwaz, op. cit.

60. Ibid.

61. Ibid.

62. Mecca and Medina, the birthplaces of Islam, are both in Saudi Arabia.

Chapter Six

1. Hammadi Benjaballah, interview by author, Tunis, 29 April 1996.

2. "Ben Ali Discusses Opposition Parties, Democracy," *FBIS-NES*, no. 29 (December 1989).

3. Samuel P. Huntington, *The Clash of Civilizations and the Remaking of World Order* (New York: Simon and Schuster, 1996).

4. Ibid., p. 114. Huntington does not feel inclined to examine the methods by which the Islamic world became familiar with Western ideas. He ignores the humiliation and impact of colonialism, and he does not take into account the many years spent in the West by most of the leading Islamists of the late nineteenth and twentieth centuries, from Sayyid Jamal al-Din al-Afghani to Sayyid Qutb and Hassan al-Tourabi.

5. The French term *integriste* literally means "one who would integrate." In this context it is applied to those who would integrate religious principles into the practice of government.

6. Jelloul Jeribi, interview by author, Tunis, 29 April 1996.

7. Fethi Howiedi, secretary of state for information, Tunisia, interview by author, Tunis, 30 April 1996.

8. Soukaina Bouraoui, interview by author, Tunis, 30 April 1996.

9. Redha Malek, telephone interview by author, 6 April 1996.

10. Mohammed Arezki Boumendil, telephone interview by author, 6 April 1996.

11. Liamine Zeroual, speech of 11 May 1996, Algérie Press Service.

12. *Financial Times,* 10 September 1997.

13. Statement issued by the AIS, 23 September 1997.

14. Such accusations against the security forces first emerged on 1 October 1997 in U.S. Senate hearings, when American academics giving evidence to the Senate Subcommittee on Near Eastern and South Asian Affairs suggested that the areas worst hit at that time by the violence were Islamist strongholds in which rival Islamists fought each other while the army stood back and failed to protect the civilians trapped in the middle.

15. The three-man mission sent on 19 January 1998 included senior foreign office ministers from Great Britain, Austria, and Luxembourg.

16. Statement issued by the European Union Council for Foreign Affairs, 26 January 1998.

17. Hassan al-Alfi, interview by author, Cairo, 1 April 1997. Al-Alfi resigned after the killing of fifty-eight foreign tourists and four Egyptians by the Gama'a al-Islamiyya at Luxor on 16 November 1997.

18. Saad Eddin Ibrahim, interview by author, Cairo, 25 April 1996.

19. This is Esposito's term. John L. Esposito, *The Islamic Threat: Myth or Reality?* 2nd ed. (New York: Oxford University Press, 1995), p. 97.

20. Youssef al-Badri, interview by author, Cairo, 20 July 1997.

21. Fouad Ajami, "The Arab Inheritance," *Foreign Affairs* 76, no. 5 (September-October 1997):133–148.

22. Ibid., 145.

23. Mohamed Sid Ahmed, interview by author, Cairo, 25 April 1996.

24. This famous line asserting one's right to choose one's own path is from the 109th sura of the Koran and has been used by secularists to confront the violent campaign of compulsion used by radical Islamist groups. In *The Message of the Qur'an,* ed. and trans. Muhammad Asad (Gibraltar: Dar al-Andalus, 1980), p. 981.

25. Rachid Mimouni, *De la barbarie en général et de l'intégrisme en particulier* (Paris: Ceres-Eddif, 1992).

26. Ibid., p. 7. My translation.

27. Ibid., pp. 165–166. My translation.

28. Dilip Hiro, *Islamic Fundamentalism,* rev. ed. (London: Paladin, 1989), p. 74.

29. Fred Halliday, *Islam and the Myth of Confrontation: Religion and Politics in the Middle East* (London: I. B. Tauris, 1996), p. 114.

30. François Burgat, *L'Islamisme en Face* (Paris: La Decouverte, 1995), p. 74. My translation.

31. Ibid., p. 78.

32. Ibid., p. 97.

33. Ajami, op. cit., 147.

34. Halliday, op. cit., p. 113.

35. Ibid., p. 119.

36. Huntington, op. cit., pp. 264–265.

37. Ibid., p. 264.

Chapter Seven

1. See note 8 below.

2. J. Spencer Trimingham, *Islam in the Sudan* (London: Frank Cass and Co., 1949), p. 195.

3. Ibid., pp. 195–196.

4. Ibid., p. 200.

5. The Koran, sura 43, verse 61, in *The Message of the Qur'an*, ed. and trans. Muhammad Asad (Gibraltar: Dar al-Andalus, 1980), p. 756.

6. Trimingham, op. cit., p. 151.

7. Ibid.

8. "Dervish" comes from the Arabic word *darwish*, which essentially means "poor," though in the context of the Mahdist state *darwish* referred to the rank and file of the Sufi orders, who became the *ansar* or "helpers"—effectively the most loyal followers—of the Mahdi.

9. The name given to the historical period of the Mahdist state.

10. Thomas Pakenham, *The Scramble for Africa, 1876–1912* (London: Abacus, 1992), p. 265.

11. Ibid., p. 544.

12. Literally, "brothers by the same father and mother."

13. P. M. Holt and M. W. Daly, *The History of the Sudan, From the Coming of Islam to the Present Day* (London: Weidenfeld and Nicholson, 1979), p. 148.

14. In December 1967, al-Azhari merged the NUP with the Peoples' Democratic Party (PDP) to form the Democratic Unionist Party, the DUP. The PDP drew much of its support from the Khatmiyya Sufi sect led by Sayyid 'Ali al-Mirghani. The DUP has ever since been regarded as the political party of the Khatmiyya much as the Umma Party is regarded as the political party of the Ansar sect.

15. Omar Hassan al-Bashir, president of Sudan, interview by author, Khartoum, 15 December 1993.

16. Hassan al-Tourabi, interview by author, Khartoum, 15 December 1993.

17. Hibir Yussuf al-Dayim, interview by author, Khartoum, 14 December 1993.

18. Baha al-Din Hanafi, interview by author, Khartoum, 13 December 1993.

19. The PAIC, or Pan-Arab and Islamic Conference, holds a biannual conference in Khartoum to discuss Islamic affairs. Hassan al-Tourabi's only official post, before he was elected speaker of the Sudan national assembly in 1996, was secretary general of the PAIC.

20. Sadiq al-Mahdi, interview by author, Omdurman, 16 December 1993.

21. The rejection of force is raised in the Koran in several different contexts: "Whoso doeth that through aggression and injustice, We shall cast him into the fire, and that is ever easy for Allah" (sura 4, verse 30); "Fight in the way of Allah against those who fight against you, but begin not hostilities. Lo! Allah loveth not aggressors" (sura 2, verse 190); "I do not worship that which you worship, and neither do you worship that which I worship. And I will not worship that which you have ever worshipped, and neither will you [ever] worship that which I worship. Unto you, your moral law, and unto me, mine" (sura 109, verses 1–6).

22. See note 21 above.

23. Mohammed al-Amin Khalifa, interview by author, Khartoum, 13 December 1993.

24. This figure and other information on the domestic policy of the NIF at this time was provided by Mohamed Ahamed Abdelgadir al-Arabab, a former provincial state minister who fled Sudan in March 1995. Interview by author, Asmara, Eritrea, 5 May 1995.

25. Hassan al-Tourabi, "The Islamic State," *Voices of Resurgent Islam*, ed. John L. Esposito (New York: Oxford University Press, 1983), pp. 245–246.

26. *Tawhid* means the unity of God and human life, which deems all public life religious and considers the purpose of public life as being the pursuit of the service of God as laid down in the religious law, the *sharia*.

27. Al-Tourabi, "The Islamic State," op. cit., p. 247.

28. Ibid., p. 249.

29. Tayeb Salih, *Season of Migration to the North*, trans. Denys Johnson-Davies (London: Quartet, 1969), p. 168.

30. Peter Rit Machar, interview by author, Ayod, Sudan, 30 March 1993.

31. Colonel John Garang, interview by author, Nairobi, 12 April 1995.

32. Hassan al-Tourabi, interview by author, Khartoum, 29 April 1995.

33. Sadiq al-Mahdi, interview by author, Omdurman, 25 April 1995.

34. This figure was provided by Baha al-Din Hanafi, director of President al-Bashir's political department.

35. Al-Tayib Zain Al-Abdin, interview by author, Khartoum, 31 May 1997.

36. Hassan al-Tourabi, interview by author, Khartoum, 3 June 1997.

37. The Oslo agreement, brokered by the Norwegian government and signed by the Palestinian Liberation Authority and Israel, established the principle that Israel would withdraw from the areas of Palestine it had occupied during the Six-Day War and would recognize the establishment of an independent Palestinian state on the West Bank and the Gaza Strip. In return, Arab states would move toward the normalization of their relations with Israel, including taking measures to allow Israel to be assured of its external security.

38. Mounir Said, interview by author, Khartoum, 30 April 1995.

39. Al-Tourabi, interview, 3 June 1997, op. cit.

40. Al-Tourabi, interview, 29 April 1995, op. cit.

41. Al-Arabab, op. cit.

42. Idriss Mohamed Idriss, interview by author, Kashm al-Girba, Sudan, 3 May 1995.

43. Sheikh Mohamed Ismael Ali, interview by author, Kashm al-Girba, Sudan, 3 May 1995.

44. Ghazi Salah Eddin Atabani, interview by author, Khartoum, 29 April 1995.

45. Interview by author, 19 April 1995.

46. Saleh Kekia, interview by author, Asmara, 6 May 1995.

47. Karim Omar, interview by author, London, 15–16 January 1997.

Chapter Eight

1. Osama Bin Laden, "Declaration of the World Islamic Front for Jihad Against the Jews and Crusaders," *Al-Quds Al-Arabi*, 23 February 1998.

2. Bernard Lewis, "License to Kill: Usama Bin Ladin's Declaration of Jihad," *Foreign Affairs* 77, no. 6, (November/December 1998):16.

3. The phrase "dialogue of civilizations" is that of President Mohamed Khatami of Iran.

4. Patrick Seale, *Asad: The Struggle for the Middle East* (Berkeley: University of California Press, 1988), pp. 160–161. The "Black September" crisis of September 1970 occurred when King Hussein of Jordan attacked the Palestinian refugee population in Jordan, with the aim of forcing Yasser Arafat and the Palestinian Liberation Organization out of Jordan. King Hussein feared that the PLO intended to seize effective power in Jordan, a country in which 60 percent of the population is Palestinian.

5. Madeleine K. Albright, U.S. secretary of state, "The Testing of American Foreign Policy," *Foreign Affairs* 77, no. 6 (November/December 1998):50.

6. UN Security Council Resolution 242 of 22 November 1967 proposed that Israel should return occupied land to the Arab countries to which it had historically belonged, in return for peace with those states.

7. The Declaration of Principles was signed in Oslo, Norway, on 20 August 1993.

8. Uri Savir, *The Process: 1,100 Days that Changed the Middle East* (New York: Random House, 1998), pp. 4–5. Uri Savir was Israel's chief negotiator in talks with the Palestinian Liberation Organization.

9. Said K. Aburish, *A Brutal Friendship: The West and the Arab Elite* (London: Indigo, 1998), pp. 30–31.

10. Albright, op. cit.

11. Samuel P. Huntington, "The Lonely Superpower," *Foreign Affairs* 78, no.2 (March/April 1999):39.

12. Ibid., p. 49.

13. See Samuel P .Huntington, *The Clash of Civilizations and the Remaking of World Order* (New York: Simon and Schuster, 1996).

14. Kasim al-Taie, interview by author, Baghdad, March 1998.

15. One U.S. dollar was then worth 1,200 Iraqi dinars.

16. Hussein Fadelrahim, interview by author, Baghdad, March 1998.

17. Edward W. Said, "Apocalypse Now," in *Acts of Aggression: Policing Rogue States* (New York: Seven Stories Press, 1999), p. 8.

18. Ibid.

19. John Mueller and Karl Mueller, "Sanctions of Mass Destruction," *Foreign Affairs* 78, no. 3 (May\June 1999):49.

20. aid, op. cit., pp. 7–9.

21. Netanyahu was defeated by the Labor Party leader, Ehud Barak. Barak won 56 percent of the votes, to Netanyahu's 43.9 percent.

22. David Hirst, *The Gun and the Olive Branch: The Roots of Violence in the Middle East* (London: Faber and Faber, 1977), p. 350.

23. Doron Rosenblum, *Ha'aretz*, 18 May 1999.

24. Interview by author, Baghdad, 14 March 1998.

25. Hosni Mubarak, president of Egypt, interview by author, Cairo, 15 February 1998.

26. Ambassador David Newton, U.S. State Department, press conference, Cairo, 17 February 1998.

27. Mubarak, op. cit.

28. UNSCOM (the United Nations Special Commission on Iraq).

29. Noam Chomsky, *World Orders Old and New* (London: Pluto Press, 1996), p. 10.

30. Noam Chomsky, "Rogue States," in *Acts of Aggression: Policing Rogue States*, op. cit., p. 15.

31. Hosni Mubarak, official statement, Cairo, 17 December 1998.

32. OIC statement, 17 December 1998.

33. Hosni Mubarak, interview with *Al Ahram*, Cairo, 1 January 1999.

34. Interview by author, Cairo, 16 January 1999.

35. Mohammed Saeed al-Sahaf, press conference, Baghdad, 13 January 1999.

36. Dispatch, Saudi Arabian News Agency, Riyadh, 14 January 1999.

37. Seale, op. cit., p. 265.

38. The same is true of Hafez al-Asad, the Syrian president, whose military campaign against the Muslim Brotherhood in 1981 escalated into a war against the movement that left thousands dead. Asad's role in the region is much more complex vis-à-vis U.S. strategy, and his vital role in the Middle East peace process has probably been the reason that the United States has refrained from daubing him a "rogue," despite his rigid opposition to Israeli manipulation of regional politics.

39. Donald C. F. Daniel and Andrew L. Ross, "U.S. Strategic Planning and the Pivotal States," in *The Pivotal States: A New Framework for U.S. Policy in the Developing World*, ed. Robert Chase, Emily Hill, and Paul Kennedy (New York: W. W. Norton and Co., 1999), p. 398.

40. Daniel Byman, Kenneth Polack, and Gideon Rose, "The Rollback Fantasy," *Foreign Affairs* 78, no. 1 (January/February 1999): p. 37.

41. Ibid., pp. 37–38.

42. Mueller and Mueller, op. cit.

43. Iraqi academic, Interview by author, Baghdad, 16 March 1998.

44. European diplomat, interview by author, Baghdad, 16 March 1998.

45. Riyadh al-Qaysi, Iraqi deputy foreign minister, interview by author, Baghdad, 16 March 1998.

46. Interview by author, Tehran, 20 September 1998.

47. See Aburish, op. cit., p. 248.

48. Ibid.

49. Osman Khalid Mudawi, interview by author, Khartoum, 26 August 1998.

50. Hassan Maki Muhammed, Dean of the Centre for Research and African Studies, International University of Africa, interview by author, Khartoum, 26 August 1998.

51. See Bin Laden, op. cit.

52. Robert Fisk, *The Independent*, 9 August 1998.

53. This was confirmed to me by a British diplomat in Khartoum.

54. This was confirmed to me by a senior Sudanese minister in Khartoum.

55. European diplomat, interview by author, Khartoum, 25 August 1998.

56. Ghazi Salah Eddin Atabani, interview by author, Khartoum, 25 August 1998.

57. Amr Moussa, press conference, Cairo, 21 August 1998.

58. President el-Bashir confirmed this at a press conference in Khartoum, 24 August 1998.

59. Hassan al-Tourabi, interview by author, Khartoum, 26 August 1998.

60. Vahe Petrossian, *Middle East Economic Digest* 43, no. 6 (12 February 1999):2.

61. Gholam Ali Koshroo, senior adviser to Iran's foreign minister, interview by author, Tehran, 19 September 1998.

62. What Mr. Koshroo refers to as the "Iraq war" was the 1980–1988 Iran–Iraq war, launched by Iraq; it is often referred to as the First Gulf War. Also, he speaks of a possible war with Afghanistan because at the time of this interview the Taleban leaders in Iran and Afghanistan were engaged in a war of words following the murder by the Taleban of several Iranian diplomats who had been stationed in the northern town of Mazar-i-Sharif. Iran had long supported the northern alliance of Afghan factions opposed to the Taleban.

63. Interview by author, Tehran, 20 September 1998.

64. Sadeq Zibakalem, interview by author, Tehran, 23 September 1998.

65. Savir, op. cit.

66. Said K. Aburish, *Arafat: From Defender to Dictator* (London: Bloomsbury, 1998), p. 262.

Conclusion

1. Muntassir al-Zayat, interview by author, Cairo, 22 April 1999.

Index

Abbas, Ferhat, 49
Abbas, Hamed, 111
Abboud, Ibrahim, 146
'Abdallahi, Khalifa, 144
Abdin, Al-Tayib Zain Al-, 158
Abdirashid, Hafez, 17
Abduh, Muhammad, 78–80, 104
Abouhalima, Mahmoud, 14
Abu Bakr, 172(n17)
Abu Zeid, Nasr Hamed, 131, 132
Advice and Reformation Committee
    (ARC), 113, 114, 115
Afghani, Sayyid Jamal al-Din al-, 76–78,
    104, 138
Afghanistan, 1–24
    aftermath of war in, 14–16
    gathering of Arab Islamists in, 3–4
    international conflict about, 22–24
    Marxist government in, 20–22
    origins of Islamist movement in, 2–3
    politics of Islam and, 5–9
    repercussions of arms supplies to,
        11–14
    Taliban aggression in, 16–20
    U.S. military support in, 9–11
Ahmed, Abu Abdallah, 100
Ahmed, Mohamed Sid, 107, 134, 136
Aideed, Mohamed Farah, 35, 37–41,
    174(n31)
AIS. See Islamic Army of Salvation
Ajaj, Ahmad, 14
Ajami, Fouad, 133, 137
Akhund, Sheikh Mohamed Omar, 16
Akhunzada, Mawlawi Abdarab, 19–20
Al-Adl wa'l Ihsane, 94–96, 97
Alasow, Abdi Ali, 42
Al-Azhar University, 82, 107, 132,
    183(n33)
Albright, Madeleine, 41
Alfi, Hassan al-, 130, 185(n17)

Algeria, 46–72
    anti-Islamists in, 61, 62, 100, 122, 128,
        135
    colonial rule in, 47–50, 54–55, 72
    elections in, 69–71, 126
    French influence in, 61, 63–64
    government upheaval in, 55–65,
        125–126
    internal violence in, 62–63, 69–70, 72,
        99–101, 123, 127–128, 185(n14)
    National Contract of, 123–124,
        178(n54)
    political campaigning in, 65–69
    war of independence in, 49–50, 64, 69
Ali, Sheikh Mohamed Ismael, 162
Ali, Siddiq Ibrahim Siddiq, 14
Amanullah, King of Afghanistan, 5, 8
Amine, Abou Abderrahmane, 71
Anya Nya movement, 146
Arabab, Mohamed Ahamed Abdelgadir al-,
    161
Arab Democratic Nasserite Party, 105
Arabia, 94–116
Arabic glossary, xiii-xiv
Arabism, 75
Arab League, 85, 160
Arab nationalism, 105
Arafat, Yasser, 136
ARC. See Advice and Reformation
    Committee
Armed Islamic Group (GIA), 59, 61–62,
    70, 71–72, 100, 123, 128, 161, 166
Arraya, al- (newspaper), 97
Arsalan, Fathallah, 95
Ashigga party, 145
Assimilation, by Muslims into European
    culture, 54, 55, 104
Association of Algerian Ulama (AUMA),
    48–50, 54, 58, 65, 74, 103
Atabani, Ghazi Salah Eddin, 152, 158,
    162, 163

221

Ataturk, Kemal, 81
AUMA. *See* Association of Algerian
    Ulama
Autocracy, 130
Awali, Mohamed, 38
Azhari, Isma'il al-, 145, 146
Azzam, Sheikh Abdallah, 2, 169(n4)

Badis, Abd al-Hamid Ibn "Ben," 49, 65, 74
Badri, Youssef al-, 131
Bangladesh, 8
Banna, Hassan al-, 74, 81–86, 109,
    169(n5), 183(n47)
Banna, Seif al-Islam al-, 109
Barre, Mohamed Siad, 34–35, 41, 44
Bashir, Omar Hassan al-, 38, 147–148,
    152, 158, 165
Bekkar, Rabia, 67
Belhadj, Ali, 61, 123
Belkhadem, Abdelaziz, 56
Ben Ali, Zein al-Abdin, 102, 117–118,
    120, 121
Ben Barka, Mehdi, 98
Benhabyles, Abdelmalek, 56–57
Benjaballah, Hammadi, 117, 118, 119, 120
Benjeddid, Chadli, 56, 57
Bhutto, Benazir, 13
Bin Laden, Osama, 2–3, 40–41, 114, 115,
    130, 163, 164, 169(n7)
Boudiaf, Mohamed, 57, 60
Boumendil, Mohammed Arezki, 125
Bouraoui, Soukaina, 121
Bourguiba, Habib, 101, 102, 117
British colonialism
    Muslim opposition to, 81, 82, 84
    Sudanese politics and, 144–145, 146
Burgat, François, 32, 54, 101, 135

Cairo, Egypt, xvi, 105
Carter, Jimmy, 10
Casey, William, 11, 171(n24)
CDLR. *See* Committee for the Defence of
    Legitimate Rights
Central Intelligence Agency (CIA), 10–11,
    12
Chaoudi, Ayachi, 62
Cherif, Gousmi, 71
Chirac, Jacques, 63–64
Christians, 110
CIA. *See* Central Intelligence Agency
Claes, Willy, 168

Clan politics. *See* Tribalism
*Clash of Civilizations and the Remaking
    of World Order, The* (Huntington),
    118
Cohen, Herman, 38
Cold War, 106, 139, 167
Colonialism
    in Algeria, 47–50, 54–55, 72
    Arab nationalism and, 106
    in Egypt, 74–75
    Islamic culture and, 50–55, 93, 184(n4)
    Islamism as response to, 103
    in Morocco, 98
Committee for the Defence of Legitimate
    Rights (CDLR), 112, 114
Communist party, 6–7, 49, 146
Community of Muslims, 24, 32, 77, 81,
    92, 106, 138, 168
Coptic Christians, 110
Courts, Islamic, 25–28, 29, 31, 42, 81,
    174(n36)
Crusades, 51, 53

Dayim, Hibir Yussuf al-, 149
Democracy, 61–62, 124–125, 148, 149,
    167
Democratic Unionist Party (DUP), 147,
    150, 186(n14)
Dere, Sheikh Ali, 25–28, 33
Dervish, 141, 144, 186(n8)
Din (Islamic way of life), 87–89
Diwani, Ahmed, 69
Dostum, Rashid, 23
Dudayev, Dzhokar, 14
DUP. *See* Democratic Unionist Party

Education
    illiteracy and, 99
    in Tunisia, 118, 119–120
Egypt, 73–93
    anticolonialism in, 74
    call to jihad in, 87–89
    cultural identity in, 74–75
    government system in, 132–134
    Islamist movements in, 89–93,
        108–112, 129–136
    Muslim Brotherhood in, 65, 81–86
    religious establishment in, 131–132
    scholarship in, 76–81, 131–132
    Six-Day War of 1967 and, 105, 107
    Sudanese relations with, 163, 164–165

Egyptian Labour Party, 107
Eid, Ali, 14
Electoral rigging, 70, 126
Elmandjra, Mahdi, 97, 98
Ennahda (Renaissance) Party, 101, 102, 117–119, 120, 121, 182(n24)
Eradicateurs, 61, 62, 100, 122, 128, 135
Eritrea, 157, 161, 162, 163
Esposito, John, 99
Ethiopia, 34–35, 157, 164
European Union, 128

Farah, Said Mohamed, 26
Farouq, King of Egypt, 84, 86, 87, 180(n33)
Farshouty, Mahmoud, 111
Fauwaz, Khaled al-, 113, 115
FFS. *See* Socialist Forces Front
FIS. *See* Islamic Salvation Front
FLN. *See* National Liberation Front
French colonialism
    in Algeria, 47–50, 175(n3)
    and interests in Sudan, 145
Fundamentalism, xvii-xviii

Gad Al-Haq Ali Gad Al-Haq, Grand Sheikh of Al-Azhar, 131
Gama'a al-Islamiyya, al-, 14, 109, 110–111, 166
Garang, John, 155, 156, 157, 158
Gaulle, Charles de, 63–64
GGC. *See* Graduates' General Congress
Ghannouchi, Rached, 101, 102–103, 119
GIA. *See* Armed Islamic Group
Globalism, 136, 138
Glossary of Arabic terms, xiii-xiv
Gordon, George, 142, 143, 144
Graduates' General Congress (GGC), 145–146
Great Britain. *See* British colonialism
Gulf War, 113–114

Haddam, Anwar, 61, 62, 71, 72, 123
Hadi, Sayyid al-, 146
Halliday, Fred, 39, 53, 135, 137
Hamas (Movement of the Islamic Society), 65–67, 126
Hamza, Mustapha, 111, 130
Hanafi, Baha al-Din, 37, 150, 152, 155
Hanafi, Hassan, 132
Harakat al-Dawla Islamiyya, 100
Hassan, Amina Ali, 25

Hassan, Sheikh Mohamed Moalim, 36
Hassan II, King of Morocco, 95, 98
Hassanyar, Amir, 21–22
HCE. *See* High Committee of State
HCS. *See* High Council for Security
Hejaz, 75, 179(n5)
Hekmatyar, Gulbeddin, 8, 13, 21
High Committee of State (HCE), 57, 60, 177(n40)
High Council for Security (HCS), 57
Hiro, Dilip, 33, 54, 134
Hodeibi, Mamoun al-, 73, 74, 90–91
Horn of Africa, 44, 174(n38)
Hourani, Albert, 51–52, 76, 81, 106
Huntington, Samuel P., xv, 118, 138–139
Husayn, Taha, 98, 106
Hussain, Sharif, 75
Hussein, Adel, 91–92, 107, 109

Ibrahim, Saad Eddin, 130
Idriss, Idriss Mohamed, 162
Ijtihad (individual reflection), 76, 77, 79, 80, 83, 85, 106, 119, 131, 176(n25)
Illiteracy, 99
Intellectuals, 8, 80. *See also* Scholarship
Inter-Services Intelligence (ISI), 9, 10, 12
Iran
    Islamic revolution in, 7
    support for Somalia from, 36–37, 41
ISI. *See* Inter-Services Intelligence
Islam
    academic study of, 51–53
    Arabism and, 75
    cultural differences within, 138–139
    European colonialism and, 50–55
    five pillars of, 170(n15)
    glossary of terms, xiii-xiv
    historical origins of, 29–32
    mystical sects of, 141–142
    political division of, 172(n17)
    popular version of, 48, 54
    scholarship and the revival of, 76–81
    Western attitudes toward, xv-xvi, 137–138
    See also Islamism; Muslims
Islambouli, Mohammed Shawky al-, 14
Islamic Army of Salvation (AIS), 61, 71, 72, 127, 128, 182(n20)
Islamic Jihad movement, 162

Islamic Salvation Front (FIS), 56, 57–59, 61, 62, 65, 66–67, 71, 72, 99–100, 120, 122–124, 126, 127–128, 161
Islamic Tendency Movement (MTI), 101
Islamism, xvii–xviii
    Arabism and, 75
    contemporary forms of, 92–93
    eradicateurs of, 61, 62, 100, 122, 128
    future of, 166–168
    governmental power and, 116, 134–136, 148–149, 151
    historical origins of, 1–2, 76–81
    Muslim Brotherhood and, 81–86
    national character of, 138–139
    political weakness of, 121–122
    secular nationalism and, 104–106, 117–121
    Western criticism of, 137–138
Israel
    founding of, 86
    Six-Day War of 1967 and, 105, 107
    territorial conflicts with, 137, 160
Issa, Hosam, 105

Jamaat-i Islami, 9, 29
Jazara Islamic group, 71
Jeribi, Jelloul, 119
Jerusalem, 137
Jess, Omar, 38
Jihad, 2, 24, 87–89, 93, 155, 162
Jihad al-Islamiyya, al-, 162
Jili'ow, Ahmed, 37
Johnson, Samuel, 51
Journalists, 61

Kabul, Afghanistan, 16, 19, 21–22
Kabul University, 8, 19, 21–22
Kafi, Ali, 60
Kashm al-Girba refugee camp, 162, 163
Kebir, Rabeh, 61, 71, 72, 122, 123, 124
Kekia, Saleh, 163
Kenya, 35
Khalifa, Magzoub al-, 158
Khalifa, Mohammed al-Amin, 152
Khan, Akhtar Abdul Rehman, 10
Khartoum University, 158, 160
Khatmiyya Sufi order, 145
Kipling, Rudyard, 22
Kitchener, Horatio Herbert, 144–145
Koran, 20, 51, 79, 85, 88, 99, 142, 152, 185(n24), 187(n21)

Lacoste, Yves, 63
Lamari, Mohammed, 122, 178(n57)

Lane, Edward, 75
Lutfi, Adil, 112

Machar, Peter Rit, 154
Madani, Abassi, 61, 65, 123, 127
Madani, Tewfik, 50
Maghreb, 48, 94–116
Mahdi, Sayyid 'Abd al-Rahman al-, 145
Mahdi, Sayyid Sadiq al-, 146, 147, 150, 151–152, 154, 156–157, 163, 166, 167
Mahdi, Sayyid Siddiq al-, 145, 146
Mahdism
    roots of, 142–143
    Sudanese politics and, 143–145
    Sufism and, 143–144
Makhzan (ruling elite), 98, 182(n4)
Malek, Redha, 62, 122, 124, 178(n61)
Manar, al- (periodical), 80
Marabouts, 48, 175(n6)
Marchand, Jean-Baptiste, 145
Marchetti, Victor, 12
Marxism, 6–7
Massari, Mohamed al-, 112–113, 114–115
Massoud, Ahmed Shah, 8, 23
Maududi, Sayyid Abul A'la, 9, 29, 30, 31, 32, 35
Mebarak, Mahiou, 60
Mecca, 33, 75, 144, 184(n62)
Mediation, 148
Medina, 184(n62)
Medinese era, 33
Mehri, Abdelhamid, 60, 64
Mekhloufi, Said, 100, 182(n19)
Mekkawi, Ibrahim al-, 14
Mengistu Mariam, Haile, 34
Mezrag, Madani, 127
MIA. *See* Mouvement Islamique Armée
Middle East, xvi, 117–139, 161
Mimouni, Rachid, 134
Mirghani, Osman al-, 150, 158
Mirghani, Sayyid 'Ali al-, 145
Mitchell, Richard, 83, 85
Modernism, 105–106
Mohamed, Ali Mahdi, 33, 37–38
Mohammed ibn Abdullah (the Prophet), 5, 7, 29–32, 51, 79, 97, 170(n15), 172(n17)
Moral education, 48
Morocco
    Islamist movement in, 94–97
    political environment in, 97–99
Mortimer, Edward, 105

Motaqi, Mullah Amid Khan, 15
Mourad, Bentounes Kelim, 46
Mourad, Sid Ahmed, 61
Mouvement de la Renaissance et de
    Renouveau, 97
Mouvement Islamique Armée (MIA), 59
Movement for a Peaceful Society (MSP),
    126. *See also* Hamas
MTI. *See* Islamic Tendency Movement
Mubarak, President Hosni, 90, 91, 129,
    130, 163
Mufti of Egypt, 79
Muhammad Ahmad ibn 'Abdallah,
    142–144, 145
Muhyadin, Sheikh Shariff Sheikh, 43
Mujahideen
    consequences of arms support for,
        11–14
    defined, 169(n2)
    lack of intellectuals in, 8
    military development of, 2, 3–4,
        171(n39)
    Somali military action by, 40–41
    Taliban ousting of, 16
    U.S. military aid to, 9–11
Mulsim World League, 9
Multiparty politics, 7, 122, 126, 146
Muslim Brotherhood, 2, 9, 65, 103,
    183(n47)
    contemporary role of, 91
    military wing of, 130
    origins and development of, 74, 81–86,
        129, 169(n5)
    political weakening of, 86–87, 90, 107,
        133
    renouncing of violence by, 109
    as Sudanese political force, 146, 147,
        149
Muslims
    Arabism of, 75
    effect of Six-Day War of 1967 on,
        107–108
    global community of, 24, 32, 77, 81,
        92, 106, 138, 168
    origins of Islamist tradition among,
        76–81
    Western attitudes toward, xv–xvi
    See also Islam

Nadwi, As-Sayyid Abul-Hassan Ali Al-
    Hasani an-, 32
Naf'i, Naf'i Ali, 153

Nahnah, Sheikh Mahfoud, 65–69, 70
Najibullah, Mohammed, 11, 15
Nasraoui, Radhia, 120
Nasser, Gamal Abdel, 87, 90, 91, 105,
    106–107
National Contract of Algeria, 123–124,
    178(n54)
National Democratic Alliance (NDA),
    157
National Islamic Front (NIF), 44, 147,
    150, 151, 152–153, 155, 156, 166
Nationalism, 105–106, 167
National Liberation Front (FLN), 49–50,
    56, 58, 60, 99, 125–126
National Unionist Party, 145
NATO. *See* North Atlantic Treaty
    Organization
Nazi Germany, 84
Nazzar, Khaled, 56
NDA. *See* National Democratic Alliance
Neofundamentalism, 92, 113
"New World Order," 136, 138
NIF. *See* National Islamic Front
Nile River, 164–165
Nimeiri, Gaafar, 147
North Africa, 117–139
North Atlantic Treaty Organization
    (NATO), 10, 167–168
Nuqrashi Pasha, Mahmud Fahmi al-, 86
Nur, Hussein Mohamed Abdul, 25, 27–28

OIC. *See* Organization of the Islamic
    Conference
Oil embargo, 108
Oklahoma City bombing, xv
Omar, Karim, 1–4, 13, 14, 15, 58–59, 61,
    100, 164
Operation Cyclone, 10, 11
Organization of the Islamic Conference
    (OIC), 37, 173(n27)
Orientalism, 52–53, 104, 181(n51)
Oslo peace accord, 159, 187(n37)
Otafi'ire, Kahinda, 163
Ottoman empire, 81, 106, 138, 142, 145
Oufkir, Gen. Mohammed, 98
Ouyahia, Ahmed, 128

PAIC. *See* Pan-Arab and Islamic
    Conference
Pakistan, 8–9, 23, 170(n19)
Palestine, 84, 86, 160
Palestinian Hamas Islamic Resistance
    Movement, 159

Palestinian Liberation Organization (PLO), 159, 161
Pan-Arab and Islamic Conference (PAIC), 150, 186(n19)
PDF. *See* Popular Defense Force
Peoples' Democratic Party of Afghanistan (PDPA), 6–7
Peshawar, Pakistan, 1, 2, 3
Pilgrimage, 75
PLO. *See* Palestinian Liberation Organization
Political Islam. *See* Islamism
Politics
    multiparty, 7, 122, 126, 146
    religion's influence on, 6–7, 134–135, 148–149, 151, 154
Popular Defense Force (PDF), 155–156, 157
Popular Islam, 48, 54
Prayer, Muslim, 75
Punishments, criminal, 27–28

Qadir, Emir Abd al-, 66, 175(n3)
Qudwany, Farid, 111
Qur'an. *See* Koran
Qutb, Sayyid, 29–30, 75, 87–90, 104, 107, 109

Rabbani, Burhanuddin, 16, 22, 23
Rafsanjani, Ali Akhbar, 38
Rahman, Sheikh Omar Abdel, 14, 111
Rally for Culture and Democracy (RCD), 62, 125
Ramid, Mustapha, 96
RCD. *See* Rally for Culture and Democracy
Redjam, Abderazak, 71–72, 100
Religion
    Algerian nationality and, 64–65
    military aggression of Taliban and, 16–20
    mystical sects in, 141–142
    origins of Islamist tradition and, 76–81
    political force of, 6–7, 134–135, 148–149, 151, 154
    scholarship and, 76–81, 82
    secular nationalism and, 105–106
Renan, Ernest, 47
Republicanism, 124–125
Rida, Rashid, 80–81, 106, 180(n21)
Rodinson, Maxine, 30

Roy, Oliver, 7, 24, 90, 92, 113
Russia
    Taliban defenses in, 23
    See also Soviet Union

Sabbawy, Mahmoud al-, 14
Sadat, Anwar al-, 14, 84, 91, 108, 110, 129
Sadi, Omar, 69
Sadi, Said, 62–63, 64, 125
Said, Edward, 50, 51, 52–53
Said, Mohammed, 71–72
Said, Mounir, 159–160
Salaf (early Muslim elders), 79, 80, 83
Salah, Zubeir Mohamed, 158
Saudi Arabia
    Egyptian relations with, 107
    Islamist movement in, 112–114
    royal family in, 113
    Sudanese relations with, 162, 163
Sayyaf, Abdul Rasul, 12
Scholarship
    academic study of Islam and, 51–53
    modern Islamist tradition and, 76–81, 114, 131
Secularism, 54, 122
Sharia (Islamic law)
    in Afghanistan, 17
    court system based on, 25–28, 29, 31, 42, 81, 174(n36)
    defined, 5, 6, 169(n8)
    Islamist movements and, 85, 89, 90, 113
    practical application of, 174(n42)
    in Somalia, 33–36, 42–45
    in Sudan, 147, 148, 153, 164
Sherchenko, Nikolai, 22
Shia Muslims, 172(n17)
Shiddo, Abel Aziz, 149, 174(n41)
Shihab (AUMA newspaper), 49
Siad, Issa Mohamed, 38
Sirri, Yasser al-, 110, 112
Six-Day War (1967), 105, 107
Socialist Forces Front (FFS), 60
Society of the Muslim Brothers. *See* Muslim Brotherhood
Somalia, 25–45
    application of Islamic law in, 33–36, 42–44
    Islamic political movement in, 36–38, 44–45

origins and evolution of Islam and,
29–32
sharia court system in, 25–28, 29
UN military action in, 38–41
Soviet Union
Egyptian ties with, 106–107
Islamist opposition to, 2, 3–4, 24
occupation of Afghanistan by, 1, 6–7,
12, 15, 170(n18)
Somali relations with, 34–35
See also Russia
SPLM. *See* Sudan Peoples' Liberation
Movement
Sudan, 140–165
foreign policy of, 159–165
government power in, 147–154,
157–158
Islamist movement in, 166–167
Mahdism in, 143–147
Ottoman influence in, 142–143, 145
political environment in, 145–147,
150–151
Sufism in, 141–142, 143, 144
support for Somalia from, 37–38, 41
war in southern, 154–159
See also National Islamic Front;
Tourabi, Hassan al-
Sudan Peoples' Liberation Movement
(SPLM), 147, 154, 155, 157, 163
Sufism
in Algeria, 48
defined, 175(n1)
Islamic opposition to, 80, 83
Mahdism and, 143–144
in Sudan, 141–142, 143, 144
Sunni Muslims, 32, 172(n17), 180(n11)
Surface-to-air missiles (SAMs), 11

Taha, Ahmed, 111
Taha, Ali Osman, 152, 158
Tajdid (religious renewal), 85, 109,
119
Takfir wa Hijra movement, 59
Tal'a al-Fath, 14
Taliban
emergence of, 16
national aggression by, 16–20
political power of, 22–24
Russian defenses against, 22–23
Tantawi, Mohammed Sayyed, 132
Tawhid (unity), 153, 187(n26)

Terrorist organizations, 130
Totalitarianism, 152
Tourabi, Hassan al-, 146, 147, 148–149,
150–151, 152, 153, 155, 156, 158,
159, 161, 165
Tribalism
Mahdism and, 143–144
origins of Islam and, 32
Somalian conflicts based on, 35–36,
42–43
Trimingham, J. Spencer, 141
Tunisia
Islamist movement in, 101–103,
117–121
modernizing reforms in, 118–119
secular education in, 119–120

Uganda, 157, 163
Umma (community of Muslims), 24, 32,
77, 81, 92, 106, 138, 168
Umma Party, 146, 147, 150
UNFP. *See* Union Nationale des Forces
Populaire
Union Générale des Travailleurs Algérien,
58
Union Nationale des Forces Populaire
(UNFP), 98
United Nations (UN), 38–41
United States
Egyptian ties with, 136
military aid to the Mujahideen by,
9–11
Somali relations with, 35, 38–41
Sudanese relations with, 157, 163, 164
Urwa al-Wuthqa, al- (journal), 76, 78

Verges, Meriem, 58
Von Grunebaum, Gustave, 32, 104

Wafd party, 84–85, 86
Wahiby, Issa Mohamed, 25–28, 42
Watt, William Montgomery, 30–31
Whirling dervishes, 141
Wilson, Charles, 171(n24)
Women
Sudanese politics and, 164
Taliban policies against, 19, 20
World Trade Center bombing, xv, 12, 13,
14, 111
World War II, 84

Index

Yassine, Nadia, 94, 95, 96, 101
Yassine, Sheikh Abdesalem, 94, 95,
    120
Yatim, Mohammed, 97
Yaya, Imam Mesuadi, 54
Young Turks, 81
Yousaf, Mohammad, 10, 11, 12
Yousaf, Ramzi Ahmed, 12, 13, 14

Zaitouna University, 119–120, 121

Zakariya, Fouad, 32
Zawhari, Ayman al-, 114
Zayat, Muntassir al-, 111
Zeroual, Liamine, 60, 63, 64, 66, 70–71,
    122–125, 128
Zeydan, Rifaat, 111
Zia ul-Haq, General, 9, 23
Zionism, 85
Zitouni, Djamel, 71–72, 182(n18)